T0125209

Fugitive Essays

Frank Chodorov

Fugitive Essays

Selected Writings of Frank Chodorov

Compiled, Edited, and with an Introduction by
Charles H. Hamilton

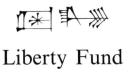

Liberty Fund

Permission to reprint from *The Income Tax* (© 1954 by Frank Chodorov), *The Rise and Fall of Society* (© 1959 by Frank Chodorov) and *Out of Step* (© 1962 by The Devin-Adair Company) granted by The Devin-Adair Company, Old Greenwich, CT 06870.

Permission to reprint "Civilization or Caveman Economy?" from the May 1940 and "Thought and the World of Action" from the January 1941 issues of *The Freeman* granted by The Henry George School of Social Science.

Permission to reprint "My Friend's Education" from the August 1954, "Reds Are Natives" from the August 1954, "A War to Communize America" from the November 1954, "How Communism Came to America" from the February 1955, "Why Teach Freedom?" from the May 1955, "The Dogma of Our Times" from the June 1956 and "Free Will and the Market Place" from the January 1959 issues of *The Freeman* granted by *The Freeman*.

Permission to reprint "What Individualism Is Not" from the June 20, 1956, issue of *National Review* granted by *National Review*.

Permission to reprint "Washington: A Psychosis" from the April 11, 1951, "Washington: American Mecca" from the June 16, 1954, and "Warfare Versus Welfare" from the January 10, 1951, issues of *Human Events* granted by *Human Events*.

Permission to reprint a previously unpublished foreword granted by Grace A. Klein.

This book is published by Liberty Fund, Inc., a foundation established to encourage study of the ideal of a society of free and responsible individuals.

The cuneiform inscription that serves as our logo and as the design motif for our endpapers is the earliest-known written appearance of the word "freedom" (*amagi*), or "liberty." It is taken from a clay document written about 2300 B.C. in the Sumerian city-state of Lagash.

© 1980 by Liberty Fund, Inc. All rights reserved, including the right of reproduction in whole or in part in any form. Brief quotations may be included in a review, and all inquiries should be addressed to Liberty Fund, Inc., 11301 North Meridan Street, Carmel, Indiana 46032-4564. This book was manufactured in the United States of America.

Library of Congress Cataloguing in Publication Data
Chodorov, Frank, 1887–
  Fugitive essays.
  Bibliography: p.
  Includes index.
1. Social sciences—Collected works. I. Hamilton, Charles H., 1946–
II. Title.
H33.C56   300   79-28720
ISBN 0-913966-72-X   HC
ISBN 0-913966-73-8   PB

              80 17 18 19 20 C 5 4 3 2 1
              17 18 19 20 21 P 7 6 5 4 3

CONTENTS

ACKNOWLEDGMENTS

For their help and encouragement as I did the research for this volume, I would especially like to thank Oscar Johannsen, Robert Schalkenbach Foundation; Robert Kephart, Kephart Communications; Edmund Opitz, Foundation for Economic Education; and Joseph Peden, Institute for Humane Studies. Paul Avrich, Bettina Bien, Leonard Liggio, Murray Rothbard, and Jack Schwartzman all helped me when I had questions. Grace Klein, Frank Chodorov's daughter, helped me to get a better sense of Frank Chodorov as a person. Susan Trowbridge listened and made sure every word was in the right place.

Charles H. Hamilton

INTRODUCTION
By Charles H. Hamilton

F rank Chodorov was by temperament and experience skeptical of the intentions of politicians and intellectuals. They wanted to change the world. And Chodorov never tired of pointing out the dangers of such obsessions: "When proponents say 'let's do something about it,' they mean 'let's get hold of the political machinery so that we can do something to somebody else.' And that somebody else is invariably you."[1] Chodorov knew that change depended on individuals taking responsibility for their own actions, not on choreographing the actions of others. For almost thirty years he sought to find and counsel those people devoted to individual freedom and a humane life. He took on "Isaiah's job."

This biblical parable is retold by Albert Jay Nock in one of his best essays.[2] The prophet Isaiah is sent by the Lord to tell the people of a decaying civilization "what is wrong, and why, and what is going to happen unless they have a change of heart

---

[1] Frank Chodorov, "Freedom Is Better," p. 396. Page citations for material reproduced here are to pages in this volume. The footnotes and the bibliography may supply additional information.

[2] Albert Jay Nock, "Isaiah's Job," in *Free Speech and Plain Language* (New York: William Morrow, 1937), pp. 248–65.

and straighten up." He didn't expect to rouse the masses to action or to convert the political powers that be; rather, in what was ultimately more important, Isaiah desired to serve the Remnant. The members of this Remnant, as the Lord explains,

> are obscure, unorganized, inarticulate, each one rubbing along as best he can. They need to be encouraged and braced up, because when everything has gone completely to the dogs, they are the ones who will come back and build up a new society, and meanwhile your preaching will reassure them and keep them hanging on. Your job is to take care of the Remnant.

When Nock wrote this essay in 1936, he saw the job going begging. A few years later, Chodorov took that job and uniquely served to maintain the tradition of what Murray N. Rothbard has called the "old American Right": that passionate belief in individual liberty which strongly opposed both the rising statist interventionism at home, and war and imperialism abroad.[3] For over twenty years, he wrote hundreds of articles, edited three magazines, and helped to edit a handful of others. With his brand of political journalism, "he deeply influenced the post-war conservative movement," as William F. Buckley once acknowledged.[4] And his important contributions still survive on the Right and in the now burgeoning libertarian movement.

A MAN MUST HAVE A CAUSE

On February 15, 1887, two poor, Russian immigrants had their eleventh child, the only one to be born in the United

---

[3] Murray N. Rothbard, "The Transformation of the American Right," *Continuum* 2 (Summer 1964): 220–31.

[4] William F. Buckley, review of *Out of Step* by Chodorov, *National Review*, December 4, 1962, pp. 446–47.

States. His name was Fishel Chodorowsky, although he was always known as Frank Chodorov. He grew up on the Lower West Side of New York City, where he helped his family with their small restaurant.

He graduated from Columbia University in 1907, and until 1937 he "wandered through the years." He taught high school for a few years. He married, and he and his wife, Celia, had two children. He ran a clothing factory in Massachusetts for a time. In 1925 he started his own small mail-order clothing firm, but it was wiped out by the Great Depression. He then held a number of sales and promotion jobs.

It was in between these jobs that Chodorov developed a passionate commitment to individualism and to the free market. Years later he was fond of saying that "a young man must have a cause."[5] He found his by accident. While working in Chicago (1912–17), he picked up a friend's copy of Henry George's *Progress and Poverty.* Assuming only that George was a fine nineteenth-century essayist, Chodorov remembers he "read the book several times, and each time I felt myself slipping into a cause."[6] That book was to give him a *Weltanschauung* that influenced all his writing.

Henry George is usually remembered for his concern over land value and the ownership of land. Land, George contended, should not be privately owned, and rent was really a social value that should not be subject to individual profiteering. This concern culminated in George's political proposal that all land rents be fully taxed—what came to be known as the single tax.

---

[5] Chodorov, *Out of Step: The Autobiography of an Individualist* (New York: Devin-Adair, 1962), p. 50.

[6] *Ibid.*

For Chodorov, the single tax was really only "a minor detail in his [Henry George's] economic and social system. "[7] Much like Albert Jay Nock, Chodorov believed in the single tax but didn't advocate it.[8] In fact, as a political solution, he questioned the idea of giving taxing power, of any kind, to the state. He saw no reason to believe that any power given to the state would be used for the good of society.

The broad strokes that George used in analyzing his world were what influenced Chodorov so much. For when *Progress and Poverty* was published in 1879, it was a stunning affirmation of the Jeffersonian and Spencerian tradition. In 1941 Chodorov put Henry George and his philosophy in that broader context:

> George is the apostle of individualism; he teaches the ethical basis of private property; he stresses the function of capital in an advancing civilization; he emphasizes the greater productivity of voluntary cooperation in a free market economy, the moral degeneration of a people subjected to state direction and socialistic conformity. His is the philosophy of free enterprise, free trade, free men.[9]

This love of liberty, this stress on the economic and social over the political, kept Chodorov close to the cause, even when, in later years, the mention of Henry George and his philosophy disappeared from his work (both because his interests had shifted and because many of the periodicals for which he wrote just would not discuss Henry George or the land question). After his debilitating stroke in 1961, on the plane back to New

---

[7] Chodorov, "Education for a Free Society," *Scribner's Commentator* (February 1941): 36.

[8] See Robert M. Crunden, *The Mind and Art of Albert Jay Nock* (Chicago: Henry Regnery, 1964), p. 36

[9] Chodorov, "Education for a Free Society," pp. 36–37.

York City, his daughter remembers his saying, in a near delirium that must have touched very close to his center, "There is only one thing, there is only Henry George."

WHEN WAR COMES

After those heady days of reading *Progress and Poverty,* Chodorov spent increasing amounts of time within the Henry George movement. Believing that his primary duty was to "teach the kids Henry George," he gravitated toward the Henry George School of Social Science in New York City. In 1937, at the age of 50, he became its full-time director. "It proved to be something that I had spent my life preparing for."[10]

With great energy, Chodorov spent five years as director, during which time he firmly established the school intellectually and financially. He loved his work and he was good at it. "I got along swimmingly for about five years, training teachers (all volunteers), setting up new courses, writing syllabi, raising money, and to my joy editing a school paper called *The Freeman.*"[11]

The Freeman, however, was more than a school paper. It offered Chodorov the opportunity to develop the editorial and writing skills that became his stock-in-trade. Founded by Will Lissner in November 1937, the paper aimed at "education in the philosophy of Henry George."[12] Authors included John Dewey, Albert Jay Nock, George Bernard Shaw, Bertrand Rus-

---

[10] Chodorov, *Out of Step,* p. 78.

[11] *Ibid.,* pp. 78–79.

[12] Contrary to what some commentators have said, this *Freeman* was not a continuation of *The Freeman* started by Albert Jay Nock and Francis Neilson in 1920. As Lissner stated in that first issue, "The paper is not a revival of the old *Freeman,* nor an attempt at it."

sell, and Francis Neilson. *The Freeman* often dealt with issues like the land question, Georgism, the evils of taxation and communism, and the importance of capitalism.

One topic above all others concerned Chodorov when he began editing and writing for *The Freeman:* the coming war. He was against war, all wars, and during the late 1930s he saw one on the horizon. Presciently, he knew war was an instrument used by politicians to enhance their power and to mask economic ills of their own making. As for intellectuals, they were weaving phrases together to "bedevil the impoverished populace."[13] These factors, Chodorov knew, would sweep the United States into war. When "Truth Faces War Hysteria," as he titled one of his editorials in the August 1940 issue, principle is the first thing to go by the board—and with it, freedom.

Chodorov refused to get involved with the emotionalism surrounding any war issue. Rather, he was constantly warning people about the effects of war (or the threat of war, which could be as bad).[14] He asked the basic, long-term questions: "How will we emerge from the emergency? What manner of life confronts us?" Sadly, "the answer that any analysis of current events brings us is that Americans of the future will be slaves of the state."[15]

Faced with war hysteria and the knowledge that war would come, Chodorov knew his task and the task of those to whom he spoke would become even more pressing. As early as November 1938, in the article "When War Comes," Chodorov wrote:

---

[13] Chodorov, "I Bring a Sword," *The Freeman* (September 1938): 2.

[14] In 1951 Chodorov wrote, "A continuing threat of war will have the same effect on our economy as a war of attrition" ("Warfare Versus Welfare," p. 370).

[15] Chodorov, "The Enemy Within," *The Freeman* (July, 1941): 194.

Those of us who try to retain some modicum of sanity will be scorned by our erstwhile friends, spit upon, persecuted, imprisoned. . . . We must steel ourselves for the inevitable. Every day we must repeat to ourselves as a liturgy, the truth that war is caused by the conditions that bring about poverty; that no war is justified; that no war benefits the people; that war is an instrument whereby the haves increase their hold on the have-nots; that war destroys liberty. We must train our minds, as an athlete trains his body, against the inevitable conflict with the powerful propaganda that will be used to destroy our sanity. Now, before it is too late, we must learn to think peace in the midst of war.[16]

The war came and Chodorov dedicated himself and *The Freeman* "to the task of educating for an enduring peace."[17] But internal conflicts at the Henry George School were to lead rapidly to his ouster. Chodorov's strong support of individualism over a more ecumenical Georgism had aroused some bad feelings. And there were other conflicts with some trustees. Finally, his antiwar editorials angered many who didn't understand his principled position. Despite the obvious support of most teachers and most readers of *The Freeman*, Chodorov was virtually evicted by the trustees while away on a trip. *The Freeman* of March 1942 announced somberly, and without explanation, "Mr. Chodorov has retired from the editorship."[18]

The war years, of course, were hard times for the individualist, antistatist, and antiwar traditions in America. What had once been a movement of some influence plummeted to its nadir, as almost everyone got on the war bandwagon. And those who, like Chodorov, stuck to their principles usually lost their jobs, or couldn't find any outlets for their writing. The war (and

---

[16] Chodorov, "When War Comes," *The Freeman* (November 1938): 2.

[17] Chodorov, "Happy New Year, Readers!" *The Freeman* (January 1942): 3.

[18] "An Announcement," *The Freeman* (March 1942): 99.

the events at the Henry George School) had deeply affected Chodorov. As he looked back on it in a letter to a friend, "it seemed to me then that the only thing for me to do was to blow my brains out, which I might have done if I had not had Albert Jay Nock by my side. Sheer willpower pulled me out of my funk."[19] Before long, however, Chodorov was to revive the old Right tradition in what was for him "the most gratifying venture of my life."[20]

IT'S FUN TO FIGHT

Out of the bleak years of World War II came the beginnings of the modern conservative movement. Chodorov was there, emphasizing the things that were dear to him: individual dignity, society, natural rights, and the free market. In November 1944 he started his own foray into personal journalism with the first issue of a four-page monthly named *analysis*. With that, and then through the mid-1950s, Chodorov "began to shape directly the intellectual development of the postwar Right . . . [especially] helping the libertarian Remnant to attain self-consciousness and intellectual coherence."[21] In 1969 M. Stanton Evans looked back on "the founding father" and said, "The Chodorov imprint is visible in every phase of conservative effort."[22]

Published from a few small rooms in lower Manhattan,

[19] "An Exile in Babylon," *Fragments* (January–March 1967): 11. This letter was written in 1951.

[20] Chodorov, *Out of Step,* p. 79.

[21] George H. Nash, *The Conservative Intellectual Movement in America* (New York: Basic Books, 1976), pp. 16, 18.

[22] M. Stanton Evans, "The Founding Father," *Ideas* (Spring–Summer 1969): 61.

analysis was, in Albert Jay Nock's estimation, "by far the best contribution to our minor literature of public affairs."[23] Although it survived until January 1951, it was never commercially successful. It never had, for instance, more than 4,000 subscribers.

Success in these things, however, is not measured in numbers alone. Rather, Chodorov contended, "It's fun to fight—when what you are fighting for stirs your imagination. . . . There is a lot of spiritual profit in being true to oneself." Furthermore, no converts were sought. Chodorov didn't believe in them and insisted that *analysis* "would not attempt to teach individualism; it would attempt to find individualists."[24] Indeed, he found many; some of the better known of this Remnant were William F. Buckley, M. Stanton Evans, Murray N. Rothbard, Edmund A. Opitz, and James J. Martin.

Publishing *analysis* was a significant financial burden for Chodorov. Times were difficult even when the rent was paid by his new friend, the well-known Thoreauvian, Leonard Kleinfeld. Close friends made a frequent habit of taking Chodorov out to dinner. In March 1951, however, he merged *analysis* with *Human Events,* a newsletter begun in 1944 by Frank Hanighen, Felix Morley, and Henry Regnery. He moved to Washington, D.C., and was an associate editor for *Human Events* until 1954. Almost monthly he wrote articles from his individualist perspective, though often on more topical subjects than had been his custom in *analysis.*

The first chance Chodorov had to develop fully his world view was during the publication of *analysis.* It was his baby:

---

[23] "A One-Man Affair," *Fragments* (January–March 1967): 7. This was a reprint of a promotional piece Albert Jay Nock wrote for *analysis* in 1945.

[24] Chodorov, "It's Fun to Fight," *analysis.* (November 1944): 1.

he "slapped it on its hopeful rump and the birthcry was anti-statism."[25] Though always a political journalist, he wrote from a basic set of principles which he took from the classical liberal tradition, from Henry George, and from the old Right tradition of Albert Jay Nock. His antistatism came from his deep-seated belief in the individual as the basic unit in society, and in the natural laws that helped to organize individual interactions. And while freedom was uniquely an emotional experience in the spirit of each person, Chodorov emphasized the social aspect of freedom, that is, the nature of the relationships that grow between people.[26]

In the social sphere Chodorov made a fundamental distinction between the economic and the political, or between society and the state. He learned this from Henry George and refined the distinction through his contact with Albert Jay Nock and through his reading of Franz Oppenheimer's *The State*.[27] Society, for Chodorov, was the free and voluntary interactions of people, and it was through these interactions that people and civilizations prospered. "Society is an economic, not a political phenomenon. . . . The marketplace makes society."[28]

The political realm was wholly different. The state, Chodorov observed, is the institutional embodiment of the political, and uses force to accomplish its ends. It adds nothing to the material or spiritual basis of civilization. Anything the state has, it has to take from the productive sectors of society. This means, Chodorov concluded, that "between the state and the individual there is always a tug-of-war: whatever power one

---

[25] Chodorov, "Let's Keep It Clean," *analysis* (October 1949): 3.

[26] See Chodorov, "The Fine Art of Plunder," *analysis* (April 1945): 3.

[27] Franz Oppenheimer, *The State* (New York: Free Life Editions, 1975).

[28] Chodorov, "After '1984'—Maybe Before," *analysis* (December 1949): 2.

acquires must be to the detriment of the other. The fiction of rendering service is fostered by the state in order that it may the better pursue its purpose."[29]

While Chodorov scorned politicians, the problem was really an attitude: an attitude toward others and toward the use of force to advance one's own ends. We were fast becoming, he once said, "a country of panhandlers."[30] Everybody sought the special privileges that the state offered only at the expense of others. Concepts of individual responsibility and voluntary cooperation dimmed and "political thought is fast crowding out all other patterns."[31] No one escaped the temptation to indulge in such privileges and no one escaped Chodorov's wrath and biting analysis of their indiscretions. Communists and socialists were clearly most interested in power and wouldn't hesitate to use the state. Chodorov also damned conservatives and many businesspeople for their support of special privileges for themselves. This made them little different from the communists and socialists. "In America it is the so-called capitalist who is to blame for the fulfillment of Marx's prophecies. Beguiled by the state's siren song of special privilege, the capitalists have abandoned capitalism."[32] This was "the crime of the capitalists."

Since politics "has destroyed every civilization man has ever built,"[33] Chodorov constantly advocated staying away from the political game. He strongly favored not voting. When, as a lark in the 1950s, he ran for the New Jersey State Senate, his campaign slogan was "Don't vote for me." Chodorov believed that

---

[29] Chodorov, "The Cardinal Crime," *analysis* (March 1949): 2.

[30] Chodorov, "Trailing the Trend," *analysis* (November 1945): 2.

[31] Chodorov, "Washington: A Psychosis," p. 46.

[32] Chodorov, "The 'Crime' of the Capitalists," p. 149.

[33] Chodorov, "A Sensible Labor Policy," *analysis* (April 1949): 1.

what was productive and creative, not to mention moral, was outside the political process. One couldn't fight the political process by joining it, so Chodorov, in all his writing, looked to the individual and education as a way to blunt the drive for privilege and collectivism.

Of course, in any society there needs to be some institutional method to protect private property and the individual's life and freedom. Chodorov called this legitimate form *government,* as opposed to the antisocial *state.*[34] It was taxation, Chodorov felt, and in particular the income tax, that transformed social and legitimate government into an antisocial state. Not only did taxes steal from producers, but they also gave the state the capital to intervene forcefully in affairs at home and abroad. Chodorov lamented the loss of the American Revolution 129 years after it had been won: in 1913 the Sixteenth Amendment installed income taxation as a permanent part of the American political landscape. This opened the floodgates of statism. In 1954 his concern led him to write *The Income Tax: Root of All Evil.* In numerous articles Chodorov sought ways to repeal the Sixteenth Amendment—a third party, states rights, or not voting. He was even a founding director of the Organization to Repeal Federal Income Taxes, Inc. It all came down to one simple belief: "Taxation is nothing but organized robbery, and there the subject should be dropped."[35]

THE COMMIE MENACE

The mid-1950s represent a watershed period for America's political consciousness. Across the spectrum, from Left to Right, anticommunism was taking hold. Within the fledgling

---

[34] See "Government *Contra* State," pp. 93–97.

[35] Chodorov, *The Economics of Society, Government, and State* (New York: Analysis Associates, 1946), p. 116.

conservative movement, Frank Chodorov and a few others tried to stem the tide of the armored cold warriors. The issue, they said, was what it had always been: the need to support individualism and to oppose statism. Communism—in both its international and domestic forms—did represent a threat, but increasing state power and diminishing individual freedom in the process of opposing communism were not answers. In fact, increasing state power to oppose communism was, ironically, one way to bring communism to America through the back door.

Chodorov made this case from his editorship of a new *Freeman*, this time published by the Foundation for Economic Education. He began his duties with the July 1954 issue, but conflict with the foundation and a long illness that made work difficult for well over a year (he was now 68) forced him to leave *The Freeman* in 1955. In his editorials and articles he tried to uphold the isolationist old Right position, as he had earlier in the *Freeman, analysis,* and *Human Events.*

In the August 1954 issue of *The Freeman,* William F. Buckley pointed out the enormous fissure developing in conservative ranks around the question, "What are we going to do about the Soviet Union?" There were, on the one hand, the "containment conservatives," concerned about communism but most concerned about the internal dangers of huge national defense budgets, conscription, etc. This was Chodorov's position. Then there were the "interventionist conservatives," who advocated a program of militant action aimed at the destruction of the Soviets as quickly as possible. Buckley prophetically concluded that "the issue is there, and ultimately it will separate us."[36]

In an editorial in that same issue, Chodorov pointed out that,

---

[36] William F. Buckley, "A Dilemma of Conservatives," *The Freeman* (August 1954): 51, 52.

in advocating interventionism against international communism, one was advocating killing people. That usually meant conquest and imperialism. It was as though these advocates thought that "the natives carry an ideological germ that threatens our way of life," and that by killing them the danger could be eradicated. Interventionists had missed the point: communism was neither a communicable disease nor a people that could just be destroyed. Communism was an idea. "It is better, therefore, to attack the idea than to attack the natives." Communism was, at base, the idea of an all-powerful state ruling over enslaved people. "That, then, is the idea that we who believe in the American tradition should try to kill, and let all natives alone."[37]

In subsequent issues of *The Freeman,* Chodorov engaged William Schlamm in a contest of will over this issue of international communism. Schlamm continually raised the specter of Soviet conquest and the duty of the United States to stamp out this menace to freedom. Just as Chodorov had warned of the coming of World War II and the consequent loss of freedom, his "well-trained nostrils" detected "the aroma of a similar stew now in the making." He reminded his readers that in any kind of war, hot or cold, the state is strengthened. Even if the war is won, the state never abdicates its newly added prerogatives. People once again lose their freedom. Statism and its threat to freedom were the crucial issues. The interventionists admitted the likelihood of a loss of freedom but they stressed the immediate danger. They were, Chodorov said, "willing to gamble with freedom. I am not."[38]

---

[37] Chodorov, "Reds Are Natives," pp. 325, 326.
[38] Chodorov, "The Return of 1940?" *The Freeman* (September 1954): 81. Also see William S. Schlamm, "But It Is Not 1940," *The Freeman* (November 1954): 169–71.

As the anticommunist feeling gathered steam, Chodorov warned that "we are again being told to be afraid." Communism was indeed a threat, but Chodorov believed it would fall of its own weight because it was economically and politically an untenable system. In any case, the United States could not be the armed guardian for the whole world. The issue was war and the necessity of avoiding it. "The important thing for America now is not to let the fearmongers (or the imperialists) frighten us into a war which, no matter what the military outcome, is certain to communize our country."[39]

The fear of international communism bred a domestic counterpart and there were increasingly loud calls for a crackdown there too. Chodorov saw beyond this immediately. If there was a problem of communists in government, Chodorov half seriously offered this solution, "How to get rid of the communists in the government? Easy. Just abolish the jobs."[40]

What bothered Chodorov most of all about the concern over domestic communism was that it was leading to the persecution of ideas. "The case against the communists involves a principle of transcending importance. It is the right to be wrong. Heterodoxy is a necessary condition of a free society. . . . Let them rant their heads off—that is their right, which we cannot afford to infringe—but let us keep them from the political means of depriving everybody else of the same right."[41] If the state were to outlaw ideas, then it could outlaw any ideas, communist *or* anticommunist. In fact, in the January 1951 issue of *analysis,* Chodorov discussed a little-known case where the government had sought to obtain the list of financial supporters

---

[39] Chodorov, "A War to Communize America," pp. 371, 379.

[40] Chodorov, "Trailing the Trend," *analysis* (April 1950): 3.

[41] Chodorov, "How to Curb the Commies," pp. 180, 182.

of an organization criticizing communist infiltration in the government. Chodorov drew the obvious conclusion: "America will not be saved by geting rid of communists. The real danger is the trend toward statism—the general attitude that condones the imprisonment of Americans for holding ideas contrary to those who wield power. "[42]

Fighting communism rested on fighting the *ideas* of communism. And, as Chodorov enjoyed pointing out, that could be embarrassing. Communism was, after all, just a form of statism. "The real traitor in our midst is the power seeker. "[43] Communists and many anticommunists were enamored of the same lure of power. The spy hunt, then, was really a heresy trial, one cult of power trying to suppress another. Anticommunism was becoming a smoke screen helping an entire gang of power seekers to strengthen the state for their own gain. As Chodorov predicted: "To put it bluntly: communism will not be imported from Moscow; it will come out of Wall Street and Main Street. It will show up as a disease internally induced by bad habits. "[44]

The legacy of this conflict over what to do about communism was, of course, a hardening of the cold-war stance within the conservative movement. Despite the efforts of Chodorov and a few others, their words seem to have fallen on deaf ears. With an ease that surprised such opposing advocates in the struggle as William F. Buckley and Murray N. Rothbard, the conservative movement became a stronghold of vehement and militant anticommunism.[45] The time was ripe for such an attitude and

[42] Chodorov, "Verboten Ideas," *analysis* (January 1951): 4.

[43] Chodorov, "Trailing the Trend," *analysis* (April 1950): 3.

[44] Chodorov, *One Is a Crowd: Reflections of an Individualist* (New York: Devin-Adair, 1952), pp. 116–17.

[45] See Nash, *op. cit.*, p. 126.

Chodorov faded away as an influence. As Murray N. Rothbard laments, "We should have listened more carefully to Frank Chodorov."[46]

ON PROMOTING INDIVIDUALISM

It was always clear to Chodorov that the ills of society came from a belief in political action and a reliance on the state. Even those with whom Chodorov would see eye to eye on the right vision of a free society were at a disadvantage if they tried to achieve their ends politically. "On the political front you are fighting a rearguard action."[47]

While he occasionally tinkered with "solutions" to problems, Chodorov's main concern was educational, to find the Remnant and to provide for it a different view of the world. The rest of it—changing the world—was the responsibility of a free and an aware populace. "One should concentrate on society and leave politics severely alone; which means education and more education, and ignoring the politicians altogether."[48]

Statism was "a state of mind, not an historical necessity,"[49] a belief in power and privilege, in opportunism, in expediency, and in action *per se*. It was in the realm of ideas that Chodorov

---

[46] Murray N. Rothbard, "The Betrayal of the American Right" (unpublished), p. 181. For a further discussion of Chodorov's views on communism and foreign policy, see Joseph R. Stromberg, "Frank Chodorov: A Libertarian's Libertarian," in "The Cold War and the Transformation of the American Right: The Decline of Right-Wing Liberalism" (M.A. thesis, Florida Atlantic University, 1971), pp. 43–51.

[47] Chodorov, "The Unimportance of Candidates," *Human Events,* January 16, 1952, p. 4.

[48] Chodorov, *Out of Step,* p. 108.

[49] "A Legacy of Value," p. 414.

mainly worked. Believing that ideas *do* have consequences, he had tried to influence ideas.

From his early days at the Henry George School, Chodorov had taught liberty. F. A. Harper, himself a great teacher, re-marked that Chodorov was one of the greatest Socratic teachers he had ever known.[50] Indeed, he is often remembered best for his teaching. At his *analysis* office, he held classes under the rubric of the Society of Individualists. And in 1950 he set to paper the words that were to found the Intercollegiate Society of Individualists. This was his last great contribution to the revival of the American Right that he had been so instrumental in fostering.

"A Fifty-Year Project" was a pamphlet that also appeared in the October 1950 issue of *analysis.* In it Chodorov tried to understand the "transmutation of the American character from individualist to collectivist." What he found was that socialism had been advanced by organizations like the Intercollegiate Socialist Society, and by students who then took up the cause. There had been no real challenge from capitalists—who often were just as socialistically inclined. And the individualists of the time remained in disarray. To combat this, a long-term project was needed to win the minds of youth. "Individualism can be revivified by implanting the idea in the minds of the coming generations. . . . The assault must be made on the campus."[51]

In the September 6, 1950, issue of *Human Events,* Chodorov reworked this pamphlet, titling it "For Our Children's Chil-dren," and called for the beginning of such a project. The article provoked quite a lot of interest, as well as a $1,000 donation from J. Howard Pew. With the help of the Foundation for Eco-

[50] F. A. Harper, "Frank Chodorov: Modern Socrates," *Fragments* (October–December 1966): 4.
[51] "A Fifty-Year Project," pp. 151, 159–60.

nomic Education, names were solicited and literature was sent to a few thousand students. The Intercollegiate Society of Individualists was formed, and within a few years over 30,000 students had received literature.

The ISI became an important part of the conservative movement in the 1950s and 1960s. And it was the high point in Chodorov's care of the Remnant:

> If there were no ISI, or something like it, the blackout of individualism would be as complete as the blackout of all culture during the Dark Ages. Future generations would indeed have to dig out of their own understanding the principle of the dignity of man, and out of bitter experience learn that the state can do no good. Those on the ISI list will probably be able to pass on to their offspring knowledge they cannot get in the classroom; that is the least gain from this effort.[52]

At the same time, Chodorov was losing favor with the now well established conservative movement. His brand of uncompromising individualism, isolationism, and free market economics was often too extreme for this adolescent movement. Chodorov himself was losing patience with the inability of these new conservatives to stick to the important principles. A movement that he had done so much to nurture, protect, and teach was becoming less and less to his liking. In a moment of exasperation he quipped, "As for me, I will punch anyone who calls me a conservative in the nose. I am a radical."[53]

THE LAST YEARS

From 1955 to 1961 Chodorov was tied to no single project. He was 68 in 1955, and those years were taking their toll. Still, he continued to write, lecture, and work on the ISI. He received

---

[52] Chodorov, "Lest It Be Forgotten," *Human Events,* August 20, 1955, p. 4.

[53] Letter to *National Review,* October 6, 1956, p. 23.

a grant from the Volker Fund to write his "autobiography," *Out of Step*. And he was close to William F. Buckley, writing as a gadfly associate editor for *National Review*. From 1957 to 1961 he went each year to teach at the Freedom School in Colorado. While there in 1961, he suffered a massive stroke that effectively ended his career. As Robert LeFevre recalled, "I have always thought that the most difficult thing Frank ever did was in that crowning effort—actually to quit. He went down fighting."[54]

The next five years were very limited ones for him. He had trouble reading and writing, and spent most of that period in a nursing home. Friends visited him. And *Fragments* magazine, almost a testament to Chodorov, was begun by a coterie of Georgist friends. On December 28, 1966, Frank Chodorov died at the age of 79.

Through his many years of writing, lecturing, and just plain talking with people, Chodorov had had his say:

> The only "constructive" idea that I can in all conscience advance, then, is that the individual put his trust in himself, not in power; that he seek to better his understanding and lift his values to a higher and still higher level; that he assume responsibility for his behavior and not shift his responsibility to committees, organizations, and, above all, a superpersonal state. Such reforms as are necessary will come of themselves when, or if, men act as intelligent and responsible human beings. There cannot be a "good" society until there are "good" men.[55]

From his work and example, we trust there are new generations of the Remnant.

Lloyd Neck, New York
November, 1978

---

[54] Robert LeFevre, "Frank Chodorov, Teacher," *Fragments* (October–December 1966): 9.

[55] Chodorov, untitled, *analysis* (July 1949): 1.

Fugitive Essays

FOREWORD

All the neighbors have fallen out and have got to calling one another horrid names, such as fascist and communist. Bitterness is in every heart and recrimination is the common habit. Under the circumstances, nobody takes time to examine the epithets hurled about, to consider their meaning or to judge their fitness. What is a fascist? What is a communist? Maybe the two are pups of the same litter, slightly different in their coloring but of the same species. No matter. As invectives they serve to divide the people into hostile camps, which seems to be the prime social purpose. It has come to the point where neutrality is inconceivable, where one who presumes to say "a plague o' both your houses" is suspect, either as to his integrity or as to his sanity.

The bitterness, as usual, follows from frustration and misunderstanding. All his life man has sought peace and prosperity. To attain that purpose he has tested one political formula after another. Each in turn has denied its promise, each bringing war and accentuating the struggle for existence, in spite of man's

---

Frank Chodorov wrote this foreword for a collection of essays he had put together. That collection was never published, and this foreword is published for the first time.

ingenuity in producing an abundance of things to live by. The
last war, bigger and more brutal than any that has gone before,
ends with but the promise of another of still greater intensity;
meanwhile, hunger stalks the world. Is this roundelay of misfortune the inevitable lot of man?

Those who call themselves, or are called, communists offer
a way out: "abolish capitalism." How? Although they will not
say so, their method is but a verbal variation of the ancient
political formula of absolutism. The danger of this is pointed
out by others, thereby automatically falling into the "fascist"
category, whose plea is to "save capitalism"; and when the
method of saving capitalism is examined, it turns out to be the
vague political scheme known as democracy, which has been
well tried and found wanting.

And here comes still another book, urging that we "try capitalism." The author, resting his case on an economic definition
of a term which is essentially economic, asserts that what has
gone by that name is not capitalism at all. If we take the trouble
to understand what capitalism is and so shape our social institutions that they will conform to this economic idea, we will
come out on top. But, he maintains, politics must be kept out.
It is not the business of politics to engage in the economic
affairs of man; its field is negative, keeping the peace, protecting life and property, meting out justice. That's all. In the
common purpose of making a living, politics is worse than a
nuisance; its intrusion must result in injustice, for, since its sole
characteristic is coercion, it is incapable of adding anything to
the economic well-being of man, and its coercive powers can
be used only to take from some and give to others. That is
injustice. This injustice, this dividing of mankind into privileged and disadvantaged classes, has always been the office of
politics, whenever it intrudes into the way men make a living,

and this is so regardless of the prevailing political form. So then, the economic maladjustments which cause friction between people cannot be corrected by any political system; the cure is in an understanding of economic principles and in ordering our social life to accord with them.

FRANK CHODOROV

Part I

The Political Mentality

The Dogma of Our Times

W hat history will think of our times is something that only history will reveal. But, it is a good guess that it will select collectivism as the identifying characteristic of the twentieth century. For even a quick survey of the developing pattern of thought during the past fifty years shows up the dominance of one central idea: that society is a transcendent entity, something apart and greater than the sum of its parts, possessing a suprahuman character and endowed with like capacities. It operates in a field of its own, ethically and philosophically, and is guided by stars unknown to mortals. Hence, the individual, the unit of society, cannot judge it by his own limitations or apply to it standards by which he measures his own thinking and behavior. He is necessary to it, of course, but only as a replaceable part of a machine. It follows, therefore, that society, which may concern itself paternalistically with individuals, is in no way dependent on them.

In one way or another, this idea has insinuated itself into almost every branch of thought and, as ideas have a way of doing, has become institutionalized. Perhaps the most glaring

This essay first appeared in The Freeman *(June 1956) and then in a slightly different form as the introduction to* The Rise and Fall of Society.

example is the modern orientation of the philosophy of education. Many of the professionals in this field frankly assert that the primary purpose of education is not to develop the individual's capacity for learning, as was held in the past, but to prepare him for a fruitful and "happy" place in society; his inclinations must be turned away from himself, so that he can adjust himself to the mores of his age group and beyond that to the social milieu in which he will live out his life. He is not an end in himself.

Jurisprudence has come around to the same idea, holding more and more that human behavior is not a matter of personal responsibility as much as it is a reflection of the social forces working on the individual; the tendency is to shift onto society the blame for crimes committed by its members. This, too, is a tenet of sociology, the increasing popularity of which, and its elevation to a science, attest to the hold collectivism has on our times. The scientist is no longer honored as a bold adventurer into the unknown, in search of nature's principles, but has become a servant of society, to which he owes his training and his keep. Heroes and heroic exploits are being demoted to accidental outcroppings of mass thought and movement. The superior person, the self-starting "captain of industry," the inherent genius—these are fictions; all are but robots made by society. Economics is the study of how society makes a living, under its own techniques and prescriptions, not how individuals, in pursuit of happiness, go about the making of a living. And philosophy, or what goes by that name, has made truth itself an attribute of society.

Collectivism is more than an idea. In itself, an idea is nothing but a toy of speculation, a mental idol. Since, as the myth holds, the suprapersonal society is replete with possibilities, the profitable thing to do is to put the myth to work, to energize its virtue. The instrument at hand is the state, throbbing with political energy and quite willing to expend it on this glorious adventure.

Statism is not a modern invention. Even before Plato, political philosophy concerned itself with the nature, origin, and justification of the state. But, while the thinkers speculated on it, the general public accepted political authority as a fact to be lived with and let it go at that. It is only within recent times (except, perhaps, during periods when church and state were one, thus endowing political coercion with divine sanction) that the mass of people has consciously or implicitly accepted the Hegelian dictum that "the state is the general substance, whereof individuals are but the accidents." It is this acceptance of the state as "substance," as a suprapersonal reality, and its investment with a competence no individual can lay claim to, that is the special characteristic of the twentieth century.

In times past, the disposition was to look upon the state as something one had to reckon with, but as a complete outsider. One got along with the state as best one could, feared or admired it, hoped to be taken in by it and to enjoy its perquisites, or held it at arm's length as an untouchable thing; one hardly thought of the state as the integral of society. One had to support the state—there was no way of avoiding taxes—and one tolerated its interventions as interventions, not as the warp and woof of life. And the state itself was proud of its position apart from, and above, society.

The present disposition is to liquidate any distinction between state and society, conceptually or institutionally. The state *is* society; the social order is indeed an appendage of the political establishment, depending on it for sustenance, health, education, communications, and all things coming under the head of "the pursuit of happiness." In theory, taking college textbooks on economics and political science for authority, the integration is about as complete as words can make it. In the operation of human affairs, despite the fact that lip service is rendered to the concept of inherent personal rights, the tendency to call upon the state for the solution of all the problems of life shows how far we have abandoned the doctrine of rights, with its correlative of self-reliance, and have accepted the state as the reality of society. It is this actual integration, rather than the theory, that marks the twentieth century off from its predecessors.

One indication of how far the integration has gone is the disappearance of any discussion of the state as state—a discussion that engaged the best minds of the eighteenth and nineteenth centuries. The inadequacies of a particular regime, or its personnel, are under constant attack, but there is no faultfinding with the institution itself. The state is all right, by common agreement, and it would work perfectly if the "right" people were at its helm. It does not occur to most critics of the New Deal that all its deficiencies are inherent in any state, under anybody's guidance, or that when the political establishment garners enough power a demagogue will sprout. The idea that this power apparatus is indeed the enemy of society, that the interests of these institutions are in opposition, is simply unthinkable. If it is brought up, it is dismissed as "old-fashioned," which it is; until the modern era, it was an axiom that the state bears constant watching, that pernicious proclivities are built into it.

A few illustrations of the temper of our times come to mind.

The oft-used statement that "we owe it to ourselves," in relation to the debts incurred in the name of the state, is indicative of the tendency to obliterate from our consciousness the line of demarcation between governed and governors. It not only is a stock phrase in economics textbooks, but is tacitly accepted in many financial circles as sound in principle. To many modern bankers a government bond is at least as sound as an obligation of a private citizen, since the bond is in fact an obligation of the citizen to pay taxes. Those bankers make no distinction between a debt backed by production or productive ability and a debt secured by political power; in the final analysis a government bond is a lien on production, so what's the difference? By such reasoning, the interests of the public, which are always centered in the production of goods, are equated with the predatory interests of the state.

In many economics textbooks, government borrowing from citizens, whether done openly or by pressure brought upon the banks to lend their depositors' savings, is explained as a transaction equivalent to the transfer of money from one pocket to another, of the *same pants;* the citizen lends to himself what he lends to the government. The rationale of this absurdity is that the effect on the nation's economy is the same whether the citizen spends his money or the government does it for him. He has simply given up his negligible right of choice. The fact that he has no desire for what the government spends his money on, that he would not of his own free will contribute to the buying of it, is blithely overlooked. The "same pants" notion rests on the identification of the amorphous "national economy" with the well-being of the individual; he is thus merged into the mass and loses his personality.

Of a piece with this kind of thinking is a companion phrase, "We are the government." Its use and acceptance are most illustrative of the hold collectivism has taken on the Amercian mind in this century, to the exclusion of the basic American

tradition. When the Union was founded, the overriding fear of
Americans was that the new government might become a threat
to their freedom, and the framers of the Constitution were hard
put to allay this fear. Now it is held that freedom is a gift from
government in return for subservience. The reversal has been
accomplished by a neat trick in semantics. The word "democracy" is the key to this trick. When one looks for a definition
of this word, one finds that it is not a clearly defined form of
government but rather the rule by "social attitudes." But, what
is a "social attitude"? Putting aside the wordy explanations of
this slippery concept, it turns out to be in practice good old
majoritarianism; what fifty-one percent of the people deem
right is right, and the minority is perforce wrong. It is the
general-will fiction under a new name. There is no place in this
concept for the doctrine of inherent rights; the only right left
to the minority, even the minority of one, is conformity with
the dominant "social attitude."

If "we are the government," then it follows that the man
who finds himself in jail must blame himself for his plight, and
the man who takes all the tax deduction the law allows is really
cheating himself. While this may seem to be a farfetched *reductio ad absurdum,* the fact is that many a conscript consoles
himself with that kind of logic. This country was largely pop-
ulated by escapees from conscription—called "czarism" a generation or two ago, and held to be the lowest form of involuntary
servitude. Now it has come to pass that a conscript army is in
fact a "democratic" army, composed of men who have made
adjustment with the "social attitude" of the times. So does the
run-of-the-mill draftee console himself when compelled to in-
terrupt his dream of a career. Acceptance of compulsory military service has reached the point of unconscious resignation

of personality. The individual, as individual, simply does not exist; he is of the mass.

This is the fulfillment of statism. It is a state of mind that does not recognize any ego but that of the collective. For analogy one must go to the pagan practice of human sacrifice: when the gods called for it, when the medicine man so insisted, as a condition for prospering the clan, it was incumbent on the individual to throw himself into the sacrificial fire. In point of fact, statism is a form of paganism, for it is worship of an idol, something made by man. Its base is pure dogma. Like all dogmas this one is subject to interpretations and rationales, each with its coterie of devotees. But, whether one calls himself a communist, socialist, New Dealer, or just plain "democrat," each begins with the premise that the individual is of consequence only as a servant of the mass-idol. Its will be done.

There are stalwart souls, even in this twentieth century. There are some who in the privacy of their personality hold that collectivism is a denial of a higher order of things. There are nonconformists who reject the Hegelian notion that "the state incarnates the divine idea on earth." There are some who firmly maintain that only man is made in the image of God. As this remnant—these individuals—gains understanding and improves its explanations, the myth that happiness is to be found under collective authority must fade away in the light of liberty.

Washington: A Psychosis

Psychology could do the country a valuable service by making a thoroughgoing analysis of the political mind. It should be done. Much of the confusion that bedevils the social body stems from the assumption that its frame of thought, its way of thinking, is identical with that of the political world, whereas even superficial observation shows that the political mind runs on tracks of its own. It is *sui generis*.

Just by way of analogy, and with no intent to be insidious, psychology recognizes the distinctive makeup of the criminal mind; it has complexes all its own, and criminal behavior is explained within the context of those complexes. In the same way, if the operations of the political mentality were clearly defined, the confusing incongruities of political behavior would fall into a meaningful pattern. It would be like opening the window of a room filled with foul air to be able to say: "What else can you expect from the political mind?"

The matter is of utmost importance at this time. Political thought is fast crowding out all other patterns, so that if it is not scientifically set apart it might cause a general mental un-

This piece appeared in Human Events *(April 11, 1951).*

balance. A community infested with gangsterism must take on the character of its dominant group, for, like Gresham's law, decadent values tend to push out of circulation the values that call for integrity. So, as the area of private life is more and more constricted by political pressures, and we are compelled by necessity to adjust ourselves to the political mentality, it is entirely possible that its pattern may supersede what we still call common sense. Assuming that political psychology is essentially an aberration, it is not inconceivable that we may all go insane and not know it.

That the politician must have an indigenous mental arrangement follows from the fact that his way of getting on in life is different from that of any other human. The impact of one's livelihood on one's psyche cannot be discounted. The bellhop in Waterloo, Iowa, will make conversation as all other bellhops do by remarking on the miserable weather; but this one will add: "It's good for the crops." In Detroit, the impending strike is the obbligato to all thought, and even the cigar-store clerk in Wall Street is conscious of Dow-Jones averages. In Washington—but we will leave that until we have explored the basic idea, that whatever circumstance determines our livelihood determines our thinking.

In that respect, the thief (used merely for illustrative purposes) is no different from any other human. The premises of his thinking may have been distorted by a phobia, but from there on his mind works as his business demands. He lives by breaking the law; his values are shaped accordingly. He cannot conceive, for instance, of a self-contained right of property. The idea is nonsensical, because experience tells him that the only inviolable property is that which cannot be got to.

To be sure, the criminal, because he has to live with himself, covers his business with an ethical cloak. He contends (like Karl Marx) that the robbery he is condemned for is common practice in all legitimate business; making a profit is only legalized thievery. Even in the matter of apprehension and punishment he finds comparison between his and legitimate business; in the latter, risks are covered by insurance, and he covers the risk of his trade by buying "protection" from complacent officials and by hiring devious legal talent. His thinking is shaped by his livelihood.

What we call the "normal" pattern of thought is so only because it is the pattern of the majority—those who live by producing goods and services. Its "principles" are made necessary by the operation of the marketplace. The merchant, the doctor, the shoemaker all have a common objective, that of satisfying the need for their services, and all their thinking is shaped by the exigencies of trade. They fall in line with community customs because that way lies acceptance of their services. The fixation of acceptance is so strong in the marketplace psychology that when an individual breaks from it he is judged abnormal; he needs "adjustment." And the values that attain top rating in the productive world—honesty, dependability, thrift, and so on—got there only because without them this world would fall apart.

We come now to the politician. He is not a criminal, by definition. Nor is he a producer, even though the textbooks on political science go to great lengths to give him credit for aiding production; their insistence on this point is indirect admission of his incapacity to contribute a single economic "good" to the marketplace. So then, if he is neither a criminal nor a producer, his mental processes must be different from both and we must look to the manner of his living for a clue.

The politician lives by taxes. It is not that his personal emoluments are derived from levies on production, but that the entire world in which he moves and finds spiritual comfort is so supported. That is more important than his livelihood, which he could, in a pinch, dig out of the marketplace. But, were taxes miraculously to be abolished, the whole political world would collapse, taking his thought pattern with it. He would most certainly suffer a mental unbalance.

Hence, taxation is of necessity a fixation in the political psyche. Yet, like all mental rigidities, it came by way of a rationalization. The institution of taxation rests foursquare on the axiom that somebody must rule somebody else. Were the notion to get around that people could manage without political power, it would be hard to make out a case for taxes. Therefore, uppermost in the thought pattern of the political cosmos is the doctrine of power. The idea of letting people alone is as far from political thinking as letting property alone is from criminal thinking. (Isn't taxation also a denial of private property?)

Now, political power is nothing but the capacity to impose one will on another, so as to bring about behavior that would not otherwise occur. The consequence of exercising such power is to inflate the ego of the one in whom it is vested. The more power the politician wields, the greater his self-esteem—and the more readily does he justify a widening of his area of power and the consequential increase in taxes. The environment he lives in compels him to think that way.

Much of the criticism of the politician stems from a misconception of the nature of his business. The principles that obtain in the social world, the one built on production, cannot apply to a world that has no interest in production, except to tax it; that world must have its own rules. Politics is, in the best sense of the word, unprincipled; it is concerned only with rulership, and experience has shown that in that trade the only valid rule of thought and behavior is expediency.

That is the clue for the suggested psychological study. Of course, the scientist would hardly be satisfied with such generalities, but would dig for the taproots of political behavior in specific cases. He would then find that there are politicians and politicians. As an instance of the differentials in the political personality pattern, it might be mentioned that Senator Truman presents a case quite different from that of President Truman. For intensified investigation, our psychologist would do well to come to Washington.

There he will find a laboratory made to order: the inevitable cocktail party. This institution plays a far more important part in Washington life than mere sociability, for it is the hatchery of much that affects the business of the nation.

Let us suppose that at one party he meets, among others, the two principal types of politician, the bureaucrat and the congressman. Present will surely be several newspapermen; they attend because they expect to pick up the thread to a headline, and they are invited because of their potential for publicity. The distaff side, being the bulk of the population, will be well represented. All present will show evidences of political-thought infection.

Although the conversation will be marked with trivialities, the investigator will quickly detect a tacit understanding; namely, that Washington is the cement that holds the country together. If our psychologist should suggest that the ordinary folk might rub along without Washington, that the legitimate functions of government could be conducted in a medium-size office building, he would freeze the assemblage into speechlessness. The mind channeled into the political pattern cannot comprehend a world without politics. The psychologist had better not advance the idea until the party is about to break up.

In the meantime, he might observe the marked difference between the demeanor of the congressman and that of the bureaucrat. The latter will display a greater sense of self-assurance; he will be soft and sanguine; he will talk with an *ex cathedra* air that only a bureaucrat can affect. And that will be so even if his job is only to take charge of the inkwells on the fourth floor of the State Department. The congressman, on the other hand, will be less sanguine but more assertive. He will display an urgency to convince and to please, characteristic of the marketplace psychology. He will show a sense of obligation and responsibility totally absent from the bureaucrat's psyche.

Perhaps the difference between the elected representative and the scion of the executive branch can be explained by the difference in tenure. The congressman is rooted in his constituency, whereas the bureaucrat has only a bureaucrat to please.

One further hint and the psychologist must go it alone. He should not overlook the barber and the taxi driver. They too will reflect the political psychology, so all-pervasive in this voteless city that one suspects it is not so much a place as a psychosis.

Washington,
the American Mecca

It's June in Washington. It's June all over the country, of
course, but to the capital city the month has special significance. It inaugurates the annual trek of gaping sightseers from
all over the country to this American mecca.

Soon the vacationing schoolteachers will be ah-ing and oh-
ing before the wondrous temples of government, while prize-
winning high school students will pay their worshipful respects
to the pompous dignitaries and official hirelings who carry on
the affairs of state. Honeymooning couples, already taking one
another for granted, will transfer their admiration and adoration
to the indicia of political power, while farmers, satiated with
the wonders of nature in their native habitats, will be propi-
tiating the gods of government in their air-conditioned apses.
In summer, it is the proper thing for Americans to come to
Washington and view with awe.

If you were to ask these visitors, they would tell you that
they came here only to admire the beauty of the town. And, to
be fair, this is a beautiful town. Why shouldn't it be? It is like
a harlot who never soils her hands with useful work, and whose

---

"Washington, the American Mecca" was one of Chodorov's articles in Human
Events *(June 16, 1954).*

only occupation, outside of harlotry, is to preen and primp—at the expense of her admirers. Washington is, and ought to be, the most beautiful city in the country; it is also the most useless.

Putting aside the aesthetic thrill which these gapers get out of the visit, they cannot but carry away with them an overpowering impression of the glory and grandeur of the government domiciled here. It must be a wondrous government that operates in this wondrous environment. And when they get back home they will tell of the invigorating, almost healing, experience of having seen the anointed and brushed the robes of greatness; even as did those who in ancient times visited Rome. They will have visited the holy of holies. And all their lives thereafter they will tell, and magnify the tale, of their almost sacred pilgrimage.

By the easy processes of the simple mind, this adoration of the domes and the masonry and the statuary will spill over to the denizens of the city—to the Pharisees and Sadducees who are integrated with the monumentalization of government. They are the bureaucrats, the truly blessed. To see them in their charmed cubicles, deeply immersed in papers, is to realize that they are different from the ordinary run of mortals, and that the difference is one not of degree but of kind. One reads sometimes of a bureaucrat who has fallen from grace, by taking a bribe or surreptitiously letting a foreign nation in on official secrets. But, a single transgression does not disprove the infallibility of the class.

There are elected officials here too, but the aura that surrounds them is not comparable with that which surrounds the bureaucrats. The former must descend from the clouds at election time and simulate the life of ordinary men. The bureaucrat always stands aloof. He is a special person, educated and trained for the priesthood, and his adeptness with the exotic rituals of government sets him off from the rest of mankind. He wields power without benefit of votes. He is anonymous, ubiquitous, indispensable. And, in a way, he enjoys immortality; administrations and congressmen come and go, but the bureaucracy goes on forever. It is the soul of that superperson called government.

The summer pilgrims who come to Washington ostensibly to see, but not unprepared to worship, are aided in their devotions by the droning guides. Perhaps it is only by dint of constant repetition, but it is a fact that these carefully trained expositors of the wonders of the national shrine develop an intonation strongly reminiscent of the ritualistic Sunday sermon. Every bit of monumentalized government is described with reverence. Stress is laid on the tradition, the historical significance, the inner meaning of each piece of stonework, until the weary minds and legs of the pilgrims are left limp with adoration, and are willing to settle on a religious acceptance of the whole thing.

There must be a purpose in all this architectural pageantry, this careful manicuring of parks and the elaborate horticulture, a purpose quite unrelated to mere aestheticism. And, judging by results, the purpose must be like unto that of the stained-glass windows and the gargoyles that adorn cathedrals: to bring the visitor into spiritual consonance with his surroundings. It is a religious purpose. This is the place where the great god government performs its miracles, this is where the "general welfare" is attended to. Here the demigods plan and direct the destinies of one hundred and sixty million mortals, here the souls of the well-taxed flock are prepared for a heaven on earth.

Politically speaking, it is good business to glamorize and glorify this modern Jerusalem. For, it is a certainty that only a fraction of the would-be worshippers get to Washington each year; and it is a certainty that each one who does partake of the religiosity of political power becomes a missionary to the folks back home. Thus, the country is made conscious of the fact that the government is great, good, glorious, and superhuman.

The debunking of Washington is the great need of the country. It is a colossal job, seeing that billions are spent each year for the specific purpose of deifying political power. But, it is a job that ought to commend itself to the young writer looking for a rather virgin field to work in. It will require the satirical skill of a Stephen Leacock, the epigrammatic ingenuity of a Charles Graham Sumner, the classical incisiveness of an Albert Jay Nock. Perhaps a Gilbert and Sullivan would be most effective.

The job should be approached from a basic premise, namely, that all the legitimate functions of the national government could be carried on, as someone has said, "in a good-sized kitchen"; surely, in not over one-tenth the floor space now occupied, and with one-tenth the present personnel. That means the country would have to be instructed in the proper functions of government—the functions for which it is designed and in which it has some competence: briefly, the dispensation of justice, cheaply, and the maintenance of order. When it goes beyond these limits, government becomes a harmful intruder into the affairs of men. There is nothing the government can do that free men cannot do better.

With that as a starting point, the debunking can proceed with ease. It can be shown that the only thing government can do when it goes beyond bounds is to confiscate private property; it cannot produce anything. Its excuse for confiscation is always that it distributes the proceeds among the "deserving poor";

the fact is that most of what it takes it keeps and spends on itself. There is no justice in that. Oh yes, it can give special privileges to certain citizens at the expense of others, which is a flagrant injustice, and when it does so its purpose is to gain support from those thus advantaged. It buys power with other people's money.

Practically speaking, the acquisition of political power is in proportion to the acquisition of economic power. Policemen (including bureaucrats) have to be paid. So, then, the power of government is dependent on the taxes it collects. The more dollars the government has to do with, the more it will do. Conversely, when the people keep their dollars, the more independent they are of the interloping government. The government, being expert in these things, is well aware of the relation of the freedom of the people to their opulence, as well as the relation of its own power to their proverty, and therefore is bent on depriving them of their dollars. It is as simple as that.

Now comes the crux of the debunking formula: What is government? It is a body of people—just ordinary mortals— whose primary purpose is to get on in life with the least possible exertion. Wielding power seems to them the way to accomplish this purpose. In that way, they are relieved of the stress and strain of the competitive world; and there is the added ego compensation which the exercise of power yields. The effect of this ego pay can be detected in the manner of even the lowliest in government service, such as post office clerks and receptionists.

This last point, that government consists of people—just ordinary mortals—who have gotten hold of power, and nothing else, needs to be widely advertised. Apologists of power like to hide that fact in the fiction that government is a superentity quite independent of its component parts, and that it has a soul of its own and a capacity for giving things which ordinary people do not have. It is a golden calf needing only worship. If people can be got to accept that paganism—that is what the annual trek to Washington is expected to do—then it is easy to put over on them any skulduggery that these mediocrities can think of.

Yes, mediocrities. There is nothing that more impresses the critical observer in Washington than the low mental level of those who presume to manage our destinies. This should not be a startling revelation; it stands to reason that a man of ability would hardly be content to bury himself in a dust-gathering pigeonhole of government. He is there simply because he is afraid of the marketplace; he is there because his nature inclines him to seek the comfort and security of his prenatal state. This should be brought out. A series of candid delineations of these personalities, sometimes called profiles, would go a long way toward cutting these self-styled demigods to size.

A debunking "movement" would be helpful. But, it needs hardly to be organized or fomented, for it would spring up automatically from a general realization that government consists of a lot of small-timers who have, by hook or crook, got hold of power and are intent on increasing their power. The development of a suspicious attitude toward all people in government would suggest the use of social ostracism as a means of keeping them in line, and that would be "movement" enough.

Suppose people were regularly to shut off their radios when a politician is on the air. Suppose they would assiduously stay away from meetings addressed by a "distinguished" personage, or, better still, would "sit on their hands" and titter at his inanities. The ego pay would be gone. Their balloons would be deflated. And those who had any ability, and some self-respect, would get out of government and start making an honest living. That would be good for society.

There is no way of keeping government within bounds but by the whip of public opinion, not that expressed at the polls, but in the arena of private life. Social ostracism, or the fear of it, would go a long way toward restraining the yen for power. If the threat were held over the politician that transgression would be met with a lack of invitations to decent people's homes, government would be clean.

If the suggestion seems farfetched, consider the conduct of village or county government. These small-town officials are of the same breed as that which infests Washington—in fact, they are no different from the ordinary run of people, equally susceptible to temptation; but they do toe the line of decency more often than do their Washington brethren. This is so not because they do not have as much to do with, in the way of taxes and power, but because their neighbors' opinion breathes hot on their necks. If the Washington official were in similar fear of social ostracism, he too might be of some service to the country.

Yes, the affairs of state would be vastly improved if the people stopped worshipping Washington. The great need of the nation is the debunking of government.

Remember Robespierre

It is agreed that you have the perfect plan—the final blueprint for the good society. It is all there; truth and justice perfectly balanced, and both supported by fundamental economics. All the parts are reinforced with natural rights. The beacon light of freedom is nicely placed at the pinnacle.

The perfect plan stands up, deductively and inductively. Your facts and figures are as irrefutable as your logic, and your charts and diagrams are most elucidating. One cannot help giving it a clean bill of health, and with enthusiasm. If it prevailed, if people were to order their affairs in accordance with the perfect plan, there is no question but that the long-sought-for good society would blossom in all its glory; no more poverty, no more war, and disharmony would vanish from this earth.

Your only job, then, is to familiarize folks with the perfect plan; its adoption must follow from a recognition of its merits. But, in this educational project you find yourself outside the field of pure thought, where you are in complete control, and must deal with people, with will and desire and prejudice and mental limitations. The people are either unwilling to consider

This was the lead article in the February 1947 issue of analysis.

the goodness you offer them, gratis, or incapable of comprehending it, and you find progress exceedingly slow. You are also confronted with opposition from vested thought. What to do now? Perhaps it would be wise to give up on the hope of participating in the millennium; the very perfection of the perfect plan is an assurance that it will keep, that in the fullness of time it will come into its own. On the other hand, you might attempt to shortcut the difficulties of education by the political method. On the theory that the end justifies the means, you might seek power to impose the perfect plan.

THE YEARNING TO GOVERN

The yearning to govern, the desire for power over others, is a most perplexing human trait. Only when it is spurred by an economic purpose does it make sense. When a man seeks political position for the betterment of his circumstances he is acting sanely, if sanity is defined as normal behavior. We call a politician corrupt when he uses his power for self-aggrandizement, but that is because we clothe politics with a fanciful myth of supernaturalness. We have but to remember man's natural tendency to satisfy his desires with the minimum of effort to realize how political power will be utilized. We call a politician corrupt when he accomplishes what we are all inclined to do, and that seems to be a perversion of values. It would be more correct to say that we are all corrupt and that the politician is merely successful.

However, the craving for power cannot always be explained in the rational terms of profit. The boy wants to be captain, not for the honorary content of the title, but because it invests him with the right to lord it over his teammates. With most fathers, governing the household is both a prerogative and a pleasure, while every wife's happiness is in proportion to the dominance she attains, by subtle means or above-board, over her husband. Few men are so rich but that a little more power over their fellow men does not flatter their egos, and no man who can command subservience deems himself poor. It would seem so much more sensible to let people alone; the exercise of power in and for itself is a thoroughly useless expenditure of effort. And most irrational of all is the desire to govern others "for their own good"—the excuse of reformers and, as history shows, the cause of great harm to reformers, reformees, and the reform.

The case of Maximilien Robespierre is most illustrative.

"THE INCORRUPTIBLE" CORRUPTED

Jean Jacques Rousseau sparked the desire to govern in many a young man of his revolutionary day. His "Rights of Man" gave the craving for political power divine sanction, while his economic, religious, and social doctrines gave it direction. Just as Marxist shibboleths turn many a noble young man toward ward-heeling and rabble-rousing and political skulduggery in general, so did the well-turned phrases of Rousseau divert promising minds from productive pursuits. One of these was Robespierre, whose first love was literature, and who gave promise of doing something in that line. The desire to do good turned into the desire for power to do good, and so he did no good at all.

The career of Robespierre is highlighted by two uncommon political experiences. First, though he rose to dictatorial power, he never used his position for his material advantage, and lived frugally all his life. Largely because of his scrupulousness in that regard he was called "the Incorruptible." Many of his bitter fights with other leaders of the Revolution centered around the fact that they acted as rational politicians, even to the point of accepting bribes from the nation's enemies. The second Robespierrist oddity is that though he protested loyalty to the ideals of Rousseau throughout his political life, he nevertheless deliberately, and with qualms of conscience, compromised these ideals when practical politics made it necessary. Thus we see that even when a politician shuns the economic possibilities of his position, even when he tries to keep faith with the ideal which first led him to seek political power, he must fail in promoting it. That is because the business of politics does not deal in ideals.

A cardinal tenet of the Rousseau creed is the inviolable right to life; therefore capital punishment is untenable. Yet, when Louis was brought to trial, Robespierre voted for the death penalty, and was impelled by his conscience publicly to proclaim the reason for this about-face. Freedom of speech and freedom of the press were sacred to Robespierre, because they were sacred to Rousseau; though he would brook no laws of suppression, he found the guillotine equally effective. When the "higher law" of the Revolution made it necessary, he suspended his democratic faith long enough to have the National Assembly arrested and some elected representatives of the people decapitated. He opposed war and waged it. And so, though Robespierre has been called "Rousseau in power," the fact is that whenever Robespierre found Rousseau an encumbrance, as he often did, he found reason enough to put him aside.

Other cases of the perversion of principle in politics are not wanting; the case of Robespierre is striking because, unlike most politicians, he seems to have been schizophrenic about it. We need not dwell on the American habit of scrapping platform promises immediately after election, for we have learned to put these promises on a par with those of a lady on the make. One would hardly have expected that sort of thing from Ramsay Macdonald, who put in a lifetime developing the ideology of the British Labour Party; yet he scuttled the whole thing, some say for "a ribbon and some pieces of silver," when he became its first prime minister. As every other socialist knows, every socialist who ever wielded a scepter whittled away some of the sacredness of Marxist principle; to millions of that creed Stalin is a Benedict Arnold, while Attlee is lower in morality than even a capitalist. It would be refreshing to learn of one case in political history in which the power sought to promote an ideal was consistently exercised in that direction.

PROMISE AND PERFORMANCE

The contradiction between political promise and performance is quite understandable when we dig into the nature of the business, breaking through the moral crust with which political institutions have surrounded themselves. When we look to beginnings we see clearly what it is all about, for then the purpose of political power was unencumbered with persiflage; the ruler and his henchman looted without ritual. Under constitutionalism the power is diffused and so is the profit; the object of administrators is to keep a balance between economic groups, leaning toward the more opulent and more powerful, for that way their own bread is buttered. Universal suffrage and representative government obscure but do not mutate the character of politics. Here the power is spread thin, and the practical art of politics consists in canalizing it for effective exploitation. Moral principle plays no part in this art, except as a ruse for enticing the miniscule pieces of power which the voters hold. Even then moral principle is mere garnishment, for the candidate relies more on his promise of "better times," fully aware that the prime motivation of the voter is economic, not moral. This conflict between economic interests, between pressure groups, continues throughout the politician's regime, and must always be his main concern; expediency (or "realism") takes precedence over principle as a matter of necessity. The first lesson the crusader in office must learn is that the crusade can wait; it always does.

And so, Robespierre in power was not sinful in betraying Rousseau. He was in error in assuming that a different course was possible.

THE POWER OF THOUGHT

To return to the perfect plan. If it is as perfect as you say it is, there is nothing you need do about it, for anything that is so sound will get around on its own power. Euclidian mathematics never had the benefit of a "movement," and entirely without legal blessing it made headway. The only way in which the law can affect the course of thought is to restrict, ban, and burn; the law can only be negative, never positive, in matters of the mind. If you look over the record of "the best that has been thought and said in the world," you will find that politics was helpful only when it got out of the way. So, if you would protect the perfect plan from pollution, your course is clearly indicated; keep it out of politics.

You will be surprised to learn, once you have decided not to politicalize it, that the perfect plan is not so perfect after all. When you were preparing it for the public arena you tactically reduced it to terms comprehensible to the lowest electoral intellect; also, for practical purposes you glossed over its deficiencies. When, however, you take it back to your private den and look it over calmly, you discover its shortcomings and go to work on them. In that you benefit yourself. It is through study and reflection that the individual puts by a profit.

The technique of perfecting an idea calls for discussion. And so you call into consultation the intellectually curious, minds which, like yours, find satisfaction in striving for an unattainable ideal. You teach and are taught. Everybody profits and, somehow, the perfect plan becomes more perfect in the getting around. Millions of years elapsed before the original wheel turned out to be an automobile, but think of the fun the countless generations had in the developing process. In like manner, that which you call the perfect plan will ultimately come into its own, maybe different in details and surely much more perfect than your present conception. You won't be here to see it in operation? What of it? You had your fun promoting the idea and should be thankful for that.

But if you insist on taking the perfect plan into politics, though it will do no good, I offer the following admonition: Remember Robespierre.

Part II

Natural Rights and Unnatural Wrongs

Source of Rights

The axiom of what is often called "individualism" is that every person has certain inalienable rights. For example, individualism holds that property *as such* obviously has no rights; there is only the inherent right of a person to his honestly acquired property . . .

The axiom of socialism is that the individual has no inherent rights. The privileges and prerogatives that the individual enjoys are grants from society, acting through its management committee, the government. That is the condition the individual must accept for the benefit of being a member of society. Hence, the socialists (including many who do not so name themselves) reject the statement of rights in the Declaration of Independence, calling it a fiction of the eighteenth century.

In support of his denial of natural rights, the socialist points out that there is no positive proof in favor of that doctrine. Where is the documentary evidence? Did God hand man a signed statement endowing him with the rights he claims for himself, but denies to the birds and beasts who also inhabit the

This article comes from chapter three of The Income Tax: Root of All Evil. *It is reprinted here as it appeared in a small pamphlet published by the Foundation for Economic Education.*

earth? If in answer to these questions you bring in the soul idea, you are right back to where you were in the beginning: How can you prove that man has a soul?

Those who accept the axiom of natural rights are backed against the wall by that kind of reasoning, until they examine the opposite axiom, that all rights are grants or loans from government. Where did government get the rights which it dispenses? If it is said that its fund of rights is collected from individuals, as the condition for their membership in society, the question arises, where did the individual get the rights which he gave up? He cannot give up what he never had in the first place, which is what the socialist maintains.

WHAT IS GOVERNMENT?

What is this thing called government, which can grant and take away rights? There are all sorts of answers to that question, but all the answers will agree on one point, that government is a social instrument enjoying a monopoly of coercion. The socialist says that the monopoly of coercion is vested in the government in order that it may bring about an ideal social and economic order; others say that the government must have a monopoly of coercion in order to prevent individuals from using coercion on one another. In short, the essential characteristic of government is power. If, then, we say that our rights stem from government, on a loan basis, we admit that whoever gets control of the power vested in government is the author of rights. And simply because he has the power to enforce his will. Thus, the basic axiom of socialism, in all its forms, is that might is right.

And that means that power is all there is to morality. If I am bigger and stronger than you and you have no way of defending yourself, then it is right if I thrash you; the fact that I did thrash you is proof that I had the right to do so. On the other hand, if you can intimidate me with a gun, then right returns to your side. All of which comes to mere nonsense. And a social order based on the socialistic axiom—which makes the government the final judge of all morality—is a nonsensical society. It is a society in which the highest value is the acquisition of power— as exemplified in a Hitler or a Stalin—and the fate of those who cannot acquire it is subservience as a condition of existence.

The senselessness of the socialistic axiom is shown by the fact that there would be no society, and therefore no government, if there were no individuals. The human being is the unit of all social institutions; without a man there cannot be a crowd. Hence, we are compelled to look to the individual to find an axiom on which to build a nonsocialistic moral code. What does he tell us about himself?

DESIRE TO LIVE

In the first place, he tells us that above all things he wants to live. He tells us this even when he first comes into the world and lets out a yell. Because of that primordial desire, he maintains, he has a right to live. Certainly, nobody else can establish a valid claim to his life, and for that reason he traces his own title to an authority that transcends all men, to God. That title makes sense.

When the individual says he has a valid title to life, he means that all that is he, is his own: his body, his mind, his faculties. Maybe there is something else in life, such as a soul, but without going into that realm, he is willing to settle on what he knows about himself—his consciousness. All that is "I" is "mine." That implies, of course, that all that is "you" is "yours"—for every "you" is an "I." Rights work both ways.

But, while just wanting to live gives the individual a title to life, it is an empty title unless he can acquire the things that make life livable, beginning with food, raiment, and shelter. These things do not come to you because you want them; they come as the result of putting labor to raw materials. You have to give something of yourself—your brawn or your brain—to make the necessary things available. Even wild berries have to be picked before they can be eaten. But the energy you put out to make the necessary things is part of you; it *is* you. Therefore, when you cause these things to exist, your title to yourself, your labor, is extended to the things. You have a right to them simply because you have a right to life.

SOURCE OF GOVERNMENT

That is the moral basis of the right of property. "I own it because I made it" is a title that proves itself. The recognition of that title is implied in the statement that "I *make* so many dollars a week." That is literally true.

But what do you mean when you say you own the thing you produced? Say it is a bushel of wheat. You produced it to satisfy your desire for bread. You can grind the wheat into flour, bake the loaf of bread, eat it, or share it with your family or a friend. Or you can give part of the wheat to the miller in payment for his labor; the part you give him, in the form of wages, is his because he gave you labor in exchange. Or you sell half the bushel of wheat for money, which you exchange for butter to go with the bread. Or you put the money in the bank so that you can have something else later on, when you want it.

In other words, your ownership entitles you to use your

judgment as to what you will do with the product of your labor—consume it, give it away, sell it, save it. Freedom of disposition is the substance of property rights.

FREEDOM OF DISPOSITION

Interference with this freedom of disposition is, in the final analysis, interference with your right to life. At least, that is your reaction to such interference, for you describe such interference with a word that expresses a deep emotion: You call it "robbery." What's more, if you find that this robbery persists, if you are regularly deprived of the fruits of your labor, you lose interest in laboring. The only reason you work is to satisfy your desires; and if experience shows that despite your efforts your desires go unsatisfied, you become stingy about laboring. You become a "poor" producer.

Suppose the freedom of disposition is taken away from you entirely. That is, you become a slave; you have no right of property. Whatever you produce is taken by somebody else; and though a good part of it is returned to you, in the way of sustenance, medical care, housing, you cannot under the law dispose of your output; if you try to, you become the legal "robber." Your concern in production wanes and you develop an attitude toward laboring that is called a slave psychology. Your interest in yourself also drops because you sense that without the right of property you are not much different from the other living things in the barn. The clergyman may tell you you are a man, with a soul; but you sense that without the right of property you are somewhat less of a man than the one who can dispose of your production as he wills. If you are a human, how human are you?

It is silly, then, to prate of human rights being superior to property rights, because the right of ownership is traceable to the right to life, which is certainly inherent in the human being. Property rights are in fact human rights.

A society built around the denial of this fact is, or must become, a slave society—although the socialists describe it differently. It is a society in which some produce and others dispose of their output. The laborer is stimulated not by the prospect of satisfying his desires but by fear of punishment. When his ownership is not interfered with, when he works for himself, he is inclined to develop his faculties of production because he has unlimited desires. He works for food, as a matter of necessity; but when he has a sufficiency of food, he begins to think of fancy dishes, a tablecloth, and music with his meals. There is no end of desires the human being can conjure up, and will work for, provided he feels reasonably sure that his labor will not be in vain. Contrariwise, when the law deprives him of the incentive of enjoyment, he will work only as necessity compels him. What use is there in putting out more effort?

Therefore, the general production of a socialistic society must decline to the point of mere subsistence.

DECLINE OF SOCIETY

The economic decline of a society without property rights is followed by the loss of other values. It is only when we have a sufficiency of necessaries that we give thought to nonmaterial things, to what is called culture. On the other hand, we find we can do without books, or even moving pictures, when existence is at stake. Even more than that, we who have no right to own certainly have no right to give, and charity becomes an empty word; in a socialistic order, no one need give thought to an unfortunate neighbor because it is the duty of the government, the only property owner, to take care of him; it might even become a crime to give a "bum" a dime. When the denial of the right of the individual is negated through the denial of ownership, the sense of personal pride, which distinguishes man from beast, must decay from disuse . . .

Whatever else socialism is, or is claimed to be, its first tenet is the denial of private property. All brands of socialism, and there are many, are agreed that property rights must be vested in the political establishment. None of the schemes identified with this ideology, such as the nationalization of industry, or socialized medicine, or the abolition of free choice, or the planned economy, can become operative if the individual's claim to his property is recognized by the government.

Economics Versus Politics

It may be that wary beasts of the forest come around to accepting the hunter's trap as a necessary concomitant of foraging for food. At any rate, the presumably rational human animal has become so inured to political interventions that he cannot think of the making of a living without them; in all his economic calculations his first consideration is, what is the law in the matter? Or, more likely, how can I make use of the law to improve my lot in life? This may be described as a conditioned reflex. It hardly occurs to us that we might do better operating under our own steam, within the limits put upon us by nature, and without political restraints, controls, or subventions. It never enters our minds that these interventionary measures are placed in our path, like the trap, for purposes diametrically opposed to our search for a better living. We automatically accept them as necessary to that purpose.

And so it has come to pass that those who write about economics begin with the assumption that it is a branch of political science. Our current textbooks, almost without exception, approach the subject from a legal standpoint: How do men make

This article comes from The Rise and Fall of Society.

a living under the prevailing laws? It follows, and some of the books admit it, that if the laws change, economics must follow suit. It is for that reason that our college curricula are loaded down with a number of courses in economics, each paying homage to the laws governing different human activities; thus we have the economics of merchandising, the economics of real-estate operations, the economics of banking, agricultural economics, and so on. That there is a science of economics which covers basic principles that operate in all our occupations, and that have nothing to do with legislation, is hardly considered. From this point of view it would be appropriate, if the law sanctioned the practice, for the curricula to include a course on the economics of slavery.

Economics is not politics. One is a science, concerned with the immutable and constant laws of nature that determine the production and distribution of wealth; the other is the art of ruling. One is amoral, the other is moral. Economic laws are self-operating and carry their own sanctions, as do all natural laws, while politics deals with man-made and man-manipulated conventions. As a science, economics seeks understanding of invariable principles; politics is ephemeral, its subject matter being the day-to-day relations of associated men. Economics, like chemistry, has nothing to do with politics.

The intrusion of politics into the field of economics is simply an evidence of human ignorance or arrogance, and is as fatuous as an attempt to control the rise and fall of tides. Since the beginning of political institutions, there have been attempts to fix wages, control prices, and create capital, all resulting in failure. Such undertakings must fail because the only competence of politics is in compelling men to do what they do not want to do or to refrain from doing what they are inclined to do, and the laws of economics do not come within that scope. They are impervious to coercion. Wages and prices and capital accumulations have laws of their own, laws which are beyond the purview of the policeman.

The assumption that economics is subservient to politics stems from a logical fallacy. Since the state (the machinery of politics) can and does control human behavior, and since men are always engaged in the making of a living, in which the laws of economics operate, it seems to follow that in controlling men the state can also bend these laws to its will. The reasoning is erroneous because it overlooks consequences. It is an invariable principle that men labor in order to satisfy their desires, or that the motive power of production is the prospect of consumption; in fact, a thing is not produced until it reaches the consumer. Hence, when the state intervenes in the economy, which it always does by way of confiscation, it hinders consumption and therefore production. The output of the producer is in proportion to his intake. It is not willfulness that brings about this result; it is the working of an immutable natural law. The slave does not consciously "lay down on the job"; he is a poor producer because he is a poor consumer.

The evidence is that economics influences the character of politics, instead of the other way around. A communist state (which undertakes to disregard the laws of economics, as if they did not exist) is characterized by its preoccupation with force; it is a fear state. The aristocratic Greek city-state took its shape from the institution of slavery. In the nineteenth century, when the state, for purposes of its own, entered into partnership with the rising industrial class, we had the mercantilist or merchant state. The welfare state is in fact an oligarchy of bureaucrats who, in return for the perquisites and prestige of office, undertake to confiscate and redistribute production according to formulas of their own imagination, with utter disregard of the principle that production must fall in the amount of the confiscation. It is interesting to note that all welfarism starts with a program of distribution—control of the marketplace with its price technique—and ends up with attempts to manage production; that is because, contrary to the expectations of welfarism, the laws of economics are not suspended by its political interference, prices do not respond to its dicta, and in an effort to make its preconceived notions work, welfarism applies itself to production, and there too it fails.

The imperviousness of economic law to political law is shown in this historic fact: in the long run every state collapses, frequently disappears altogether and becomes an archaeological curio. Every collapse of which we have sufficient evidence was preceded by the same course of events. The state, in its insatiable lust for power, increasingly intensified its encroachments on the economy of the nation, causing a consequent decline of interest in production, until at long last the subsistence level was reached and not enough above that was produced to maintain the state in the condition to which it had been accustomed. It was not economically able to meet the strain of some immediate circumstance, like war, and succumbed. Preceding that event, the economy of society, on which state power rests, had deteriorated, and with that deterioration came a letdown in moral and cultural values; men "did not care." That is, society collapsed and drew the state down with it. There is no way for the state to avoid this consequence—except, of course, to abandon its interventions in the economic life of the people it controls, which its inherent avarice for power will not let it do. There is no way for politics to protect itself from politics.

The story of the American state is instructive. Its birth was most auspicious, being midwifed by a coterie of men unusually wise in the history of political institutions and committed to the safeguarding of the infant from the mistakes of its predecessors. Apparently, none of the blemishes of tradition marked the new state. It was not burdened with the inheritance of a feudal or a caste system. It did not have to live down the doctrine of "divine right," nor was it marked with the scars of conquest that had made the childhood of other states difficult. It was fed on strong stuff: Rousseau's doctrine that government derived its powers from the consent of the governed, Voltaire's freedom of speech and thought, Locke's justification of revolution, and, above all, the doctrine of inherent rights. There was no regime of status to stunt its growth. In fact, everything was *de novo*.

Every precautionary measure known to political science was taken to prevent the new American state from acquiring the self-destructive habit of every state known to history, that of interfering with man's pursuit of happiness. The people were to be left alone, to work out their individual destinies with whatever capacities nature had endowed them. Toward that end, the state was surrounded with a number of ingenious prohibitions and limitations. Not only were its functions clearly defined, but any inclination to go beyond bounds was presumably restrained by a tripartite division of authority, while most of the interventionary powers which the state employs were reserved for the authorities closer to the governed and therefore more amenable to their will; by the divisive principle of *imperium in imperio* it was forever, presumably, deprived of the monopoly position necessary to a state on the rampage. Better yet, it was condemned to get along on a meager purse; its powers of taxation were neatly circumscribed. It did not seem possible, in 1789, for the American state to do much in the way of interfering with the economy of the nation; it was constitutionally weak and off balance.

The ink was hardly dry on the Constitution before its authors, now in position of authority, began to rewrite it by interpretation, to the end that its bonds would loosen. The yeast of power that is imbedded in the state was in fermentation. The process of judicial interpretation, continued to the present day, was later supplemented by amendment; the effect of nearly all the amendments, since the first ten (which were written into the Constitution by social pressure), was to weaken the position of the several state governments and to extend the power of the central government. Since state power can grow only at the expense of social power, the centralization which has been going on since 1789 has pushed American society into that condition of subservience which the Constitution was intended to prevent.

In 1913 came the amendment that completely unshackled the American state, for with the revenues derived from unlimited income taxation it could henceforth make unlimited forays into the economy of the people. The Sixteenth Amendment not only violated the right of the individual to the product of his efforts, the essential ingredient of freedom, but also gave the American state the means to become the nation's biggest consumer, employer, banker, manufacturer, and owner of capital. There is now no phase of economic life in which the state is not a factor, there is no enterprise or occupation free of its intervention.

The metamorphosis of the American state from an apparently harmless establishment to an interventionary machine as powerful as that of Rome at its height took place within a century and a half; the historians estimate that the gestation of the greatest state of antiquity covered four centuries; we travel faster these days. When the grandeur of Rome was at its grandest, the principal preoccupation of the state was the confiscation of the wealth produced by its citizens and subjects; the confiscation was legally formalized, as it is today, and even though it was not sugarcoated with moralisms or ideologically rationalized, some features of modern welfarism were put into practice. Rome had its make-work programs, its gratuities to the unemployed, and its subsidies to industry. These things are necessary to make confiscation palatable and possible.

To the Romans of the times, this order of things probably seemed as normal and proper as it does today. The living are condemned to live in the present, under the prevailing conditions, and their preoccupation with those conditions makes any assessment of the historic trend both difficult and academic. The Romans hardly knew or cared about the "decline" in which they were living and certainly did not worry about the "fall" to which their world was riding. It is only from the vantage point of history, when it is possible to sift the evidence and find a cause-and-effect relationship, that a meaningful estimate of what was happening can be made. We know now that despite the arrogance of the state the economic forces that bear upon social trends were on the job. The production of wealth, the things men live by, declined in proportion to the state's exactions and interferences; the general concern with mere existence submerged any latent interest in cultural and moral values, and the character of society gradually changed to that of a herd. The mills of the gods grind slowly but surely; within a couple of centuries the deterioration of Roman society was followed by the disintegration of the state, so that it had neither the means nor the will to withstand the winds of historic change. It should be noted that society, which flourishes only under a condition of freedom, collapsed first; there was no disposition to resist the invading hordes.

The analogy suggests a prophecy and a jeremiad. But that

is not within the scope of this essay, the hypothesis of which is that society, government, and the state are basically economic phenomena, that a profitable understanding of these institutions will be found in economics, not in politics. This is not to say that economics can explain all the facets of these institutions, any more than the study of his anatomy will reveal all the secrets of the human being; but, as there cannot be a human being without a skeleton, so any inquiry into the mechanism of social integrations cannot bypass economic law.

From God or the Sword?

I s the state ordered in the nature of things? The classical theorists in political science were so persuaded. Observing that
every agglomeration of humans known to history was attended
with a political institution of some kind, and convinced that in
all human affairs the hand of God played a part, they concluded
that the political organization of men enjoyed divine sanction.
They had a syllogism to support their assumption: God made
man; man made the state; therefore, God made the state. The
state acquired divinity vicariously. The reasoning was bolstered
by an analogy; it is a certainty that the family organization,
with its head, is in the natural order of things, and it follows
that a group of families, with the state acting as overall father,
is likewise a natural phenomenon. If deficiencies in the family
occur, it is because of the ignorance or wickedness of the father;
and if the social order suffers distress or disharmony it is because the state has lost sight of the ways of God. In either case,
the paterfamilias needs instruction in moral principles. That is,
the state, which is inevitable and necessary, might be improved
upon but cannot be abolished.

This article comes from The Rise and Fall of Society.

Accepting *a priori* the naturalness of the state, they sought for the taproot of the institution in the nature of man. Surely, the state appears only when men get together, and that fact would indicate that its origin is lodged in the complexity of the human being; animals have no state. This line of inquiry led to contradictions and uncertainties, as it had to because the evidence as to man's nature lies in his moral behavior and this is far from uniform. Two men will respond differently to the same exigency, and even one man will not follow a constant pattern of behavior under all circumstances. The problem which the political scientists with the theological turn of mind set for themselves was to find out whether the state owed its origin to the fact that man is inherently "good" or "bad," and on this point there is no positive evidence. Hence the contradictions in their findings.

The three thinkers along these lines with whom we are most familiar, although they had their forerunners, are Thomas Hobbes, John Locke, and Jean Jacques Rousseau. As a starting point for their speculations, the three of them made use of the same hypothesis, that there was a time when men were not politically organized and lived under conditions called a "state of nature." It was pure assumption, of course, since if men ever roamed the face of the earth as thoroughgoing isolationists, having no contact with one another except at the end of a club, they never would have left any evidence of it. There must always have been at least a family organization or we would not be here to talk about a state of nature.

At any rate, Hobbes maintained that in this prepolitical state man was "brutish" and "nasty," ever poised at the property and person of his neighbor. His predatory inclination was motivated by an overweening passion for material plenty. But, says Hobbes, man was from the beginning endowed with the gift of reason, and at some point in his "natural" state his reason told him that he could do better for himself by cooperating with his fellow "natural" man. At that point he entered into a "social contract" with him, by the terms of which each agreed to abide by an authority that would restrain him from doing what his "nature" inclined him to do. Thus came the state.

Locke, on the other hand, is rather neutral in his moral findings; to him the question of whether man is good or bad is secondary to the fact that he is a creature of reason and desire. In fact, says Locke, even when he lived in his natural state, man's principal concern was his property, the fruit of his labor. His reason told him that he would be more secure in the possession and enjoyment of it if he submitted himself to a protective agency. He therefore entered into a social contract and organized the state. Locke makes the first business of the state the protection of property, and asserts that when a particular state is derelict in that duty it is morally correct for the people to replace it, even by force, with another.

Looking into the state of nature, Rousseau finds it to be an idyllic Eden, in which man was perfectly free and therefore morally perfect. There was only one flaw in this otherwise good life: the making of a living was difficult. It was to overcome the hardships of natural existence that he gave up some of his freedom and accepted the social contract. As to the character of the contract, it is a blending of the will of each individual with that of every other signatory into what Rousseau calls the general will.

Thus, while the three speculators were in some disagreement as to the nature of man, where the seed of the state was to be found, they nevertheless agreed that the state flowered from it.

It should be pointed out that this attempt to find an origin of the state was not their prime purpose, that each of them was interested in a political system of his own, and that each deemed it necessary to establish an origin that would fit in with his system. It would not serve our present purpose to discuss their political philosophies, but it is interesting to note that each was fashioned to fit the exigencies of the times, giving rise to the suspicion that their theories as to origin were similarly influenced. Their common prepossession was that the state is in the natural order of things, and Hobbes gives it divine sanction. In that respect they followed tradition; early Christian speculation on the state referred to its ideal as the "City of God," and Plato spoke of his state as something "of which a pattern is made in heaven."

Modern political science passes up the question of origin, accepts the state as a going concern, and makes recommendations for its operational improvement. The metaphysicians of old laid the deficiencies of a particular state to ignorance or disobedience of the laws of God. The moderns also have their ideal, or each political scientist has his own, and each has his prescription for achieving it; the ingredients of the prescription are a series of laws plus an enforcement machinery. The function of the state, it is generally assumed, is to bring about the good society—there being no question as to its ability to do so—and the good society is whatever the political scientist has in mind.

In recent times a few investigators have turned to history for evidence as to the origin of the state and have evolved what is sometimes called the theory of the sociological state.

The records show, they observe, that all primitive peoples made their living in one of two ways, agriculture or livestock raising; hunting and fishing seem to have been sidelines in both economies. The requirements of these two occupations developed clearly defined and different habits and skills. The business of roaming around in search of grazing land and water called for a well-knit organization of venturesome men, while the fixed routine of farming needed no organization and little enterprise. The phlegmatic docility of scattered land workers made them easy prey for the daring herdsmen of the hills. Covetousness suggested attack.

At first, the historians report, the object of pilferage was women, since incest was taboo long before the scientists found reason to condemn the practice. The stealing of women was followed by the stealing of portable goods, and both jobs were accompanied by the wholesale slaughter of males and unwanted females. Somewhere along the line the marauders hit upon the economic fact that dead men produce nothing, and from that observation came the institution of slavery; the herdsmen improved their business by taking along captives and assigning menial chores to them. This master-slave economy, the theory holds, is the earliest manifestation of the state. Thus, the premise of the state is the exploitation of producers by the use of power.

Eventually, hit-and-run pilferage was replaced by the idea of security—or the continuing exaction of tribute from people held in bondage. Sometimes the investing tribe would take charge of a trading center and place levies on transactions, sometimes they would take control of the highways and waterways leading to the villages and collect tolls from caravans and merchants. At any rate, they soon learned that loot is part of production and that it is plentiful when production is plentiful; to encourage production, therefore, they undertook to patrol it and to maintain "law and order." They not only policed the conquered people but also protected them from other marauding tribes; in fact, it was not uncommon for a harassed community to invite a warlike tribe to come in and stand guard, for a price. Conquerors came not only from the hills, for there were also "herdsmen of the sea," tribes whose hazardous occupation made them particularly daring on the attack.

The investing people held themselves aloof from the conquered, enjoying what later became known as extraterritoriality. They maintained cultural and political ties with their homeland, they retained their own language, religion, and customs, and in most cases did not disturb the *mores* of their subjects as long as tribute was forthcoming. In time, for such is the way of propinquity, the ideational barriers between conquered and conquerors melted away and a process of amalgamation set in. The process was sometimes hastened by a severing of the ties with the homeland, as when the local chieftain felt strong enough in his new environment to challenge his overlord and to cease dividing the loot with him, or when successful insurrection at home cut him off from it. Closer contact with the conquered resulted in a blending of languages, religions, and customs. Even though intermarriage was frowned upon, for economic and social reasons, sexual attraction could not be put off by dictum, and a new generation, often smeared with the bar sinister, bridged the chasm with blood ties. Military ventures, as in defense of the now common homeland, helped the amalgam.

The blending of the two cultures gave rise to a new one, not the least important feature of which was a set of customs and laws regularizing the accommodation of the dues-paying class to their masters. Necessarily, these conventions were formulated by the latter, with the intent of freezing their economic advantage into a legacy for their offspring. The dominated people, who at first had resisted the exactions, had long ago been worn out by the unequal struggle and had resigned themselves to a system of taxes, rents, tolls, and other forms of tribute. This adjustment was facilitated by the inclusion of some of the "lower classes" into the scheme, as foremen, bailiffs, and menial servitors, and military service under the masters made for mutual admiration if not respect. Also, the codifying of the exactions eventually obliterated from memory the arbitrariness with which they had been introduced and covered them with an aura of correctness. The laws fixed limits on the exactions, made excesses irregular and punishable, and thus established "rights" for the exploited class. The exploiters wisely guarded these rights against trespass by their own more avaricious members, while the exploited, having made a comfortable adjustment to the system of exactions, from which some of them often profited, achieved a sense of security and self-esteem in this doctrine of rights. Thus, through psychological and legal processes that stratification of society became fixed. The state is that class which enjoys economic preference through its control of the machinery of enforcement.*

The sociological theory of the state rests not only on the evidence of history but also on the fact that there are two ways by which men can acquire economic goods: production and predation. The first involves the application of labor to raw materials, the other the use of force. Pillaging, slavery, and

* This brief summary of the historical background of the sociological theory suggests Old Testament stories of the conquest of Canaan by the Israelites, the history of England and the Roman Empire. However, the principal proponents of this theory, Gumplowicz and Oppenheimer, were more interested in the origin of the state than in its development, and they dug into the records of early tribes all over the world; wherever they looked they found that the political organization began with conquest.

conquest are the primitive forms of predation, but the economic effect is the same when political coercion is used to deprive the producer of his product, or even when he accedes to the transfer of ownership as the price for permission to live. Nor is predation changed to something else when it is done in the name of charity—the Robin Hood formula. In any case, one enjoys what another has produced, and to the extent of the predation the producer's desires must go unsatisfied, his labor unrequited. It will be seen that in its moral aspect the sociological theory leans on the doctrine of private property, the inalienable right of the individual to the product of his effort, and holds that any kind of coercion, exercised for any purpose whatsoever, does not alienate that right. We shall take up that point later.

Incidentally, at first glance this theory seems to bear a resemblance to the dictum of Karl Marx that the state is the managing committee for the capitalistic class. But the resemblance is in the words, not in the ideas. The Marxian theory maintains that the state in other hands—the "dictatorship of the proletariat"—could abolish exploitation. But the sociological theory of the state (or the conquest theory) insists that the state itself, regardless of its composition, is an exploitative institution and cannot be anything else; whether it takes over the property of the owner of wages or the property of the owner of capital, the ethical principle is the same. If the state takes from the capitalist to give to the worker, or from the mechanic to give to the farmer, or from all to better itself, force has been used to deprive someone of his rightful property, and in that respect it is carrying on in the spirit, if not the manner, of original conquest.

Therefore, if the chronology of any given state does not begin with conquest, it nevertheless follows the same pattern because its institutions and practices continue in the tradition of those states that have gone through the historic process. The American state did not begin with conquest; the Indians had no property that could be lifted and, being hunters by profession, they were too intractable to be enslaved. But the colonists were themselves the product of an exploitative economy, had become inured to it in their respective homelands, had imported and incorporated it in their new organization. Many of them came to their new land bearing the yoke of bondage. All had come from institutional environments that had emerged from conquest; they knew nothing else, and when they set up institutions of their own they simply transplanted these environments. They brought the predatory state with them.

Any profitable inquiry into the character of the American state must therefore take into account the distinction between making a living by production and gaining a living by predation; that is, between economics and politics.

Government *Contra* State

This necessarily brief summary of the distinction between these political institutions will serve, it is hoped, to interest the reader in further investigation. The distinction is based on historical evidence and is supported by the principles of political economy. The best argument for this distinction is in Our Enemy the State, *by Albert Jay Nock. The interested reader will also find the following helpful:* The State, *by Franz Oppenheimer;* The Man Versus the State, *by Herbert Spencer;* The Perplexed Philosopher, *by Henry George.*

Over his fireplace, even before there were vigilantes or sheriffs, the frontiersman kept a ready musket. It was standard equipment for the protection of life and property. It was his government.

That is to say, government arises from the innate sense of the right to life and the related right to property. The right to life is an indisputable axiom; it inheres in the individual by the necessity of existence. But the right to life is a meaningless abstraction until it is translated into the possession and enjoy-

This piece first appeared in analysis *(February 1946).*

ment of things which make life possible, beginning with food, raiment, and shelter. The undisturbed possession and enjoyment of things which give existence substance and reality are called the right of property.

When I say that I have a right to life I mean that all the elements which center in my person—body, soul, faculties and acquired characteristics—are an integral to which no other person can show a natural title. When I labor to produce anything, I contribute part of "me" to the thing produced; it came into being because of "me." The sense of attachment to that thing may arise from the necessity of existence; I feel that it is mine not only because I made it but because I need it. At any rate, the relationship between things and persons which we call property rights is rooted in the indisputable right of the person in himself.

Labor, therefore, is the moral basis of property rights. Labor, however, involves exertion, and exertion brings on a feeling of weariness and irksomeness. We seek to avoid it; we try to satisfy our desires with the least expenditure of labor. We are not interested in working *per se;* we are interested in enjoyment. Therefore, the getting of something "for free"—that is, without giving up any labor in return—is appealing to our instinct. This conflict between desire and the aversion to labor goes on in all of us; in that sense there is a thief in every one of us. That is why the frontiersman keeps a government—a musket—over his fireplace.

However, the more time the frontiersman puts into protecting his life and property, the less time he has for enjoying life and producing property. Protection is a necessary nuisance. His neighbors are of like mind, and as soon as there are enough of them to make it possible they hire a policeman, a specialist with the musket, to relieve them of the nuisance end of their business. They vest in him the authority necessary to maintain that peace and tranquillity which are conducive to the production of property.

There is a threat to life and property also in the hazard of fire; to ward against this danger a volunteer fire department arises. And again, as this business of putting out fires interferes with the prime business of producing goods and services, a specialist in firefighting is hired by the group. Other overall jobs come up as the community grows, jobs which would be done on a volunteer basis by each of the producers where the population is sparse. Every one of these overall, community jobs arises from the concern of the individual in his life and property, and is a job well done to the extent that his private enterprise is thereby promoted.

Government, then, is a specialized service arising out of community life. It owes its existence to the individual's interest in himself. Its specific job is to maintain the peace necessary to productive enterprise. Its related job is that of providing such services as may enable each of the specialists in the community to carry on more efficiently. And that's all. It is a negative specialty, operating only as occasion for its services arises. Whether as policeman, judge or street cleaner, government adds nothing to the general fund of wealth directly. It is negative and neutral; it is an agent, not a principal; it is a servant, not a master.

The distinctive characteristic of government is that in performing its functions it may have recourse to the use of coercive authority. Its particular attribute is power, vested in it by the producing specialists for the specific purpose of maintaining a condition necessary to their production. But that very protective measure is a danger to all the producing specialists, because it can be used against them. The firearm which the frontiersman turns over to the constable may be used to rob him of his property. When it is so used, when the government becomes predatory rather than protective, it ceases to be a service; it is the state.

Going back a bit, the moral basis of political authority is the right of life and the related right of property. But when that political authority is so exercised as to deny these basic rights, it divests itself of all ethical validity; and that is so even if those who so exercise the political authority surround themselves with law, custom, and a desire to do good. Just as a surgeon's scalpel becomes in fact a dagger when it is used with the intent to kill, so when the exercise of political authority deprives the individual of his rights it ceases to be a service and becomes a disservice.

The state—those in whom the political authority is vested and who use it for other than protective purposes—justifies its action by invoking a "higher law." That is, it substitutes for the rights of the individual the rights of the clan, the community, the nation. But whence come the rights of these collective fictions? We are told that God made man, but nowhere is it asserted He also fathered an empire, or a village. That which we call "soul" is a private affair and no way of transferring it to another person or group of persons has been discovered. Hence the idea that a number of people, acting together, have a right which supersedes the rights of the individual is pure fantasy, and one which, as experience shows, has been invented to no good purpose.

This is not to say that those who advance this idea are inherently wicked, or are more wicked than the rest of us. They may be motivated by the noblest of intentions, their hearts overflowing with the milk of human kindness. Nevertheless, when they speak of "my country, right or wrong," or "Deutschland über alles," or the abolition of private property for the furtherance of the general good, they advance the false notion of a "personal" state. There is no such thing; only individuals exist. And the idea is decidedly at variance with the concept of rights, for it assumes that the individual is subservient to the collectivity, as to both life and property.

Far from being a person, the state is a group of persons who have acquired the power vested in government and make use of it in such a manner as to deprive the individual of his right to life and property. The state is historically grounded in conquest. The purpose of conquest is exploitation. Exploitation is any means of getting goods and services without rendering an equivalent in exchange—that is, any method of "getting something for nothing." The state by virtue of the power of government which it acquires, perpetuates the purpose of conquest; by legal methods it regularizes the exploitation of the producer, in favor of the nonproducer, and by an elaborate system of education it obfuscates the immoral relationship and even covers the exploiters with an aura of respectability.

The state is divided into two groups, those who wield political power and those who benefit by it. That is what we mean by the phrase "the state within the state." The keystone of this predatory structure is the power of taxation. Taxation is the regularized method of extracting property from producers for the benefit of the political arm of the state; the revenue enables it to maintain its administrative and executive machinery, particularly the military, and to induce acquiescence through its system of indoctrination. The more it taxes the stronger it becomes and, as a consequence, the weaker the power of resistance that may be brought to bear against it.

The beneficiaries of state power are the privileged classes. The greatest privilege which the state can confer is that of collecting rent from users of the earth. As all production consists of the application of labor to land, the owners of mines, franchises, and other choice spots are in a position to demand a permission-to-live price. Since nobody would of his own free will pay this price, which is in reality akin to tribute, force must underlie its payment; this the state supplies. Although this fact has been lost in the limbo of land laws, it shows up clearly when we trace title deeds to their source: force or fraud. Nobody can put to property in land the moral title test of "I made it."

Whenever necessary to maintain or strengthen its position, the political arm of the state will hand out other privileges, and each group which thus secures for itself a means of enjoyment without labor becomes a supporter of its benefactor. In recent times we have seen how the state will shore itself up by handing out the dole privilege to the "underprivileged" who have been taxed and rack-rented out of the opportunity of earning a living for themselves. As political power is incapable of producing a thing, the privileges handed out amount to the taking of production from some and giving it to others; this is the essence of exploitation, the object of conquest.

The distinction between government and state, then, is in the use to which political coercion is put. When it is used negatively, for the protection of life and property, with which must be included the adjudicating of disputes among citizens, it is a service; when it is used positively, in the interests of one group of citizens, including politicians, against the interests of other groups, it is a disservice. In the one case it makes for harmony, in the other it is the cause of discord.

Civilization or Caveman Economy?

I have been asked to talk about international trade. I shall begin by talking about civilization, that thing which, we are being told, is on the brink of destruction. For I believe that there is a definite relationship between the processes of civilization and the mode of exchange called international trade.

What is civilization? There have been many definitions of this concept, ranging from those that are purely material to those that are exclusively cultural. To define this word properly, let us examine how we use it. In a general way, we think of civilization as the customs, education, political methods, religion, technical knowledge, and so forth, prevailing at any given period of history, or on some part of the inhabited globe. Perhaps all of these characteristics can be grouped under the term "mores."

We speak of Greek civilization and have a concept of a certain development in arts or the philosophical contributions of the early Greeks. We speak of Egyptian civilization and conjure up an idea of pyramids and angular forms, magnificent courts and corresponding slavery. Japanese civilization of the eighteenth

Chodorov gave this talk to the Kiwanis Club in New York City, and it was broadcast over WMCA. It first appeared in The Freeman *(May 1940).*

century connotes something different from Japanese civilization of the twentieth century.

Yet there must be something indigenous to all civilizations,
and the only way we can isolate this common denominator is
by a process of elimination, by imagining a complete absence
of civilization.

Let us assume that our pre-civilization ancestor, the caveman, provided all of his satisfactions by his own efforts; that
is, he caught the fish he ate, he hunted so that he could have
meat and raiment for himself, he alone provided the cave dwell-
ing which he shared with no one except his mate; and if he had
any idea of entertainment, it was necessary for him to entertain
himself. The very first impulse of man is to seek those satisfactions which enable him to live; and since our caveman shared
none of his products with his fellow man, it was only by his
own labor that he could live.

This caveman's satisfactions must have been quite simple.
He could not have satisfactions which required a complexity
of effort. In other words, he was a "jack-of-all-trades and master of none."

In due time it must have occurred to him that if he concentrated upon one of these trades, let us say fishing, while his
neighboring caveman concentrated upon the making of such
clothes as they both wore, both could be more proficient—each
would produce more. But in order for such specialization to be
possible, it was necessary for these two cavemen to arrange for
some method of exchange. In all probability, it occurred to
these original men that they must trust each other. The fishing
caveman who brought his excess fish to his tailoring neighbor
must have agreed to give fish on the promise of the other that
when the latter finished the desired loincloth he would deliver
it to the fisherman.

We see, then, that both markets and credit are necessary for specialization. We cannot possibly have division of productive labor unless the specializations can be exchanged; for if one man who makes shoes finds that there is no way to dispose of his shoes, he would starve to death unless he quit concentrating upon shoemaking and went to work on food production.

Civilization at bottom is merely a mode of living together. The reason for men living together in a community is that each one, trying to satisfy his desires with the least effort, finds that in a community not only is there greater production through division of labor, but, even more important, the community is itself a market for the exchanges.

Gregariousness may have a psychological interpretation, but economically it is merely the expression of the individual's desire to find satisfactions. The more people there are in a community, the larger the market, the easier trade becomes, and, therefore, the greater is the number of specialized arts.

For instance, it is only in a large city that an operatic star finds a market for her services. So highly developed an entertainment machine as the Yankee baseball club could not be developed in, let us say, Broken Bow, Oklahoma. There could not be an automobile factory making a thousand machines a day unless there were one thousand buyers a day. We find that where specializations have been most highly developed, there are the greatest number of people, and, consequently, the most facile market.

I think we can fairly state, then, that civilization started when the art of trade was discovered. At first the specializations are necessarily confined to immediate necessities, such as food, raiment, and shelter. But with his immediate desires satisfied, man seeks higher gratifications, and soon the system of the market enables some people to become priests, troubadours, traveling entertainers, healers.

Thus, the exchange of goods with which civilization starts develops into an exchange of services and ideas. Without a market the doctor could not develop and trade his skill for the necessities of life. Without a market, there would be no lawyers, no actors, no professors; we would all have to be as self-sustaining as the caveman.

Every increase in trade facilities aids in the spreading of cultural values; and, contrariwise, every interference with trade results in a corresponding retardation of cultural progess. In other words, the freer the trade, the greater the advance in civilization, and the more restrictions there are on trade, the surer will be the retrogression of civilization.

We have never had free trade, and I use that word in the sense not only of trade between peoples of various countries, but also of trade between peoples of the same country. We have never permitted the absolutely free exchange of productive specializations, free of political regulations, free of taxes, free of privilege. Therefore, we have never been completely civilized.

And since trade has never been absolutely free, production has never been free. For interference with the market is interference with production. When a market is restricted by government control, by government levies, or by monopoly, the result on exchanges is the same. When I go to market with my bushel of onions and am waylaid on the road by a tax collector who takes from me a portion of my onions, and then by someone else who because of a legal privilege deprives me of more of my onions, I cannot expect to get as many potatoes from you in exchange for my depleted stock. You do not have compassion upon me and give me the same number of potatoes even though

I give you less onions; I simply haven't the goods to pay for your potatoes and I go home with less than I started out with.

And since you have not sold me all your potatoes, you take your surplus stock home, and you don't grow so many next season; that is, you are out of a job. Interference with the market, by regulation or by privilege, therefore has the tendency to cut down production, or employment.

Any difficulties placed in the way of production have an effect on those cultural values which are the marks of advanced civilizations. For it must be remembered that it is not until material needs are satisfied that these cultural values make their appearance. When man is struggling merely to live, he does not develop an appreciation for art. And as this struggle becomes more intense and more general, interest in thought diminishes in proportion. Thus we see that handicaps on production as well as on exchange retard the progress of civilization.

War is a complete denial of freedom of the market. In the first place, warriors do not produce. Their specialty is destruction. The goods they destroy are produced by workers who get nothing in exchange except a promise to pay, some time in the future. This repayment may be made to their children and children's children, by production in the future. For all debts are liquidated ultimately with goods or services. Now, then, if warriors destroy production wihout bringing to market something in exchange, it is obvious that the producers have less for themselves, and the processes of a free market are therefore denied. Whenever—by any technique—I am deprived of my production, my power to trade is to that extent limited.

Embargoes, blockades, quotas, inflation, sinking of ships, all of the methods of war, have for their purpose the interference with the exchange of goods for goods. They are avowedly a denial of trade, and trade is synonymous with civilization.

More important, from the ultimate point of view of mankind, than even the destructive activities of war are the tendencies to isolate peoples completely from one another mentally and spiritually. The technique of modern warfare is complete isolation before as well as during the war.

It is the business of the government which prepares you for war to teach you to hate. It is the business of the government which prepares you for war to teach you not to trade with certain peoples because they have bad "ideologies." It is the business of the government which prepares you for war to prevent information coming to you which might predispose you kindly toward the people whom you will be called upon to kill. It is the business of war to break down that free exchange of goods, services, and ideas which is indigenous to all civilizations at all times.

You have no doubt observed that in dealing with the interrelated questions of trade and civilization, I have not distinguished between international trade and internal trade. There is none. What difference is there, essentially, in the exchange of goods between a New Yorker and a Vermonter and the exchange of goods between a New Yorker and a Canadian? Does a political frontier inherently make a man a bad customer? When Detroit sells an automobile to Minnesota, the debt is eventually liquidated by a shipment of flour; and if the automobile is sold to Brazil, the sale is completed with a shipment of coffee. Nationality, color, race, and religion are of no consideration in any of these exchanges. These characteristics become of importance only where the war technique has become an integral part of our political system.

Trade, internal or international, is the harbinger of goodwill

among men, and peace on earth. The opposite of trade is isolation, and isolation is a mark of decadence, of a return to a
caveman economy. If it is good for America to isolate itself
from other countries, economically and culturally, it is good
for New York to isolate itself from Connecticut, for Manhattan
to isolate itself from the Bronx, for every man to isolate himself
from his neighbor. Just as individuals specialize in occupations,
so do nations, and usually the specializations are determined
by superior natural resources or the development of special
skills. It is no reflection on the United States that Australian
wool has been a staple longer than that grown on American
sheep. But it is a reflection on American intelligence that
America makes it difficult for us to get this better wool, just as
it is a reflection on the intelligence of Australians that they
impose on themselves difficulties in the getting of our superior
automobiles.

Isolation and self-sufficiency are war techniques. Both ideas
derive from the stupid concept of war as the reason for and goal
of national existence. Both, therefore, are tendencies toward
decivilization. And in the final analysis, the isolation and self-
sufficiency idea is merely national caveman economy.

In closing I want to point out to you businessmen that it is
your duty to emphasize the dignity and importance of trade in
our national life. In the early days of the science of political
economy it was taught that trade is a necessary evil—that it is
not productive. This erroneous theory, first enunciated by the
French physiocrats and later developed by the Marxists to the
point where they pontifically declared all exchange occupations
to be parasitical, is not yet quite deleted from all of our books
on economics; lately our political thinking has evidenced some
traces of it.

One of the contributions to economic thought developed by

the foremost American economist, Henry George, was that exchange is part of production—that the salesman and the banker have as much to do with production as the man at the machine. For, said George, the object of production is consumption, and a thing is not produced until it reaches the consumer. Therefore, any specialist who aids in the distribution of things is a producer of things. As the number of our specializations increases, a larger army of distributors is necessary. The market becomes more important, and the jobber, retailer, advertiser, and common carrier become greater and greater factors in our productive machinery.

And the size and the freedom of the market are the measuring sticks of civilization.

Free Will and the Marketplace

F ree will is the starting point of all ethical thinking and it plays an equally important part in the business of making a living. If man were not endowed with this capacity for making choices, he could not be held accountable for his behavior, any more than could a fish or a fowl—an amoral being, a thing without a sense of morals. So, if man were devoid of this capacity, his economics would be confined to grubbing along on whatever he found in nature. It is because man is capable of taking thought, of making evaluations and decisions in favor of this or that course, that we have a discipline called economics.

In making his ethical choices, man is guided by a code believed to have the sanction of God; and experience has shown that the good life to which his instinct impels him can be achieved only if he makes his decisions accordingly. The Ten Commandments have been called the Word of God; they can also be described as natural law, and natural law has been described as nature's way of applying means to ends. Thus, we

This article is an adaptation from an address Chodorov gave before an American Farm Bureau conference in Madison, Wisconsin, in October 1958. It was originally printed in The Freeman *(January 1959).*

say that nature in her inscrutable ways has determined that water shall always run downhill, never up; that is a natural law, we say, because it is without exception, inevitable, and self-enforcing. Therefore, when we decide to build ourselves a house, we set it at the bottom of the hill so as to avail ourselves of a supply of water. If we put the house at the top of the hill, nature will not cooperate in our obstinacy and we shall not have any water in the house; unless, of course, we discover and make use of some other natural law to overcome the force of gravity.

That is to say, nature is boss and we had better heed her teaching when we make decisions or we shall not achieve the ends we desire. But, her teaching is not freely given; we must apply ourselves diligently to a study of her ways to find out what they are. The prerequisite for a successful investigation is to admit that nature has the secret we are trying to uncover; if we begin by saying that in this or that field nature has no laws, that humans make their own way without reference to nature, we shall end up knowing nothing.

If, for instance, we discard the Ten Commandments, declaring them to be mere man-made conventions changeable at will, we end in chaos and disorder—evidence that we are on the wrong track. Likewise, if we declare that God in His infinite wisdom chose to disregard economics, that in ordering the world he overlooked the ways and means for man's making a living, that in this particular field man has to work out his own formulas, we will end up with a poor living.

"ECONOMICS" WITHOUT PRINCIPLES

And that is exactly what has happened in the study of economics; many experts in this field are of the opinion that nature can tell us nothing about the business of making a living; it is all a matter of human manipulation. That is why economics is so often a meaningless hodgepodge of expediencies, leading us to no understanding and no good end. I might add that the incongruities of ethical life, such as divorce, juvenile delinquency, international friction, and so on, are largely the result of the current conceit that there is no warrant for ethics in nature, no positive laws for moral behavior; but that is another subject.

I shall try to present some evidence that nature has her own rules and regulations in the field of economics, indicating that we had better apply ourselves to learning about them if we would avoid the obviously unsatisfactory results from relying on man's ingenuity. Come with me into the laboratory of experience, which is the source of much understanding.

THE FIRST PIONEER

Let us cast our mind's eye back to the time when there was no Madison, Wisconsin, or any other city west of the Alleghenies, when only the seed of a later social integration was planted here—when a lone frontiersman decided to settle on this spot of earth. The primary consideration which influenced his decision was the possibility of making a living here. He selected what later became Madison because the land was fertile, water was plentiful, the forests abounded with wood for his comfort, meat for his sustenance, and hides for his raiment. This was the workshop from which he could expect good wages for his efforts. Without benefit of economic textbooks, he hit upon a couple of economic laws: (1) production, or wealth, consists of useful things resulting from the application of human labor to natural resources; (2) wages come from production.

These laws, these precepts of nature, are still in force and always will be despite the efforts of some "experts" to rescind them. Often the yearning for manna from heaven obscures the fact that only by the application of labor to raw materials can economic goods appear, but the yearning is so strong that men ask government to play God and reproduce the miracle of the wilderness

Government, of course, can produce nothing, let alone a miracle; and when it presumes to drop manna on its chosen people, it simply takes what some produce and hands it over to others; its largess is never a free gift. And as for wages, they still come from production, even though there are sectarians who maintain that wages come from the safety vaults of a soulless boss. The consequences of disregarding these two dictates of nature are too well known to call for discussion.

Returning to our first pioneer, his initial wages are meager. That is because he is compelled by the condition of his existence to be a jack-of-all-trades, proficient in none. He produces little and therefore has little. But he is not satisfied with his lot for, unlike the beasts in the forest or the fish in the sea, man is not content merely to exist.

And here we hit upon a natural law which plays a prime role in man's economic life: he is the insatiable animal, always dreaming of ways and means for improving his circumstances and widening his horizon. The cabin built by the pioneer to protect himself from the elements was castle enough in the beginning; but soon he begins to think of a floor covering, of pictures on the wall, of a lean-to, of a clavichord to brighten his evenings at home, and, at long last, of hot- and cold-running water to relieve him of the laborious pumping. Were it not for man's insatiability, there would be no such study as economics.

A NEIGHBOR ARRIVES

But the things the pioneer dreams about are unattainable as long as he is compelled to go it alone. Along comes a second pioneer, and his choice of a place to work is based on the same consideration that influenced his predecessor. What wages can he get out of the land? However, as between this location and others of equal natural quality, this one is more desirable because of the presence of a neighbor. This fact alone assures a greater income, because there are jobs that two men can perform more easily than can one man alone, and some jobs that one man simply cannot do. Their wages are mutually improved by cooperation. Each has more satisfactions.

Others come, and every accretion to the population raises the wage level of the community. In the building of homes, in fighting fires and other hazards, in satisfying the need of entertainment or in the search for spiritual solace, a dozen people working together can accomplish more than twelve times what each one, working alone, can do. Still, the wage level of the community is rather low, for it is limited by the fact that all the workers are engaged in the primary business of existence on a self-sustaining, jack-of-all-trades basis.

At some point in the development of the community it occurs to one of the pioneers that he has an aptitude for blacksmithing; and if all the others would turn over to him their chores in this line, he could become very proficient at it, far better than any of his neighbors. In order for him to ply this trade the others must agree to supply him with his needs. Since their skill at blacksmithing is deficient, and since the time and effort they put into it is at the expense of something they can do better, an agreement is not hard to reach. Thus comes the tailor, the carpenter, the teacher, and a number of other specialists, each relieving the farmers of jobs that interfere with their farming. Specialization increases the productivity of each; and where there was scarcity, there is now abundance.

The first condition necessary for specialization is population. The larger the population the greater the possibility of the specialization which makes for a rising wage level in the community. There is, however, another important condition necessary for this division of labor, and that is the presence of capital. The pioneers have in their barns and pantries more than they need for their immediate sustenance, and are quite willing to invest this superfluity in other satisfactions. Their savings enable them to employ the services of specialists; and the more they make use of these services the more they can produce and save, thus to employ more specialists.

This matter of savings, or capital, may be defined as that part of production not immediately consumed, which is employed in aiding further production, so that more consumable goods may become available. In man's search for a more abundant life he has learned that he can improve his circumstances by producing more than he can presently consume and putting this excess into the production of greater satisfactions.

RESPECT FOR PROPERTY

Man has alway been a capitalist. In the beginning, he produced a wheel, something he could not eat or wear, but something that made his labors easier and more fruitful. His judgment told him what to do, and of his own free will he chose to do it. That makes him a capitalist, a maker and user of capital. The wheel, after many centuries, became a wagon, an automobile, a train, and an airplane—all aids in man's search for a better living. If man were not a capitalist, if he had chosen not to produce beyond requirements for immediate consumption—well, there would never have been what we call civilization.

However, a prerequisite for the appearance of capital is the assurance that the producer can retain for himself all he produces in the way of savings. If this excess of production over consumption is regularly taken from him, by robbers or tax collectors or the elements, the tendency is to produce no more than can be consumed immediately. In that case, capital tends to disappear; and with the disappearance of capital, production declines, and so does man's standard of living.

From this fact we can deduce another law of nature: that security in the possession and enjoyment of the fruit of one's labor is a necessary condition for capital accumulation. Putting it another way, where private property is abolished, capital tends to disappear and production comes tumbling after. This law explains why slaves are poor producers and why a society in which slavery is practiced is a poor society. It also gives the lie to the promise of socialism in all its forms; where private property is denied, there you will find austerity rather than a functioning exchange economy.

THE TRADING INSTINCT

The possibility of specialization as population increases is enhanced by another peculiarly human characteristic—the trading instinct. A trade is the giving up of something one has in order to acquire something one wants. The trader puts less worth on what he possesses than on what he desires. This is what we call evaluation.

It is not necessary here to go into the theory, or theories, of value except to point out that evaluation is a psychological process. It springs from the human capacity to judge the intensity of various desires. The fisherman has more fish than he cares to eat but would like to add potatoes to his menu; he puts a lower value on fish than on potatoes. The farmer is in the opposite position, his barn being full of potatoes and his plate devoid of fish. If an exchange can be effected both will profit, both will acquire an added satisfaction. In every trade—provided neither force nor fraud is involved—seller and buyer both profit.

Only man is a trader. No other creature is capable of estimating the intensity of its desires and of giving up what it has in order to get something it wants. Man alone has the gift of free will. To be sure, he may go wrong in his estimates and may make a trade that is to his disadvantage. In his moral life too he may err. But, when he makes the wrong moral choice, we hold that he should suffer the consequences, and hope that he will learn from the unpleasant experience.

So it must be in his search for a more abundant life. If in his search for a good life the human must be allowed to make use of his free will, why should he not be accorded the same right in the search for a more abundant life? Many of the persons who would abolish free choice in the marketplace logically conclude that man is not endowed with free will, that free will is a fiction, that man is merely a product of his environment. This premise ineluctably leads them to the denial of the soul and, of course, the denial of God.

Those who rail against the marketplace as if it were a den of iniquity, or against its techniques as being founded in man's inhumanity, overlook the function of the marketplace in bring-

ing people into closer contact with one another. Remember, the
marketplace makes specialization possible, but specialization
makes men interdependent. The first pioneer somehow or other
made his entire cabin; but his son, having accustomed himself
to hiring a professional carpenter, can hardly put up a single
shelf in a cabin. And today, if some catastrophe should cut off
Madison from the surrounding farms, the citizens of the city
would starve. If the marketplace were abolished, people would
still pass the time of day or exchange recipes or bits of news;
but they would no longer be dependent on one another, and
their self-sufficiency would tend to break down their society.
For that reason we can say that society and the marketplace are
two sides of the same coin. If God intended man to be a social
animal, he intended him to have a marketplace.

TRADERS SERVE ONE ANOTHER

But, let us return to our imaginary experiment. We found
that as the pioneer colony grew in numbers, a tendency toward
specialization arose. It was found that by this division of labor
more could be produced. But this profusion from specialization
would serve no purpose unless some way were found to dis-
tribute it. The way is to trade. The shoemaker, for instance,
makes a lot of shoes of various sizes, but he is not interested
in shoes *per se;* after all, he can wear but one pair and of one
particular size. He makes the other shoes because other people
want them and will give him in exchange the things he wants:
bread, raiment, books, whatnot—the things in which his interests naturally lie. He makes shoes in order to serve himself,
but in order to serve himself he has to serve others. He has to
render a social service in order to pursue his own search for a
more abundant life.

In our lexicon we refer to a business undertaking by the

government as a social service; but this is a misnomer, because we can never be certain that the service rendered by the government business is acceptable to society. Society is compelled to accept these services, or to pay for them even if unwanted. The element of force is never absent from a government-managed business. On the other hand, the private entrepreneur cannot exist unless society voluntarily accepts what he has to offer; he must render a social service or go out of business.

Let us suppose that this shoemaker is especially efficient, that many people in the community like his service and therefore trade with him. He acquires what we call a profit. Has he done so at the expense of his customers? Do they lose because he has a profit? Or, do they not gain in proportion to the profit he makes? They patronize him because the shoes he offers are better than they could make themselves or could get elsewhere, and for that reason they are quite willing to trade with him. They want what they get more than they want what they give up and therefore profit even as he profits.

If he goes wrong in his estimate of their requirements, if he makes the wrong sizes, or styles that are not wanted, or uses inferior materials, people will not patronize him and he will suffer a loss. He will have no wage return for the labor he puts in and no return for the capital—the hides and machinery—which he uses in making his unwanted product. The best he can do under the circumstances, in order to recoup some of his investment, is to hold a bargain-basement sale. That is the correlative of profits—losses.

No entrepreneur is wise enough to predetermine the exact needs or desires of the community he hopes to serve and his errors of judgment always come home to plague him. But, the point to keep in mind is that when an entrepreneur profits, he does so because he has served his community well; and when he loses, the community does not gain. A business that fails does not prosper society.

The marketplace not only facilitates the distribution of abundances—including the abundances that nature has spread all over the globe, like the coal of Pennsylvania for the citrus fruit of Florida, or the oil of Iran for the coffee of Brazil—but it also directs the energies of all the specialists who made up society. This it does through the instrumentality of its price indicator. On this instrument are recorded in unmistakable terms just what the various members of society want, and how much they want it. If the hand on this indicator goes up, if higher prices are bid for a certain commodity, the producers are advised that there is a demand for this commodity in excess of the supply, and they then know how best to invest their labors for their own profit and for the profit of society. A lower price, on the other hand, tells them that there is a superfluity of a certain commodity, and they know that to make more of it would entail a loss because society has a sufficiency.

The price indicator is an automatic device for recording the freely expressed wishes of the community members, the tally of their dollar ballots for this or that satisfaction, the spontaneous and noncoercive regulator of productive effort. One who chooses to tamper with this delicate instrument does so at the risk of producing a scarcity of the things wanted or an overabundance of unwanted things; for he disturbs the natural order.

BENEFICIARIES OF COMPETITION

One more social function of the marketplace needs mentioning. It is the determinant of productive efficiency, provided, of course, it is permitted to operate according to the unimpeded motive power of free will. In the primitive economy we have been examining, one shoemaker can take care of the shoe needs of the community. Under those conditions, the efficiency of that server is determined by his skill, his industry, and his whim. He alone can fix the standard of the service he renders his customers, or the prices he charges. Assuming that they can go nowhere else for shoes, their only recourse if they do not like his services or his prices is either to go without or to make their own footwear.

As the community grows in size, another shoe specialist will show up to share the trade with the first one. With the appearance of a second shoemaker the standard of efficiency is no longer determined by one producer. It is determined by the rivalry between them for the trade of the community. One offers to fix shoes "while you wait," the other lowers his prices, and the first one comes back with a larger assortment of sizes or styles. This is competition.

Now the beneficiaries of the improved services resulting from competition are the members of society. The more competition and the keener the competition, the greater the fund of satisfactions in the marketplace. Oddly enough, the competitors do not suffer because the abundance resulting from their improved efficiency attracts more shoe customers; "competition," the adage holds, "is good for business."

If, perchance, one of the competitors cannot keep up with the improving standard of performance, he may find himself out of business; but the increased productive activity resulting from the competition means that there are more productive jobs to be filled, and in all likelihood he can earn more as a foreman for one of the competitors than he could as an entrepreneur. Even those physically unable to care for themselves and dependent on others are benefited by competition; when there is an abundance in the marketplace, charity can be more liberal.

IMMUTABLE LAWS PREVAIL

I am not attempting here a complete course in economics. What I have tried to show is that in economics, as in other disciplines, there are inflexible principles, inevitable consequences, immutable laws written into the nature of things. Exercising his free will, man can attempt to defy the law of gravitation by jumping off a high place; but the law operates without regard for his conceit, and he ends up with a broken neck.

So, if the first pioneer had set up with force of arms a claim to everything produced in the Madison area, other pioneers would not have come near, and the community known as Madison would never have been born. Or, if he could have collected tribute, also by force of arms, from every producer in the area, he would have driven prospective specialists to places where private property was respected. If the first shoemaker had established himself, with the help of law, as a monopolist, barring competition, the shoes that Madisonians wore would have been of poor quality, scarce, and costly; the same result would have followed any legal scheme to subsidize his inefficiency at the expense of taxpayers. If early Madisonians had decreed to abolish the marketplace with its price indicator, specialization and exchange would have been thwarted and the economy of Madison would have been characterized by scarcity.

The laws of economics, like other natural laws, are self-enforcing and carry built-in sanctions. If these laws are either unknown or not heeded, the inevitable eventual penalty will be an economy of scarcity, a poor and uncoordinated society. Why? Because the laws of nature are expressions of the will of God. You cannot monkey with them without suffering the consequences.

One Worldism

F ive years ago the organization of the United Nations was ushered into the world as the guarantor of peace. It has failed. Despite that obvious fact, there are many whose faith in some sort of a superstate as an instrument of peace is unshaken, and who lay the failure of the UN to the limitations put upon it by the autonomy of its members. That is to say, they believe in peace through authoritarianism; the more authoritarian, the more peace.

History cannot give this faith the slightest support. The glory that was Rome did not prevent its parts from coming into conflict with one another, or from rising up against the central authority. Even our American coalition of commonwealths came near breaking up in war, and uprisings have all but disintegrated the British Empire. Centralization of power has never been a guarantor of peace. On the contrary, every such centralization has been accomplished by war and its career has been one long preoccupation with war.

The best that can be said of any coalition of states is that it can keep smoldering fires from breaking out only so long as none of its members can exercise control over the others. It can

"One Worldism" originally appeared in analysis *(December 1950) and was subsequently excerpted in* The Freeman.

maintain an armed truce. The UN has not done even that, simply because no one state has shown sufficient strength to take control. The two most powerful members have been in contention since its beginning and are now poised for a test of arms to determine the issue. Nothing else is more certain than that the rivalry of these two powers will shortly reach the breaking point, that the UN shall collapse or shall be succeeded by another coalition in which one or the other will be on top.

The UN—it is moonshine to think otherwise—consists of two hostile camps, one held together by the American dollar, the other by fear of the Soviet army. Neither law, morality, nor ideology is a cementing influence. If the American dollar is withdrawn the West will break up, its members entering into new alignments dictated by expediency; if the Soviet power shows weakness, Titoism will splinter the Red empire.

In short, it is evident now—even as it was to any one with some familiarity with the history of alliances—that the high moral purpose written into the charter of the UN charter is but a fairy tale. World peace is not to be achieved through this monstrosity. Like the League of Nations which it succeeded, or the Holy Roman Empire, or any of the political coalitions in the history of the world, the UN is incapable of giving the world peace simply because it rests on the unsound assumption that peace is a function of politics. The fact is that peace and politics are antithetical.

When we look into the nature and substance of peace, and make comparison with the business of politics, we see how silly is this faith in the superstate. It is as irrational as the religions of totemism, animism, or fetishism. It is another magic religion, in which the hope of man for a better life rests on the mystic powers of an inscrutable authority, which must be propitiated into seeing things as man sees them. Just as primitive man sought the answers to all his questions in the totem pole, so does modern man look to political power to solve the problems of life. In both cases we have the same flight from self-reliance, the same escape from individual responsibility, the same mother complex. That is the only way one can explain this blind faith in the efficacy of political power. The superstate idea is the most advanced form of this religion. The psychological identity of primitivism and statism is only obscured by the ritualism of charters, constitutions, and protocol.

SOCIETY IS PEOPLE

Peace is the business of society. Society is a cooperative effort, springing spontaneously from man's urge to improve on his circumstances. It is voluntary, completely free of force. It comes because man has learned that the task of life is easier of accomplishment through the exchange of goods, services, and ideas. The greater the volume and the fluidity of such exchanges, the richer and fuller the life of every member of society. That is the law of association; it is also the law of peace.

It is in the marketplace that man's peaceful ways are expressed. Here the individual voluntarily gives up possession of what he has in abundance to gain possession of what he lacks. It is in the marketplace that society flourishes, because it is in the marketplace that the individual flourishes. Not only does he find here the satisfactions for which he craves, but he also learns of the desires of his fellow man so that he might the better serve him. More than that, he learns of and swaps ideas, hopes, and dreams, and comes away with values of greater worth to him than even those congealed in material things.

Society has no geographical limits; it is as big as its marketplace, its area of exchanges. The Malayan and the American are automatically enrolled in the same society by the exchange of rubber for a jukebox, and even the difficulties of language are overcome when a New Yorker confronts a Chinese menu. South American music became the idiom of the North American dance floor because automobiles are swapped for coffee and bananas. Society is the organization of people who do business with one another.

The law of association—the supreme law of society—is self-operating; it needs no enforcement agency. Its motor force is in the nature of man. His insatiable appetite for material, cultural, and spiritual desires drives him to join up. The compulsion is so strong that he makes an automobile out of an oxcart, a telephone system out of a drum, so as to overcome the handicaps of time and space; contact is of the essence in the marketplace technique. Society grows because the seed of it is in the human being; it is made of man, but not by men.

The only condition necessary for the growth of society into one worldism is the absence of force in the marketplace; which is another way of saying that politics is a hindrance, and not an aid, to peace. Any intervention in the sphere of voluntary exchanges stunts the growth of society and tends to its disorganization. It is significant that in war, which is the ultimate of politics, every strategic move is aimed at the disorganization of the enemy's means of production and exchange—the disruption of his marketplace. Likewise, when the state intervenes in the business of society, which is production and exchange, a condition of war exists, even though open conflict is prevented by the superior physical force the state is able to employ. Politics in the marketplace is like a bull in the china shop.

POLITICS IS FRICTION

The essential characteristic of the state is force; it originates in force and exists by it. The rationale of the state is that conflict is inherent in the nature of man and he must be coerced into behaving, for his own good. That is a debatable doctrine, but even if we accept it the fact remains that the coercion must be exercised by men who are, by definition, as "bad" as those upon whom the coercion is exercised. The state is men. To cover up that disturbing fact, the doctrine of the superpersonal state is invented; it is more than human, it exists distinct from the people who staff it. That fiction is given plausibility by clothing it with constitutions, laws, and litanies, like "my country right or wrong." A religion of authoritarianism is built up around an idol.

But, ritual does not give divinity to a golden calf. The hard fact remains that the priesthood of the state is just men, and the coercion it employs reflects its human capacities and frailties. The "priests" cannot get away from those limitations. Whatever "badness" is in them will show up in their use of force. They are not made "good" by the power to impose their will on other men.

Getting down to the facts of experience, political power never has been used for the "general good," as advertised, but always has been used to further the interests of those in power or those who can support them in this purpose. To do so it must intervene in the marketplace. The advantages that political power confers upon its priests and their cohorts consist of what that power skims from the abundance created by society. Since it cannot make a single good, it lives and thrives by what it takes. What it takes deprives producers of the fruits of their labors, impoverishes them, and this causes a feeling of hurt. Intervention in the marketplace can do nothing else, then, than to create friction. Friction is incipient war.

Now, if the business of the state is to cause friction within any given segment of society, any one country, by what logic can it be shown that a world-state will prevent friction? If a small state is an evil, as the one-worlders insist, why should a big state be a good? Can an institution that is essentially antisocial be made prosocial by enlargement? No matter how high the totem pole it is not God.

Reason and fact are at great disadvantage in confronting blind faith, and those who worship at the shrine of authoritarianism will not be shaken by argument. Yet, one cannot help asking how the superstate will employ its army; the worshippers admit that an army is necessary to its proper functioning. The army will certainly be used to suppress something, to stop some people from doing something that to them seems good. For instance, there are many people in the world who practice polygamy, some who practice polyandry, and a few who go in for monogamy. Will the omniscient priesthood of the superstate use its army to enforce a uniform conjugal practice? In that case, of course, friction will result.

Or, if it is decided that the world has too much oil—the "overproduction" theory—will the army be sent to Texas or to Iran to shut down the "excess" wells? When such frictional situations are brought up, the devotees of authoritarianism answer that everything will be resolved by the "democratic" process—a process that has never stopped war.

ONE WORLD—ONE MARKETPLACE

One worldism is not an impossible ideal; but, it is not attainable through the medium of political power. On the contrary, the organization of the world into a single society—which is what the one-worlders really want—can be accomplished only if people can rid themselves of the fetish of authoritarianism. If men could come to a belief in themselves, if they could lose faith in the golden calf of politics, if they could once reach the maturity of manhood, the law of association would do the rest. It is not necessary to plan or build a world society; it is only necessary to remove the obstructions to its growth, all of which are political and all of which stem from faith in authoritarianism.

Our own country furnishes an illustration. In the beginning, before Americans had been completely converted to this political paganism, it was stipulated that their marketplace should be as large as the country; the erection of trade barriers between the component commonwealths was prohibited. As the frontiers of the country were extended the marketplace grew apace and, in time, goods, men, and ideas moved without hindrance from the Atlantic to the Pacific, from Mexico to Canada. Therefore, an American society grew up. It was not planned; it grew. Several times the little separate political establishments set up blocks to trade at their respective borders, causing friction, but on the whole their efforts were frustrated by the spirit of free trade. (It might be well to mention, in passing, that the prime cause of the Civil War was protectionism, which is a dogma of authoritarianism.)

Let us look at a contrary example. Europe, which, outside of Russia, compares in size with the United States, is cross-checked with tariff barriers, and Europe has been a battlefield for centuries. Political particularism has prevented the flowering of a European society. It is impossible for such a thing to get going in an area darkened by passports and customs regulations. Time and again the doctors of political science have prescribed some sort of political union for the ills of Europe, on the assumption that such a union will be followed by a customs union. Quite the contrary; the borders between countries lose all meaning if the peoples can "do business" with one another; which is another way of saying, if the states get out of the way of society. No political union can set up a society in Europe; that can only come from uninhibited "higgling and haggling" in a common marketplace.

If their senses were not dulled by their idolatry, the one-worlders could draw a sound conclusion from these two examples; namely, that the only way to a world society is through free trade. This does not mean that free trade alone would guarantee world peace, for there are other political institutions that make for frictions; but, it would go a long way. After all, if the customer is always right, how could he be an enemy?

Part III

Why We Have Socialism

About Socialism and Socialists

I was a shaver of ten or twelve when, on doing errands for my father, I ran into Grand Street. That was, and is, a thoroughfare in downtown New York, but in those days it was an institution, made so by a number of establishments along the street called "coffee saloons." These, I presume, served other foods, but when I patronized them in the afternoons they purveyed only mugs of coffee and hunks of cake. The customers, or habitués, seemed to be less interested in eating and drinking than in arguing the metaphysical notions of Karl Marx or Kropotkin.

Each of these establishments acquired a character of its own, deriving from the particular ideology advocated by its clientele, or from an interpretation of that ideology enunciated by some self-appointed pundit who had got a following. There was at least one "saloon" which only the true believers frequented, their principal pastime, aside from discussing moot questions in Marxist "science," being to castigate the revisionists, who held forth in another "saloon." The latter, who called themselves Social Democrats, spent most of their time proving to

This article appeared as chapter 8 of Out of Step.

one another the correctness of the reforms they had concocted; incidentally, they must have been right, for most of the reforms were later taken over by the Democrats and then by the Republicans. But, on the whole, these socialists were evolutionary, rather than revolutionary; they dreamed of the day when capitalism shall have decayed, from its internal deficiencies, when a mere push from the proletariat will topple it. They were willing to let the immutable forces of history do the job, and contented themselves with talking; there was little inclination to help the forces of history along. That was long before Lenin came along with his doctrine of dynamism.

There are very few of the Grand Street type of socialists around these days, either in this country or in Europe, except, perhaps, in the Kremlin. Gone are the doctrinaires, the "scientific" socialists, with whom I delighted to argue on the campus of Columbia College, or whom I heckled on the soapbox in Union Square, New York. They have disappeared not only because the measures they advocated have largely been accepted and have been institutionalized, but more so because their theoretical position has been undermined by experience. There are therefore few to say a good word for the laboriously manufactured labor theory of value, or to give even lip service to the Marxist many-worded theory of surplus value, which was the keystone of his theory of exploitation, which in turn was the basis for his indictment of capitalism. The Russian "experiment" has shown that the state can be built on the bones of the proletariat, as well as on the bones of capitalists, and his "withering away of the state" theory has gone the way of all his notions. There is nobody to argue with, and all the hours I put into *Das Kapital,* for the purposes of dialectic, now seem to have been wasted. Too bad, for I did have a good time with these socialists.

But, that is the way of empirical knowledge: it makes a mess of theories confidently advanced by long-winded economists and ivory-tower social scientists. Capitalism, without benefit of a theory, and operating solely on the mundane profit motive, has disproven Marx on every point. To be sure, the economists of the Austrian school had done in the labor theory of value— that the value of a thing is determined by the amount of labor put into producing it—by showing that value is entirely subjective and has no relation whatever to labor; but capitalists did it in their own way; when people wanted a thing and were willing to pay for it, the capitalists made it, and when there was no demand for a thing it simply was not made. That is to say, the consumer puts a value on what he wants. The surplus value theory had it that capitalists paid labor subsistence wages and retained as profits all that labor produced above this subsistence level; but capitalism proved that wages come out of production, and that the more capital is used in production, the greater the output of labor and therefore the greater its rewards. Capitalism has raised wages, not lowered them, as Marx predicted. So much so, that the worker with a washing machine and an automobile has lost every vestige of "working-class consciousness." He even plays golf.

It took capitalism almost a hundred years to demolish "scientific" socialism by the pragmatic method, but it did so thorough a job of it that *Das Kapital* has been laid to rest without a requiem. Even the nationalization of industry, once given the top priority of all socialistic programs, has lost its appeal. In England, the labor unions, which furnish the bulk of the finances for the Labour Party, have given up on nationalization for two reasons: first, in a strike against privately owned industry the government can be called in as a mediator, and the government can always, for political reasons, be counted on to favor the strikers, while a strike against a nationalized industry is in fact a strike against the government, or a revolution, with questionable results; second, the inefficiency of a bureaucratically controlled industry is too evident to warrant even discussion. The German socialists, heretofore the most valiant of Marxist protagonists, have declared that nationalization is to be resorted to only if it advances "socialistic ends"; otherwise, industry can be left in private hands. The fact of the matter is that the condition of the workers has so improved under a free economy that they do not relish any change, and the theoretical socialists, anxious for votes, have had to change their theory to suit their following.

So, what is socialism without Marx? I put that question to an official of the French Socialist Party and received this answer: "Marx could not have anticipated the great technological advances of the past century and, therefore, while his theories were correct in his day they do not apply to present conditions. Nevertheless, Marx did much for the working-class movement in his time and he still gives our movement direction and inspiration." That is to say, there is no theoretical position for socialists, no postulates to guide them, and they must "play it by ear." As a matter of necessity they are reduced to expediencies and have therefore become mere politicians, not revolutionists. In every country the socialists have become office seekers, aiming to get hold of the reins of government by parliamentary methods, and for no other purpose than to enjoy the prerogatives and perquisites of office. Power for the sake of power is their current aim.

Well, how does one acquire power in a country ruled by popular suffrage? By promising the electorate all their hearts desire and by being more profligate with promises than the opposition. Thus, socialism has become mere welfarism, and with welfarism comes control of the national economy. But, while Marxism aimed to control the economy for the purpose of destroying capitalism, modern socialism seems bent on controlling the economy for the sake of control; even advocating something called a "mixed" economy, partly free and partly controlled.

In short, socialists everywhere have adopted the program of American "liberals." In Europe, those of the socialistic persuasion still maintain their allegiance to the name, since there the word *liberal* still retains its original meaning, as defining one who would remove laws, not proliferate them, while the socialistically minded in this country have perverted the word into its opposite meaning. But the European socialist and the American liberal are both energumens for government intervention in the affairs of men, both have an overpowering desire for power, and both offer to buy votes with tax money. The programs and the tactics of the two are identical. And neither has any theoretical position, any philosophy of either government or economics, by which they can be judged. Both are opportunistic.

Returning to Grand Street; at that age I could not follow the reasoning—if it can be called reasoning—of the various pundits who held forth in these "saloons," but I did acquire a dislike for socialists that has hung onto me ever since. A child is guided by his instincts, which are packaged in its little brain when he comes into this world. Just as his bundle of muscles may be developed along certain lines, or his senses sharpened by practice, so may his instincts (or temperament, if you wish) be refined or trained by education; but, trained or untrained, the original stock manifests itself in his reaction to his environment, and this reaction remains constant. That is why there are, in degree of devotion or adherence to doctrine, all kinds of

Catholics or Jews, and all sorts of Democrats or Republicans. That is what we mean when we say that the boy is a "born" mathematician or a "born" politician. His instinct inclines him toward a given body of thought, and no amount of argument or education can wean him away from it. He will drift toward that body of thought no matter what influences are brought to bear upon him simply because of an intuitive, built-in inclination toward it.

Socialists are born, not made. (And so are individualists.) In a way, the basic urge toward socialism is in all of us, since every one of us is inclined to impose our set of values on others; we seek to "improve" the other fellow up to our own particular standards. But, most of us will try to "elevate" the other fellow and, meeting resistance, will give it up as a hopeless job. The socialist, however, has an intuitive urgency for power, power over other people, and proceeds to bolster this urgency with an ethic: he seeks power for a humanitarian purpose. He would "elevate" all mankind to his ideal. Since the individual does not wish to be "elevated," and lays claim to something called rights, the socialist undertakes to prove that the individual does not exist, that an amorphous thing called "society" is the only fact of reality, and proceeds to impose his set of values on this thing. Having made this discovery—that society is something greater than the sum of its parts, with an intelligence and a spirit of its own—the socialist dons his shining armor and sets forth on a glorious adventure for its improvement. He works for the "social good"—which is what he wanted to do since first he became aware of his instinct.

I have never met a dedicated socialist who did not deem himself a leader—if not at the top of the revolution, then at least as commissar of toothpicks in the ninth ward. He is not a replaceable part of the thing called society, but was destined, at birth, to be a regulator of this thing. This desire for power is quite common, even among nonsocialists, but while others seem willing to win their spurs according to the rules of the marketplace, the socialist claims the scepter because he has a mission. He is of the anointed. In this respect, the socialist is no different from the millions of bureaucrats who now infest the social order; the bureaucrat is, like the socialist, a ruler by natural selection.

Environment or education has little to do with the making of a socialist. He may come from a wealthy home, where all his training should incline him toward capitalism, or he may come from the slums. In point of fact, many of the leaders among the socialists, those who do most to advance the cause, are inheritors of great fortunes accumulated under capitalism. It is sometimes claimed that their urgency to destroy the system stems from a sense of guilt; they feel, according to this theory, that they are not entitled to the riches they have inherited, that the riches stemmed from an iniquitous system, and are impelled by this sense of guilt to dedicate themselves to the destruction of the system. I do not hold with this theory, and I point to the fact that only a few of these scions of great wealth become socialists, while the great majority put their money to productive enterprise or consume it in luxurious living. These few were born with an innate compulsion to socialism. There is no other way to account for their idiosyncrasy.

Education merely supplies the words and ideas that fit in with the primordial inclination of the socialist. He will accept at face value all the theories, all the figures and charts supporting his preconceived notions, and will reject offhand any argument or data that support the idea of individual freedom. You cannot teach anybody anything that he does not in a real sense already know. A class of freshmen can be subjected to all the litanies of the socialistic creed; the majority will take in what they are taught for the purpose of getting a passing grade, but a minority will thrill to the instruction, while a still smaller minority will in their hearts reject it. Those who respond favorably to the instruction came intuitively prepared to do so, while those who find it repulsive were likewise instinctively opposed to it. On the other hand, give a course in classical economics, or teach a group the meaning of natural rights, and some, though they have absorbed all the words of freedom, will come away entirely unconvinced. Some emotional blocking prevents the ideas from taking root. And this is also true of all the collectivistic professors; they read all the books which the individualist holds most dear, but the reading leaves them cold to the ideas; they are collectivist because nature inclined them toward collectivism.

It is true that by far the majority of our educators are socialists. But this follows not from the fact that they were educated in the creed, but that most of those who go into the pedagogical business are by nature inclined toward it. Teaching is by general acclaim a noble profession, getting that reputation from the fact that its practitioners generously and without expectation of monetary rewards undertake to inculcate values in the young. But, it is also a profession that is removed from the disciplines of the marketplace and as such appeals to those who find these disciplines distasteful; they have no liking for the higgling and haggling of the marketplace, no inclination to enter the competitive field. Since our educational system is largely dominated by government, and is therefore monopolistically controlled, it attracts those who favor that kind of control; that is, it has a lure for the socialistically minded.

Our current crop of college professors was attracted to the profession during the New Deal. Then it was that President

Roosevelt welcomed into the bureaucracy a host of professors bent on trying out, at the taxpayers' expense, some ideas on "social betterment" which they had whittled out of words, and the opportunity thus offered to "do something about it" attracted a number of young men and women (because they were inherently socialists) to teaching; it seemed the right way to get into the bureaucracy, where one could help fix up the world. That is really where they belong, in the bureaucracy, for that is where one gets clean away from the marketplace. However, vast as is the bureaucracy there is not room in it for all the professors, and many do not have even the solace of temporary employment on government projects; most must remain on campuses for the rest of their lives, and they make the best of it by imposing on their students the values acquired during their own student days. They are still New Dealers; in fact, they inherited the instinct.

One more bit of evidence to support my thesis that socialism is intuitive, not acquired, is my experience with ex-socialists and ex-communists. I have known a number of them and, with one exception, though they had dropped theoretical socialism they were all for government intervention; even that one exception was for our undertaking a "preventive war" with Russia. All of them were intellectually honest men and rejected Marx on the basis of evidence and the dictates of logic; all of them were revolted by the immoralities of Sovietism. Yet, they could not accept wholeheartedly the principles of laissez-faire economics, nor could they subscribe to the idea of negative government. They held to the notion that government ought to intervene in the marketplace, for the "social good," that political power could be exercised for the benefit of mankind. They were socialists in spite of themselves. They gave the impression that if only they were in command, socialism would work out all right. Other doxies were heterodox, but theirs was orthodox.

Since socialism is so well institutionalized, since it is the going order, introduced through democratic methods, it might be claimed that almost all, or at least the majority of the people, are socialists. That is not so. The average person is not the least bit interested in any ideology, being content to get along as best he can under any conditions imposed on him. To be sure, almost everybody is enticed by the prospect of something for nothing, and since that is what our socialists—calling themselves liberals—offer, almost everybody is willing to go along with their programs. Taking a gift does not, however, entail acceptance of the donor's philosophy. The proletarian and the plutocrat will both accept a handout without regard to consequences, thinking only of immediate enjoyment and disregarding the motives of the donor; welfarism does not commit the welfaree to any ideology.

In point of fact, it is the human capacity for adjustment that the socialist counts on to advance his cause. He lures the unsuspecting public by his offer of something for nothing and when they become inured to its acceptance, so that they consider it a right," he proceeds to burden them with additional gifts, the acceptance of which becomes easier with each new donation. His motive is to institute a regime of statism, in which a bureaucracy regulates the market, plans the economy and regiments the people. But, he gets there by degrees, basing his program on the capacity for adjustment, rather than on the conscious acceptance of his ideal. That is how our "social security" scheme has developed; starting in 1935 with old-age "insurance" for a limited number of persons, it has widened its coverage, increased the emoluments, compelled others to come under its aegis, and, of course, increased taxes; it will shortly include medical services for oldsters, from which will come socialized medicine for all.

I have seen welfarism introduced as a temporary measure, intended for relief of the masses during the depression, and have watched it grow into a permanent policy of the nation, so much so that even to question it is to draw down on oneself the opprobrious name of reactionary. In twenty-five years it has come to pass that one out of every six Americans is the recipient of government handouts of some kind, and the number is growing. To be sure, the very beneficiaries of the system pay for what they are getting, in taxes and in inflation, and they pay in addition the cost of administrating the collection and distribution of the largess. Of course, it has all been done by the democratic process, by voting into office men of a socialistic bent, and, democracy being what it is, the process of socializing the country cannot be stopped. A people can vote themselves into slavery, though they cannot vote themselves out of it.

The "Crime" of the
Capitalists

More than a century ago Karl Marx prophesied the collapse of capitalism and the advent of socialism. In the stars of history were written two theories which foretold the inevitable. These theories he called the "concentration of capital" and "increasing misery."

The theories and the prophecy are worked out in great detail over hundreds of pages of fine print, but briefly they come to this: private property contains within itself the seed of its own destruction; this is its exploitative character. The laborer is robbed of his product by way of the surplus value inherent in capitalism, and the capitalist cannot consume all that he confiscates; hence a burdensome abundance accumulates. There is nothing the capitalist can do about it, for the surplus comes from the very nature of private ownership. When the owners try to unload in the market, domestic or foreign, a competitive contest takes place. The large capitalists eliminate the smaller. Those who have much have more thrust upon them. This centralization of capital makes capitalism in time a top-heavy

"The 'Crime' of the Capitalists" was posthumously published in Ideas *(Spring–Summer 1969). It is a reworking of an article Chodorov published in* analysis *(November 1945) under the title "Why We Have Socialism."*

structure, ready to topple over at the first good push. Meanwhile, the lot of the workers becomes progressively worse; their desperation drives them eventually to revolt. The revolt must prosper because this vast army, enlarged by demotions from the capitalist class, is "disciplined, united, organized, by the very mechanism of the process of capitalist production itself." At the right moment—Marx expected it in his lifetime— "the knell of capitalist property sounds. The expropriators are expropriated."

A century should be time enough to test these theories. And the evidence of this period, even as a number of his followers admit, hardly supports them. Instead of an increasing concentration of capital, the figures show a constantly expanding class of capital owners; instead of intensified misery, the lot of the proletariat has vastly improved, even if the general wage level seems out of kilter with the general increase in production. These "scientific" theories, like others by which Marx hoped to lift socialism out of dreamy utopianism, have been knocked awry by facts, and his prophecy, based on these theories, seems to have been the vision of an armchair revolutionist.

And yet, it happens that Marx did hit upon an eventuality. Private capitalism is indeed slipping, while socialism is stepping along.

At this point, we ought to attempt, at least, a formulation of a general definition of socialism. The task is complicated by the lack of agreement among socialists themselves as to what the term means. To some it is a goal, to others it is a system of revolutionary tactics; it is an end in itself, it is a means toward another end, and on what that ultimate end may be there are opinions; in truth, it must be said that to the vast majority of its devotees socialism is the undefined "good society" of which mankind has dreamed since the beginning of time. Since no all-inclusive definition is possible, the best that can be done is to find among the various shadings of doctrine some common thread of thought. And that is: the public ownership and operation of the means of production and exchange. This, of course, will not satisfy all, if any, groups. Some will take umbrage at the word "public" and demand that "social" be substituted; the lack of a social goal in this definition will shock many, though the inclusion of a specific goal would raise a howl of dissension; many socialists demand a limit to public ownership, while others would leave nothing but personal articles in the hands of the individual. However, the common denominator is inclusive enough to make a working definition.

Public ownership of capital, no matter what it may ultimately lead to, comes to state capitalism. Capital is inanimate. Somebody must produce, make use of and look after it. If private persons are prevented by police power from accumulating and employing capital, the job must be undertaken by or under the supervision of political persons, that is, if there is going to be any capital—and that, however one tries to camouflage the fact, is state capitalism. Nor is it anything else if the regime is instituted without the use of prohibitory laws, as when private enterprise is wiped out in a competitive struggle with state-owned capital because it is under the handicap of supporting its competitor with taxes.

Only in Russia, its satellites, and China, now that the German and Italian machines have been smashed, is outright and unequivocal state capitalism a going concern. England is on the way to adopting it; while the present regime proposes to monopolize only certain forms of capital, the question which experience will decide is whether the intrusion of the state into one phase of the economy can stop at that predetermined point. The odds are against it, simply because in a highly specialized economy every industry impinges on many others, and the state must find it necessary to go into businesses related to those already nationalized. Even in America, long a sanctum of free enterprise, state capitalism is proceeding apace. There is no other way to describe federal ownership and operation of vast hydroelectric plants or the government's entry into the housing business or its extensive banking enterprises. In almost every country in the world the state has acquired monopolies of particular forms of capital and the trend is very definitely toward a widening of the practice. So that, if the statement that socialism is with us seems to be hyperbole, it is only so in point of degree; the seed has been planted, the soil is fertile and rapid growth seems inevitable.

But—if Marx's theories have proven to be fallacious—how is it that his prophecies of state capitalism are being fulfilled? Who is to blame? The answer is ironic but undeniable.

Between those who worship at the temple of capitalism and those who, to propitiate the gods of socialism, scorn that edifice, there are points of essential similarity; that is, similarity in essential articles of faith. For instance, a tenet common to both is that only under the aegis of the state is economic betterment to be found. The bitterest hater of socialism is as quick to call on political power to help him out of an economic morass as is the avowed socialist. Those unions which reject communism (for practical discussion, communism must be regarded as a socialistic sect) and those which openly espouse it are both in favor of a partnership with political power; hard-headed businessmen and visionary pink professors join in asking the government to tax and spend the country into prosperity; protectionism, socialized medicine, unemployment insurance, social security, full-employment legislation, farm subsidies, and all manner of political cures for economic ills find support

in the opposing camps. The difference between the two sim-
mers down to the question who shall control the power of the
state; both are committed to the doctrine of more bread through
more police.

Capitalists will demur at this statement and protest that the
cardinal prayer in their litany is individualism. Yet when you
parse this prayer you find it is only a supplication for privilege.
Privilege from whom? The state, the source of all privilege.
Privilege for whom? Themselves, of course. Privilege against
whom? Those who, deprived of access to the source of power,
are put under compulsion to give up part of their production to
those who have been favored by the state. Every privilege involves an advantage, and every advantage predicates a disadvantage. Therefore, the individualism about which the going
capitalism prates is a decidedly one-sided arrangement. It is
quite the opposite of that equality of rights and opportunities
which is the keystone of true individualism.

When we consider the history of what is called capitalism
we see that its principals never concerned themselves only, or
even mainly with private ownership of the means of production
and exchange. At the inception of the laissez-faire economy in
the eighteenth century, the rising class of entrepreneurs put
forth every effort to acquire for themselves a preferred position
comparable to that occupied by the nobility; the task of producing goods and services for exchange has always been secondary and unwanted. Slavery, patents, franchises, protective
tariffs, cartels, subsidies, land grants—any monopolistic avoidance of the demands and risks of competition has been and is
the hope and the goal of the businessman. He is a capitalist
only by necessity; his ambition is to be a monopolist. Since
every privilege amounts to getting something for nothing, no
privilege can be self-enforcing. Taking property always requires

force, and legalized force is the most expedient. The sovereignty of the state, backed by general acquiescence, is the source of privilege. It is the gangster's gun made shiny by the law.

The state, however abstract it may seem, is composed of human beings whose motivations are typical of the race. Their only price for granting a privilege is a further increment of power. Patents require a patent office, tariffs call for an extensive customs service, land grants demand a register's office. Every privilege granted by the state enlarges its working force, its power, and its income by way of additional tax levies. Capitalists have rarely objected to all this; the cost of maintaining a bureaucracy is an inconsequential charge against profitable privileges, and is in the main met by taxes on producers anyway.

As it went about peddling privilege for grants of power, the state could not restrict its clientele to a specially selected group; that is, not after constitutionalism effected a diffusion of its strength. Feudalism had kept everything running smoothly by limiting privilege and political power to a well-circumscribed group. When the growing class of industrialists broke through this crust they demanded a share in the political power. Their economic strength made it impossible to hold them in subjection, and by the use of such shibboleths as "no taxation without representation" and "the rights of man" they managed to wangle their way into a partnership with the rulers. There the *nouveaux riches* held on, emulating their feudal predecessors by using political power to their advantage. They instituted the mercantilist system of creating scarcities so that the worker would have to give up more to them for the needs of life. To the privileges of the feudal landowners were added the privileges of the industrialists. Both classes, knowing how they came by their affluence, were intent on depriving the clamoring crowd of access to that power. But the crowd could not be denied forever, and when at long last it became a participant in power, by way of the vote, it soon learned its economic possibilities.

And so, as the suffrage was extended the state's customers increased in number and ferocity. Privilege was added to privilege with dizzy profligacy; the capacity of production to meet the price was ignored in the wild scramble for something "for free." Meanwhile, this siphoning of production involved an increasing overhead cost, thus further depleting the economy, while the administrative agency became stronger and bolder by the wealth and power thus put into its hands. It met the disaffection arising from a lowering economy by adding another group to its roster of privilege, another tax levy to its fiscal strength. Just as it relieved "infant industries" of foreign competition with a protective tariff, which added to its coffers, so it provided medical care for the indigent at the price of so-called social-security taxes; it subsidized the railroad magnates and the impoverished farmers with equanimity, and blithely put the costs on production. What else could it do? Nor could it carry out its assignments without an increase in its collecting and dispensing personnel, whose keep must also be provided for by producers.

As I have pointed out on numerous occasions, socialism is the end-product of an economy sucked dry by privilege. It is the political control of an economy so weakened by political intercession that it cannot stand up on its own feet. When the remuneration for productive effort is insufficient to warrant the expenditure, when rent, royalties, subsidies, and doles, to say nothing of the enforcement costs, absorb so much that sustenance becomes precarious and the incentive for capital accumulation disappears, then the state takes over and tries to make a go of it. It is not necessary here to discuss the causes of the periodic paroxysm known as the "depression"; it should be pointed out, however, that during such times the transference of economic power from producer to politician is accelerated, for it is then that the bewildered public is most susceptible to the most impossible promises. Nor need we go into the subject of war to show how this political upheaval gives impetus to the socialistic trend, not only by the new coercive instruments it puts into the hands of the state, but more so by the correlative economic power conferred on the politician; the financing of war through loans, to mention but one instance, creates a privilege class most intimately concerned with the state's power of levying taxes.

Socialism creeps up on society. It need not come by way of revolution, as Marx predicted. The bolsheviks in Russia and the fascists in Italy did take over the economies of their respective countries with a fanfare of arms, but in Germany it was initiated with legality and in England it is going through the parliamentary mill in due order. In America the state is becoming the one and only capitalist quite peacefully, making its way to the seductive strain of "the better life." And, in those countries where state capitalism became an accomplished fact as well as in those countries where it promises to come into its own, the proletarian revolution was and is absent. A few intellectuals made Russia what it is, while the Nazis and fascists owed their success to the support of middle-class industrialists. In England the privileged classes have taken to the idea of selling out their holdings to the state, and in America it is the so-called capitalist who is to blame for the fufillment of Marx's prophecies. Beguiled by the state's siren song of special privilege, the capitalists have abandoned capitalism. In doing so they may well have made inevitable that day in the not-so-distant future when their dearly bought privileges will be swept away as the state formally takes the means of production into its own hands. How right Lenin was when he said that the capitalist would sell you the rope with which you intended to hang him if he thought he could make a profit on the sale.

A Fifty-Year Project

C ame 1950, and the Sunday supplement writers had something new to engage their talents. The achievements of the human race, particularly the American branch of it, during the first half of the twentieth century made good copy. Every accomplishment of note, in science, art, industry, or sports, received proper notice. Except one. And that one achievement of the last fifty years is far more startling, far more important from the long-term point of view, than anything the literary gentlemen paid their respects to. It was the transmutation of the American character from individualist to collectivist.

The replacement of the horse and buggy by the automobile is startling enough; but is it as startling as the contrast between Cleveland and Truman? This is not to compare one president with the other, but to point out the remarkable change in the character of the people presided over. Cleveland's remark that the government could not take care of the people who took care of it was made because Americans thought that way; today, the

This article was originally written for and published in pamphlet form by the National Council for American Education. I have reprinted here the version Chodorov published in analysis *(October 1950). A different version appeared in* Human Events *and was the impetus for the founding of the Intercollegiate Society of Individualists. It was also reprinted in* Out of Step.

handout principle of government is accepted by all good Americans, from pauper to millionaire. At the beginning of the century the tradition of individualism that had held up since the Revolution was still going strong; by 1950, only the physical composition of the individual remained, for his character had been well washed out by the caustic of socialism.

Anybody can make a machine, but the unmaking of a national character is the work of genius. The accomplishment is too great to be ignored. A study of just how it was done is in order, and it ought to be undertaken at once, before the American individualist becomes a subject for speculative archaeology. There are still some living remnants of the species, and traces of the way they behaved and thought have not yet been entirely obliterated. A thorough analysis of the character transformation may well serve the twenty-first century in its disillusionment; and it may help them find their way back to a sense of freedom; provided, of course, such a work should escape the bonfire of past values that always lights up the road of socialism.

AN IMPORTANT CHAPTER

At least one chapter of the book should deal with how the collectivist seed was implanted in the soft and fertile student mind forty-odd years ago. That's how it all began. Collectivism is, after all, only an idea, and the usual way of acquiring an idea is by learning. The followers of Marx are fond of saying that socialism is an inevitable product of the forces of history; but, this manure of inevitability is the fertilizer they use to aid the idea of socialism in taking root and sprouting after it is planted. If the thing was to come anyhow, why have they been so assiduous in spreading the idea? Why did they bother to organize students' socialist clubs when socialism was "in the nature of things"?

Just how socialism first invaded the campus is not recorded. Perhaps a student or two became infected at some street corner and brought it in. The glorious promise of socialism gave it easy access to the idealistic adolescent mind, insufficiently fortified by reason or experience. At eighteen, one is ready to take up for every underdog, real or imaginary, and the opportunity to remake the world is most inviting. Very few students, however, paid much attention to the importation when it first appeared; one had enough to do to get over the difficult hurdles of the rigid curriculum that prevailed in those days. Besides, one had to prepare oneself for the arduous task of meeting the problems of the world as an individual. It was then taken for granted that one's way in life called for industry and self-improvement; politics and a government job, including an army career, were for the unfit only; you got an education so that you could the better take care of yourself, not society. While that tradition prevailed, socialism made little headway on the campus.

The idealistic pretensions of socialism did capture a few hearts, while its vibrant and challenging slogans fed the nascent revolutionary flame of youth. Their intellectual vanity was flattered by the "scientific" claims of socialism; they knew all about surplus value, which the others did not understand, and that made them an elite. The "science" was aided and abetted by such fighting words as "workers of the world unite, you have nothing to lose but your chains," and the knight-errant of the fuzzy chin was aroused to the full. Truth to tell, those who espoused socialism were among the most imaginative, volatile, and articulate students; the fact that they were ignored or derided by their classmates simply added to their ardor, for it fed the sense of superiority that makes for martyrdom. They made some headway with a few who could not break into the fraternities or could not make the athletic teams.

CONVERSION WITHOUT UNDERSTANDING

In those early days the socialistic students were unorganized. They were held together by the bond of the unwanted. Their principal occupation was mutual conversion. When they got hold of a possible proselyte, they put him to a disadvantage by the ready speeches got out of their extracurricular reading, mostly pamphlets, and the prospect was overpowered, if not convinced. They attracted some attention by their self-assurance and by their audacity, which was their purpose in the first place. But, on the whole, they cut little figure on the campus; far less, let us say, than did the few students of Oriental origin who came to American colleges before World War I.

Not long after the Brest-Litovsk treaty, the organized socialistic student group began to appear and the apparatus of proselytizing was set up. Unauthorized posters advertising "noted" speakers adorned the official bulletin boards, and often the promise of enlightenment was supplemented with the assurance of refreshments. Conversion through the media of dances and punch was found to be even more effective than through literature and argument. The membership of these clubs grew.

Between the two world wars the socialists got going on their "inevitable" idea in dead earnest; they pushed it along with all the organizational ingenuity they possessed, and they possessed plenty. Lenin had taught them that one need not wait on the slow process of evolution; history could be hurried. The process of expedition consisted in the marshaling of the mass-mind behind an idea, whether understood or not; in fact, the less understood the better, for thinking might retard the action to which the historical forces are amenable. The teaching of "scientific" socialism was suspended and the necessity of "dynamism" was emphasized. Action for the sake of action was all that counted. Marx was spoken of and revered, but far more important than an understanding of what he taught was the doctrine of solidarity and the policy of movement.

The organizers paid special attention to the mass-mind on the campus, the mind that would eventually make the rules for other people to live by. Their efforts here were aided by the disillusionment that followed the war with the Central Powers. Taking advantage of this frame of mind among the students, the socialists set themselves up as the "prophets of pacifism," conveniently overlooking the militancy preached by Marx. Many a student became a socialist—that is, joined a socialist club—simply because he was opposed to war; which was all right with the doctrinaire leadership, whose goal was numbers, not understanding.

To make trouble for trouble's sake is a fundamental of socialist strategy, and the students' clubs followed that principle in campus affairs at any and all occasions. Their *esprit de corps* was thus improved. Nothing favored their purpose more than involvement in a strike, and they looked upon one in the neighborhood with great favor. It gave them an opportunity to harangue the crowd, pass out leaflets, do picket duty, charge the police, and get themselves arrested and martyrized. It was a lark to be sure, but a lark glamorized with a "noble" purpose. Active participation in some labor trouble was a cementing influence far more effective than intellectual agreement. It was a demonstration of the superiority of the group over the individual.

CAME THE NEW DEAL

By the time the New Deal came upon us these college socialists were well organized. They had become intercollegiate
in scope. At national conventions the boys and girls settled all
the problems of mankind, national and international, present
and future. They debated and resolved, resolved and debated,
and went back to their respective campuses thoroughly exalted.
They attracted attention, and among those attracted were sons
of the detested capitalistic class, boys who were thrilled by the
prospect of expiating the sins of their fathers on the altar of the
"public good," meanwhile flattering their egos by the attendant
publicity. Money to carry on the crusade was thus easier to
come by.

The effects of three decades of organization and propaganda
soon became evident. Thousands of graduates of these socialistic clubs had gone out into the world. It was natural that they
should enter those fields in which ideas and opinions are the
main stock-in-trade, and where training in organizational methods comes in handy; the teaching profession, labor unions,
social work, law and politics, and, most important, the publishing business. Working themselves into positions of importance, they eased the way for a supporting cast of their own
kind. Jobs for the faithful became plentiful; for nonbelievers
the opportunities became scarcer and scarcer. Since the third
decade of the century, therefore, a pedagogue of known individualistic inclinations has found employment increasingly difficult, and an antistatist writer simply has no market for his
wares. If a book of that type does get into print, thanks to a
venturesome publisher, it is given short shrift by the reviewers,
most of whom came out of the socialistic college environment,

and its chances for wide reception are thus choked off; on the other hand, any kind of socialistic bilge is boosted into a masterpiece. The clan takes care of its own.

The New Deal was a product of this extracurricular work in the colleges. When the "emergency" hit President Roosevelt, he had nobody to turn to for advice but the graduates of these socialistic clubs. The businessmen, the men who concern themselves with the making and selling of things, were in the main devoid of any knowledge of fundamental economics, and too bewildered by the turn of events to be of much use in the situation. The loudmouthed theoreticians were more sanguine; besides, the books they had had published qualified them as experts. It would be interesting to know how many of the professors who came to the aid of Mr. Roosevelt had been associated with socialistic groups in their college days; that would throw light on the transmutation of the American character.

The apparatus of the New Deal was most favorable for the "inevitable" idea, for it provided the sustenance necessary for effective propaganda work. No longer were the socialist workers dependent for their living on voluntary contributions; the taxpayer now fed them well, and they worked the better on full stomachs. Today, a bright young man cannot afford to entertain individualistic ideas, assuming that he happened on them in some dust-covered book, because such ideas carry a decided economic disadvantage. The best jobs go to those most loyal to the new Americanism.

HELP FROM THE ENEMY

The character of a nation is the way it thinks. American thought in 1950 is collectivistic because the seed of that kind of thinking was well planted in its most receptive minds during the early years of the century. What we have now is the fruit of careful and assiduous husbandry.

The climate of the times favored the socialists. They could point up the manifest injustices and incongruities that had developed under the prevailing system of private property, which made no distinction between productive effort and political privilege. The growth of monopolies, and the ruthlessness of their practices, presented an easy indictment of private property as a whole. It was a damaging indictment and the heart of youth was so touched that examination was precluded. The fact that monopoly is a product of politics, and that socialism is nothing but a political scheme, did not occur to them, and the monopolists were in no position to bring up the matter. Socialism, of course, proposes to substitute public for private monopoly, claiming that, with the "profit motive" gone, the evils inherent in monopoly would be wiped out. The inference is that under socialistic management monopoly would be an instrument for good only; which is a variation of the "chosen people" doctrine, and that catered to the conceit of the neophyte socialists.

Then, the obvious incongruity of the "boom and bust" economy helped the socialistic idea along, particularly as it came up with a plausible explanation and a cure; the going capitalism offered neither. Again, the recurrence of war under capitalism was a condemnation that youth could understand, and since socialism insisted that it had a preventive it was accepted sight unseen. Youth loves, never analyzes, a panacea.

Abysmal ignorance of their own philosophy, plus a smug complacency, put the practicing capitalists at a disadvantage in meeting the challenge of youth. They had been in the driver's seat too long to believe dislodgment a possibility. Somewhere hovering over their cloudy heads, but not bothering them at all, were the ideas of Locke, Adam Smith, Jefferson, and the other libertarians of the past two centuries; these were like heirlooms gathering dust in a closet and never taken out for examination or appreciation. The only economic ideas the capitalists had a working acquaintance with were those conducive to the piling up of profits, like protective tariffs and other special privileges. As for the doctrine of natural rights, which is the foundation of capitalistic thought, it meant nothing to them but the right to exploit their fellow man. Preoccupation with the business of making money, by any and all means, dulled whatever intellectual capacity they might have had. The best they could offer to inquiring youth was their own affluence as a demonstration of the excellence of the status quo, which youth could see was far from excellent.

IDEAS HAVE CONSEQUENCES

Under the circumstances, the idea of socialism took root and flourished. The question now, at the half-century mark, is whether it is destined to crowd out the remaining vestiges of individualism in the American culture. It would seem so. But socialism is only an idea, not an historical necessity, and ideas are acquired by the human mind. We are not born with ideas, we learn them. If socialism came to America because it was implanted in the minds of past generations, there is no reason for assuming that future generations will come by that idea without similar indoctrination; or that the contrary idea cannot be taught them. What the socialists have done can be undone, if there is a will for it. But, the undoing will not be accomplished by trying to destroy established socialistic institutions. It can be accomplished only by attacking minds, and not the minds of those already hardened by socialistic fixations. Individualism can be revivified by implanting the idea in the minds of the coming generations.

So then, if those who put a value on the dignity of the individual are up to the task, they have a most challenging opportunity in education before them. It will not be an easy or quick job. It will require the kind of industry, intelligence, and patience that comes with devotion to an ideal. And the only reward they can hope for is that by the end of the century, the socialization of the American character will have been undone.

Things being as they are, perhaps the job should begin by going after the preadolescent mind, even in the kindergarten grade. The socialists, it might be recalled, did not neglect to turn nursery rhymes to their use, and since the advent of the comic book, the communists (or advanced socialists) have employed this medium of indoctrination. But that is a specialized effort that could well be deferred until the college mind, the mind that will soon enter the active arena, is taken care of. The assault must be made on the campus.

WRITE OFF THE FACULTY

Assault is the proper word, and the proper attitude, for the proposed job. The possibility of winning over the faculty to the individualistic idea might as well be dismissed aforehand, simply because the professorial mind is by and large beyond redemption; it is both the effect and the cause of the condition that is to be corrected. Here and there a welcome atavism will be found, but it will be rare, and the safe thing to do is to write off the faculty. That tactic, moreover, will find favor with the students, particularly those endowed with the gift of intellectual curiosity; to be able to controvert the dicta of the professor is always a sophomoric delight. To win the student over to the idea of individualism it is necessary to equip him with doubts regarding the collectivistic doctrines insinuated into the lecture room or into his textbooks. If the suggested undertaking should apply itself to a refutation of the "adopted" texts, especially in the fields of economics, social science, and government, a veritable revolution could be started on the campus in short order; the vulnerability of these texts is all too obvious to even superficial examination.

The apparatus for initiating the project suggests itself. It would consist of a lecture bureau, manned by a secretariat and a corps of lecturers. The business of the bureau would be to arrange for lectures on or near the selected campuses. The lecturers—probably difficult to find these days—would have to be acquainted with socialistic theory as well as with the literature of individualism, for since the purpose is to uproot the trend of thought, the student would have to be impressed with its inadequacies. Whatever the subject matter of the lecture, the doctrine of the primacy of the individual, as against the supremacy of the social order, must be emphasized; thus, the student will learn to recognize in the classroom or textbook the insidious implication that the social order and its political establishment take precedence over the individual. Every lecture must contain a challenge.

It is unnecessary, in throwing out the suggestion, to detail an entire program. Once started, the project would develop a momentum of its own; the students would see to that. It might be suggested, however, that the lectures be followed up with the organization of Individualistic Clubs and an intercollegiate affiliation. Prizes for essays on individualism would do much to stimulate thought; and a publication offering an outlet for articles would be a necessity. Out of these activities would come an *esprit de corps* based upon conviction and enthusiasm for a "new" idea. The individualist would become the campus radical, just as the socialist was forty years ago, and the aura of the "intellectual elite" would fall on him.

Is the effort worthwhile? To which one offers as answer another question: What in life is more worthwhile than the pursuit of an ideal?

Part IV

Communism and America

Let's *Teach* Communism

This is a defense of our universities. As they open their doors for another year of business they teach under a widespread suspicion of teaching communism. The suspicion is unsupported by fact; it is pure witchcraft. There is reason to believe that some in the faculties *advocate* communism, but none *teaches* it. The distinction is important. To illustrate the point, in the field of religion there are many who are intellectually incapable of comprehending Christianity, and therefore of teaching it, but who are quite adept at advocating (preaching) it. So with communism; it is a pattern of ideas following from basic assumptions, and unless one has made a critical examination of these assumptions one is incapable of evaluating the superimposed ideas. Our colleges are debarred from examining the basic assumptions of communism because, as I will attempt to show, these basic assumptions are part and parcel of what is called capitalism, the going order, and it would hardly do to bring this fact to light.

If it is the business of universities to expose students to ideas, they are not doing the job properly if they neglect to include

This article first appeared in analysis *(September 1949) and was reprinted as chapter 8 of* One Is a Crowd.

in their curricula a course in communism, simply because as a system of thought, a philosophy, communism is in the ascendancy these days. A graduate ought to be thoroughly at home with the ideas he has to live with, he ought to understand the basic postulates of his ideological environment. It might be difficult to dig up professors able to brush aside the seductive phrases of communism so as to get to its roots, seeing how the subject is beclouded with war hysteria, and expedience might tell against the introduction of such a course of study. This is regrettable. For, lacking the opportunity to investigate communism, the students will come away from their education with the popular notion that it is indigenous to an "enemy" nation or an "inferior" people. To illustrate the kind of course I have in mind—this is *not* an application for a job; perish the thought!—I present herewith a few samples of communist theory that are equally the marrow of current "true Americanism." At random, we will begin with a conception of wages.

It is an axiom of communism that wages are a fraction of production given to the workers by those who own the means of production. Boiled down to its essence, this idea can be expressed in three words: capital pays wages. But, is that so in fact? If we define capital as the tools of production, this conception of wages becomes silly, for an inanimate object is incapable of paying anything. If, as the communists do, we include in the definition the owners of capital, we are faced with another *reductio ad absurdum:* competition between these machine owners for the services of machine users automatically fixes the level of wages; capitalists are without the means of affecting the ups and downs of that level.

The capitalist, of course, speaks of the wages he "pays." But, he is quick to point out that the wages do not come out of his capital, but are derived from the sale of his products; if the market does not absorb the output of his plant he ceases to be a "payer" of wages. This means that the envelopes he hands out to his employees are filled by the consumers, and these are, in large part, the workers themselves. Thus, the employer of labor is labor, and the wage earner is the wage payer. It follows that the general level of wages is determined by the general level of production—leaving out, for the moment, any purloining—and neither capital nor capitalist has any part in fixing it.

It follows also that political power can in no way affect an increase in wages; nor can capital by itself do so. Wages can go up only as a result of increased production, due to an increase in population or improvement in the skill and industry of the current population. That elemental fact will be admitted even by professors of economics, and it is possible that some legislators will recognize it. Yet, if you dig into some standard economics textbooks or examine the labor legislation of our land you will find ideas that stem from the communist notion that capital pays wages and that the hardheaded capitalist keeps them low. A minimum-wage law, for instance, is based on that notion; the law assumes that cupidity is at the bottom of the marginal worker's low income; the capitalists must be compelled to disgorge. All of which is silly, for the legally enforced increase is simply passed on to the consumer, unless it can be absorbed by increased production arising from technological improvement. Yet, in the course I suggest, it would have to be pointed out that minimum-wage laws—that all legislation dealing with labor-employer relations—are concessions to the communist conception of wages.

Our immigration-restriction laws pay homage to this idea, for these laws, translated into economics, simply say that there are just so many jobs that capitalists have at their disposal, that any increase in the working population will lower the wage level by simple division; the idea that the immigrant makes his own wages is rejected offhand. Birth control is likewise advocated as a means of raising the wage level, and Malthusianism borrows all its economics from communism. And, if you go to the bottom of our "social welfare" enthusiasm you will find the capital-culprit notion.

Space does not permit an examination of all the facets of current thought traceable to this basic bit of communism, but it is evident that the proposed course could do quite a job on it.

This brings us to the communist indictment of private property. The inherent power of capital to fix the level of wages will be used by its owners to defraud the laborers. They will see to it that the laborers receive just enough to keep them alive and on the job, retaining all above that level for themselves. Here communism introduces the doctrine of natural rights, although it denies that doctrine vehemently later on; it says that the laborers have an absolute right in all that is produced by virtue of the energy put into production; energy is a private possession. If this is so, then what the capitalist keeps for himself amounts to robbery. The word generally used is *exploitation*. This iniquitous arrangement brings on a host of evil social consequences and should therefore be stopped. How? By outlawing private capital. Everything that is produced should belong to the community as a whole (which, by the way, is a flat denial of the original right of the laborer to his product), and the state, acting for the community, must be made sole owner and operator of all capital. The state, particularly when manned by communists, will have no interest in exploitation and will pay wages in full.

The holes in that indictment are many and serious, and we

can leave it to our professor in communism to point them out. It would then be incumbent on him also to point out that capitalism, in practice, accepts the indictment in large chunks. A number of institutions have grown up under capitalism that are obviously concessions to the charge brought against it by communism. The absorption by the state of large parts of the electric power business was facilitated by moral fustian about the "power trust," while political participation in the banking, housing, insurance, and several other businesses is justified on the inadequacies, if not villainies, of private capital. Thus, while capitalism carries on its word battle with communism, it pays its adversary the high compliment of accepting its doctrine in practice.

Our professor of communism could, and should, emphasize this point by an analysis of taxation, particularly the direct kind. Income taxes unequivocally deny the principle of private property. Inherent in these levies is the postulate that the state has a prior lien on all the production of its subjects; what it does not take is merely a concession, not a right, and it reserves for itself the prerogative of altering the rates and the exemptions according to its requirements. It is a matter of fiat, not contract. If that is not communist principle, what is? The professor would have to point that out. And he should, in all conscience, show that the considerable amount of capital now owned and operated by the "capitalistic" state was siphoned out of pockets of producers by means of taxation.

But right here the professor would find himself in a mess of trouble. On the other side of the hall the professor of taxation and the professor of political science would be telling their students that the right of property is conditional, not absolute, that the owner is in fact a trustee answerable to society as a whole. They would deny that this is a concession to communist principle; but it is. The professor of philosophy would pitch in with an outright rejection of the theory of natural rights, asserting that what we call rights are but privileges granted to his subjects by the sovereign. The board of trustees would also take notice; the university and its supporters hold a lot of government bonds which are dependent on the power of taxation, and it would hardly do to question the propriety of this power. And, if the professor presumed to point out that communism is quite consistent in advocating taxation as a means of destroying private capital, he would have the whole house of respectability on his head.

A few more topics that our course in fundamental communism should touch upon—and then we can close up shop.

Reverting to the concept of natural rights—basic in capitalistic thought—we find that its taproot is the will to live. Out of this primordial desire for existence comes the idea that no man may lay claim to another man's life. How does that idea line up with military conscription? It doesn't, and the only way you can logically support conscription is to invoke the communist principle that the right to life is conditioned by the needs of the state.

Take the subject of monopoly. Communism makes much of it, although by a strange twist of logic it sees in state monopoly all the virtues lacking in private monopoly. Capitalism, in theory at least, equally condemns monopoly, on the ground that any restriction of competition lowers the general level of production and is a deterrent to human aspirations. An examination of the anatomy of monopoly reveals that its vital organ is the power to restrict production, and the source of this power is the state. Without some law favorable to its purpose every monopoly would disintegrate. Hence, the very fact of monopolies under a regime of capitalism—sometimes called "free enter-prise"—lends support to the communist assertion that the state is a committee managing affairs for the benefit of monopolists.

In discussing monopolies the class would most certainly hit upon the topic of exploitation; that is, any legal means for getting something for nothing. Having disposed of the unten-able proposition that the ownership of capital is in itself a means of exploitation, the professor, being a man of intellectual in-tegrity, would be compelled to admit that the object of monop-oly is exploitation, and that the state, in establishing the special privileges which spawn monopolies, is the guilty one. He might go so far as to declare the state—even the "dictatorship of the proletariat"—the only exploitative factor in any economy.

And so on and so on. In dissecting communism and exposing its vital parts to view, this proposed course would demonstrate the unpleasant truth that capitalist practice too often squares with communist theory. That might prove disquieting to the established departments of law, social science, history—to say nothing of the mahogany office up front. It might also disturb the students, inured as they are to a quasi-communist quasi-capitalist environment.

Under the circumstances, no college could entertain the idea of introducing into its curriculum a course in communism, and the charge that they are teaching the subject is unfounded. That they make concessions to communist theory in many of their courses is true, but that is a requirement put upon them by the as-is capitalism. And I might add that I have no fear of being asked by any college president to offer the proposed course.

Commies Don't Count

The Chamber of Commerce of the United States is as fretful as a rooster whose harem is being eyed by a rival. Its agitation is recorded in a report, "approved unanimously by the board of directors," titled *Communist Infiltration in the United States,* with the subtitle, in red ink, *Its Nature and How to Combat It.* The thing is well done and is worth the quarter asked for it; that is, if you are not familiar with what is going on along those lines.

When you read this pamphlet you get the idea that these communists are a pretty bad lot, unscrupulous, ruthless, lying, and altogether Machiavellian. No doubt they are. I would not know; the few communists I have come into contact with have irritated me with their stupid vulgarity and I therefore try to avoid them. They do not concern me. Why does the Chamber of Commerce of the United States interest itself in them? The pamphlet suggests purely patriotic motivation. It warns the reader that what the communists hope to impose on him violates the institutions collectively called Americanism. One wishes the Chamber had supplemented its report with a detailed description of the Americanism it is anxious to preserve. Lacking

This appeared in analysis *(December 1946).*

such a description, we must supply one from our knowledge of the inclinations of all chambers of commerce which flourish or have flourished in these United States.

WHAT THE COMMIES WANT

Putting that aside for the moment, let us consider what these communist fellows want. Their ultimate aim, about which they are unequivocal, regardless of the methods by which they hope to attain it, is to establish a committee of men who by virtue of their control of the political machinery of the country would order the private and public affairs of all citizens. They claim that such a committee would bring to us that full measure of happiness for which men have always yearned. That the claim is subject to doubt is unimportant; the goal of centralization of power is what we are concerned with. The Chamber of Commerce says that this in itself is very bad.

Considering the nature of political power, we must agree with the Chamber. Political power has always been the instrument by which those who control it have feathered their nests at the expense of those upon whom that power is imposed. In economic terminology this process of getting something for nothing is called exploitation. The seed of exploitation is the human inclination to satisfy desires without expending labor, and we must conclude that all humans, you and I, are exploiters at heart. The crude, uncertain and dangerous method of exploitation is taking by force; the sophisticated method is taking by means of a recognized privilege. The privilege way is better because it achieves regularity through common adulation of the law, on which the privilege is based, and has the further advantage of being supported by the physical force at the command of the political power which created it. Thus, the veterans could overpower the artisans and merchants of the community and take the goods they want; or, they can apply to the Congress, using their votes as a bribe, for a regularized grant of goods.

The communists claim that their kind of committee will not use political power in this historic way. It is a claim which we must, on the basis of all the evidence, dismiss out of hand; it is predicated on the assumption that the communist is *sui generis,* different in kind from all other men. That partakes something of the miraculous, and until the miracle is seen we shall have to assume that the communistic political committee will operate as all political committeemen have always operated; they will take care of themselves and their friends. The only difference between it and the others is that its exercise of power will be without limit, and that means that the committee will dispose of the entire national output as they see fit. All privilege will be centered in those who control political power. In that respect it will be different from the American procedure, wherein various pressure groups share in the munificence of political power. It will be monolithic rather than pluralistic exploitation.

In either system those who produce the goods and services by which they hope to live are defrauded; assuming, of course, that the producer has a right to enjoy the products of his labors. The difference between the two seems to lie in the extent and incidence of fraud. That's all.

The unhorsing of privilege can be effected only by a revolt against political power *per se,* and for that enterprise the people who make up chambers of commerce show no passion. They engage in no movement for the abolition of taxes, without which the state would fold up, and one is justified in assuming that they do not wish this to happen; the state has proven itself a valuable ally. They make no demand for the abolition of all subventions, but, rather, are feverishly lobbying Congress and the local politicians for every conceivable tax aid their cupidity can invent. The purpose and practice of every organization of businessmen—industrialists, bankers, farmers, and now laborers—have been to secure from political power some economic advantage for its members. Hence, the current fretfulness about the communists must be laid to the fear of competition in the control of political power.

COMMUNISM VIA AMERICANISM

The essence of communism is the concentration of political power. That will come about, is coming about, in the historic American way; that is, by the outright sale to political power of big chunks of social power in return for privilege. It is a matter of trade pure and simple. This bargaining between privilege and power is so characteristic of our public affairs that it must be accounted an essential of Americanism. The very inception of our centralized government was attended by an urgency to transform worthless Continental money, held largely by patriotic speculators, into purchasing power by means of federal excise and tariff taxes. Tradition has conveniently obscured the fact that our Constitution was framed by the "rich and well-born," on the doctrine that only such are entitled to govern. For about a hundred years thereafter a favorite Americanism was the granting of monopoly land privileges to various groups whose support at election time was the *quid pro quo;* the more important groups got title to the more important forest and mineral resources; the less influential, like the Grand Army of the Republic, had to be satisfied with homesteads. The rise of railroad empires is a prime lesson in Americanism, while the protective tariff swindle runs it a close second. More recently, centralized power has battened on various "relief" grants, such as handouts to the indigent, parity prices for farmers, aid to educational institutions, and so on; by all of which the membership of American chambers of commerce has profited.

Looking ahead just a little bit, perhaps not more than a year or two, we can discern a development in Americanism which will bring us to the brink of the communistic goal. Industry will force the politician into business by demanding of him a guarantee against capital losses, if not an assurance of dividends. The present situation in the coal industry is a signpost. The industry was taken over by the government when its owners refused to operate it at a loss. The government then concluded the contract with the labor union, and since the owners have refused to assume this obligation, the operation of coal mines became a sovereign function of government. Meanwhile, be it noted, the stocks of the corporations taken over by the government have maintained comparable market values. That is to say, the capital of the coal companies has not been impaired; the owners know that the government cannot force them to absorb losses incurred by its operation; and if they recover their business, any deficit due to operations in the interim will be made up by a tax grant. That is why the stocks of these corporations hold up.

HOW IT WILL COME ABOUT

Time was when Americanism shook at its foundations at the mere suggestion of government intervention in the field of business, except as a benefactor. But now this step is looked upon with complacency, if not as good Americanism. An airline company actually invites the government to take over its business when the squeeze between fixed rates and wage demands leaves nothing in the way of a return on capital. That seems to be the latest in Americanism. The next step is as straight as the crow flies. Industry will proposition government as follows: regulate us, fix prices, fix wages, if you will, but for the sake of 100 percent Americanism guarantee us some rate of return, or at least assure us against losses. It is not outside the range of possibility that the government will respond by establishing insurance of stock values, similar to the insurance of bank deposits. This will facilitate a transition to the British scheme of translating stocks into government bonds. Either as guaranteed stocks or as bonds, the support comes from taxation. Therefore the holders have a vested interest in government and, having in mind the preservation and perpetuation of their incomes, must skill themselves in the business of politics. They will perforce become the controlling committee. Thus the communistic goal of centralization will be achieved by means of on-the-barrel Americanism.

The commies don't count. That miserable crew of Moscow-led slaves have neither the strength nor the skill to push themselves into a position of predominance. They present no competitive force. But they may, and probably will, hasten centralization by creating a fear of it. We have an historic precedent to go by. In 1786, Captain Daniel Shays, a soldier of the Revolution, organized the debt-ridden farmers of Massachusetts and marched them against the government of the commonwealth. This violence galvanized the privileged classes into action against the dissatisfaction which was current throughout the colonies, and the result was a demand for strong government. There is reason to believe that the cause of Hamiltonian centralization was advanced by "Shays' Rebellion," and that but for the clamoring of the mob for relief from taxation and mortgaged indebtedness, the substitution of the Constitution for the Articles of Confederation might not have been effected. Whenever the mob starts acting up, the privileged citizenry comes to the aid of political power. Never have these people asked for a decomposition of political power. That being so, the clamoring of the Chamber of Commerce against the threat of communism is more of a portent of centralization than the antics and the slogans of the commies.

How to Curb the Commies

The trial of the communists in a New York court may have some educational value. The "sensational" evidence will be informative to those completely ignorant of Marxist-Leninist doctrine. That such ignorance should obtain, however, is not the fault of the communists, for they have made it a point these past hundred years to inform the world of their revolutionary intentions. They never made any bones about it. Their profuse literature is, as a whole, a call to arms; not only is the proletariat urged to get into the proper revolutionary frame of mind, but broad outlines as to strategy and even tactical details are offered in their manuals. The communistic cabal has never been secretive. Hence, one having the slightest acquaintance with their literature cannot get excited about the court "revelations"; the best the newspaper accounts offer in the way of interest is the counterespionage of the FBI, which brings the story up to the true-detective level.

From what has thus far transpired it seems that the communists look upon the trial as another opportunity to advertise their wares. They never miss a point. Should the accused be

"How to Curb the Commies" appeared in the May 1949 issue of analysis.

judged guilty (which they fervently hope), an attempt will be made to turn the higher courts into publicity agencies, and if in the end the eleven should be sent to jail they will serve the cause of communism by their martyrdom. The dupes, the proletariat now contributing liberally toward the cost of the defense, will be properly fired by such a turn of events. Hence, the juridical affair, whatever its outcome, must be put down to the profit side of their grand campaign.

As the defendants assert, the evidence being adduced indicates that their ideas are on trial, that they are being prosecuted for harboring thoughts deemed inimical to the public welfare. Even if it is proven that they have conspired to overthrow the government by force, the fact remains that conspiracy itself is only an idea. People of like mind agree to do this or that, but until they act, separately or in concert, the agreement remains an idea. If the communists are convicted of conspiring to bring about revolution, the judgment is long overdue, for ever since Marx gave them the *Communist Manifesto,* in 1848, the communists have been at it—by their own admission.

The case against the communists involves a principle of freedom that is of transcending importance. It is the right to be wrong. Heterodoxy is a necessary condition of a free society. When two people are in disagreement, both may be wrong, but both cannot be right. The very fact that I reject communism indicates that it is, from my point of view, erroneous; if I judged it to be sound, I would accept it. It would then cease to be "wrong" and would become "right." However, the important thing is not the wisdom I display in the choice of ideas but the right to make a choice. It is important to me, for the freedom of selection is necessary to my sense of personality; it is important to society, because only from the juxtaposition of ideas can we hope to approach the ideal of truth.

Whenever I choose an idea and label it "right," I imply the prerogative of another to reject that idea and label it "wrong." To invalidate his right is to invalidate mine. That is, I must brook error if I would preserve my freedom of thought. When I presume to be in possession of "absolute truth," and maintain that those who disagree with me not only are in error, but are wickedly or sinfully so, I lay myself open to similar judgment; in the end, then, the "absolute truth" becomes a matter of power to constrict thought.

If there is anything characteristic of America, and for which Americans can be thankful, it is that it is an area in which thought has been permitted to run riot. To be sure, our history is not free of political efforts to put limits on what people may think. Men have been legally punished for holding theological concepts at variance with those of the ruling group; for being atheists; for objecting to war; for believing that they have a right to buy and sell in the open market; for condemning slavery; for advocating birth control; for teaching the theory of evolution; for harboring art values that in the eyes of the law constituted obscenity. In every case, the authorities sought to get at ideas by inflicting punishment on those who held them; in every case, freedom of thought was the issue. It is to the credit of the American genius for freedom that ultimately the right to think as one wishes prevailed, even though too often some were made to suffer for it. Somehow the citadel of thought has held firm, and the right to be wrong has added something to human dignity.

The issue is up again. Is it wise, is it safe, to punish those who advocate communism? Granted that this doctrine is in itself a vicious denial of human dignity, the issue is not the doctrine but the right to hold it. If men are punished for espousing communism, shall we stop there? Once we deny the right to be wrong we put a vise on the human mind and put the temptation to turn the handle into the hands of ruthlessness.

But, it will be asserted, a primary tenet of communism is this very denial of free thought; if its advocates come into power they would do harm to all who entertain ideas contrary to their "line." That is true. On that point too the communists have been explicit; their insistence on the "absolute truth" of their doctrine puts any divergence from it in the category of sinful and dangerous error, not to be tolerated. It is known that when they are in power they are more ruthless in attacking unorthodoxy than was the Holy Inquisition. It is also a known fact that their doctrine undergoes the mutations dictated by political exigency and is therefore orthodox only as it serves those in power. The danger, to those who hold freedom as the highest good, is not the ideas the communists espouse but the power they aspire to. Let them rant their heads off—that is their right, which we cannot afford to infringe—but let us keep from them the political means of depriving everybody else of the same right.

This is hardly a difficult job; in fact, the tactic by which they hope to climb to power is extremely vulnerable. In the lingo of prizefighting, they telegraph their punches. They have never made a secret of the fact that their plan of attack on society consists of the use of the labor movement, and particularly its strike technique, to foment riots, to attack property and violate life, so that under cover of confusion they may take over the reins of government. Hence, the curbing of the communists can be effected by the exercise by the government of the only function for which it has any competence, the only justification of its being: the protection of life and property. If this function, this duty, were punctually and relentlessly performed at all times, and especially during strikes, the communists would be as harmless as a high school debating team.

Illustrative of the way a few policemen, instructed to do their duty, can frustrate the communist method is the story of a recent taxicab strike in New York. There is no evidence that the communists had a hand in this affair; nevertheless, it demonstrates how to reduce their offensive method of harmlessness. A self-appointed union leader went through the usual procedure of stirring up trouble: meetings, a demand, a strike vote, a call upon the 12,000 operators to quit work. It was all done in the apple-pie order characteristic of a commissar-led venture. The city government, however, sensed that it would be politically profitable to do its duty in this case; it decided to protect life and property. Perhaps this decision was dictated by the manifest unpopularity of the strike among the cabdrivers, one-third of whom are in business for themselves and the rest are partially on their own. At any rate, the police protection afforded the operators and their customers reduced violence to a few isolated incidents. Life and property were safe. Within a week all the city's taxicabs were doing business as usual, and the strike instigator was reported to have skipped town.

Contrast this taxicab strike with the 1934 rumpus, also in New York. At that time a "liberal" mayor of the city, courting the labor vote, did not proffer protection of life and property. Even within sight of policemen (who were reported to have turned their backs upon such incidents), taxicabs were overturned and drivers were beaten up. Hoodlums invaded their homes and applied persuasive treatment. The engineers of the strike achieved their purpose, of course, but only because the city government was derelict in its duty. Had they been communists, bent on the major strategy, had the strike involved a number of industries and a couple of hundred thousand workers, they could have taken over the government, lock, stock, and barrel.

The strike, regardless of all rationalization, is an organized attack on life and property. It is a miniature war. Theoretically there can be a peaceful strike, but actually there is no such thing. Violence is an essential part of its technique. Those workers who would prefer to continue working are intimidated or beaten into conformity by shock troops, often mercenaries in the pay of the leaders. The right to work, which is the right to live, is denied to all who would take the jobs vacated. Meanwhile, the right of property is invalidated in that capital is compelled to remain idle, its value to diminish; the owners are forcibly prevented from employing their capital. The sit-down strike, in which the strikers take physical possession of the plant, is an outright violation of property rights, and the picketline is a prelude to the destruction of property. The strike, presumably a protest against prevailing wage rates or working conditions, is in fact an instrument of force directed against life and property. So long as it is permitted to operate as such, the government is remiss in its duty.

That is the obvious fact. Whether workers profit by the strike, whether wages are raised or working conditions are improved, is beside the present point, which is that the strike technique plays right into the hands of the communists. Were they deprived of it, their whole revolutionary program would go awry and they could enjoy their palaver to their hearts' content. The menace of communism will not be removed by investigations, by legal prosecution, or by legislation outlawing its advocates;

all such measures are dangerous in that they open the way to attacks on freedom of thought. To curb communists the government has all the power it needs or ought to have. If the communists succeed, it will be only because the politicians, by neglecting their duty to society, become their accomplices.

How Communism Came to America

If all the card-carying members of the Communist party in the United States were put in jail or deported, it would have little or no effect on the growth of communism in America. True, members of the party are especially dangerous because most of them have pledged allegiance to a foreign government. But so far as advancing the principles of communism is concerned, they are not nearly as effective as the average Republican or Democrat who professes to hate communism and all it stands for.

That's a strong statement! Proof? Reach for your dictionary and turn to *communism:* "Any system of social organization involving common ownership of the means of production, and some approach to equal distribution of the products of industry." This, of course, is to be done through and by the authority and force of government.

How much communism do you believe in and support? The so-called average American is currently demanding that about one-third of the nation be communized, when measured by the government's tax take; one-fourth when measured by government's ownership of land; more than one-fourth when measured

Chodorov wrote this editorial for the February 1955 issue of The Freeman.

by government's ownership of total national wealth other than land; almost one-fourth when measured by government's production of electricity; about nine-tenths when measured by government's ownership of school and subsidies to education; better than one-half when measured by government's share of the earnings from industry; and so on and so on.

Ah! you say, but democratic ownership and controls by government in America aren't true communism; when you say communism, you mean the dictatorial program laid down by Karl Marx in his *Communist Manifesto* in 1848.

Okay, reach for that document and read: "We have seen . . . that the first step in the revolution by the working class is to raise the proletariat to the position of the ruling class; to win the battle of democracy. The proletariat will use its political supremacy to wrest, by degrees, all capital from the bourgeoisie; to centralize all instruments of production in the hands of the state."

Mark well the phrases "to win the battle of democracy" and "to wrest, *by degrees,* all capital." No revolution there! While we have been passing laws against those who might advocate the violent overthrow of the government, the real threat to freedom in America—democratic government ownership and controls—has leaped to new heights.

But let us refer again to the communist program as laid down 107 years ago by Marx and Engels in their *Communist Manifesto:* "These measures will, of course be different in different countries. Nevertheless, in the most advanced countries the following will be pretty generally applicable." Then they list the long-time objectives of communism. Among them are government ownership of land, a heavy progressive income tax, abolition of inheritance rights, a national bank, government ownership or control of communication and transportation facilities, state-owned factories, a government program for soil conservation, government schools, and free education.

How many of these planks of the *Communist Manifesto* do you support? Federal Reserve Bank? Interstate Commerce Commission? Federal Communications Commission? Tennessee Valley Authority? The Sixteenth (income tax) Amendment to our Constitution? The inheritance tax? Government schools with compulsory attendance and support?

Did the card-carrying communists bring any of these to America? Remember, these ideas were generally repudiated in the United States of 1848 when Marx recommended them. Would any of them disappear if the party members were imprisoned or deported?

But maybe you would prefer to consult the works of a modern American communist, rather than an old European one. Well, how about Earl Browder, the former leader of the Communist party in America? In a 1950 pamphlet, "Keynes, Foster, and Marx," he lists twenty-two items which "express the growth of state capitalism . . . an essential feature of the confirmation of the Marxist theory." Among them are the following governmental actions: deficit financing, insurance of bank deposits, guaranteed mortgages, control of bank credits, regulation of installment buying, price controls, farm price supports, agricultural credits, RFC loans to business, social security, government housing, public works, tariffs, foreign loans.

How many of these measures—which a leading communist identifies as Marxist—do you oppose? All of them? Half? Would any of them disappear as a result of jailing the communists?

The opening sentence of this editorial is: "If all the card-carrying members of the Communist party in the United States were put in jail or deported, it would have little or no effect on the growth of communism in America." Government ownership and government controls have come to America because we the people have demanded them, not because the communists brought them from Russia. We can rid ourself of the communism of government ownership and government controls—and return to private ownership and a free market—any time we want to.

That's the question! Do the American people want to return to the responsibilities of freedom of choice? Do many of us really desire to return to the original American concept of a strictly limited government? I believe we do—fundamentally—and that we will yet turn back before it's too late. But if I'm wrong in this hope and belief, at least let's not blame the communists for our own rejection of freedom and responsibility. Let's put the blame where it belongs—on you and me and other Americans who have avidly accepted the subsidies of a paternalistic government while self-righteously professing to detest the communistic principle of government paternalism.

Part V

Why Don't You Propose Something Constructive?

On Saving the Country

A friend writes: "Let the socialists have the damned country, it isn't worth saving."

But, I am not for saving the country. I am not for saving anybody—but myself. That's as much as I feel able to try, and it's the only job of salvation that a fellow can undertake and expect positive results. Trying to impose salvation on another is an impossible conceit and in the final analysis comes to imposing my will on his, which is something quite different from saving him.

It might be advisable right here to define this "saving" business. The obvious question one must put to the fraternity of country savers is, What do you want to save it from? For saving implies the avoidance of an evil. The communists are out to save the country from capitalism, the Republicans from the Democrats, the anti-Semites from the Jews, the white Protestants from the Negroes and the Catholics, while the "liberals"—God save their kindly hearts—are busy combating a heterogeneous host of evils which are taking the country to perdition. Each reformer diagnoses the country's case differently and then proceeds to go to bat for his particular curative pill.

This short piece appeared in analysis *(January 1945).*

It never occurs to the reformer that people have a right to be left alone, or even to be wrong. When a person finds complete satisfaction in the common groove of thought, is not inclined to question or investigate its soundness, self-improvement is impossible; any attempt to disturb his equanimity is a form of sadism. The businessman who finds complete contentment in his bank balance, the worker to whom his squalid tenement is castle and his beer is the nectar of life, the professor who has achieved heaven via the degrees attached to his name—why bother them? If they are not edifiable, they are at least satisfied.

The panaceamonger has no intention of permitting people to enjoy their adjustment to what he considers error. He is for saving them, come hell or high water, and toward that noble end he proceeds to practice mental mayhem. The fact is, as anyone who has watched this breed will testify, he actually derives pleasure from torturing his victims. Mesmerizing them with his ancient-mariner glare, he dins his cacophonous phrases into their numbed brains until any latent capacity for reason is completely gone, buries them in leaflets, and struts off with all the joy of life. He will not let ignorance continue along its blissful ways because his personal delight is in peddling "the truth."

Let us consider the concept of freedom, for that is the glorious goal toward which, regardless of their contradictory diagnoses and conflicting therapeutics, all reformers would lead us. Putting aside any idea of freedom in the abstract, we see that freedom is what people become accustomed to. Some years ago this was brought to my attention in a striking way. I was driving in a western state where, at that time, anybody who had the price of an automobile was a qualified driver. There was an accident. Following the ritual I had become accustomed to in the East I pulled out my driver's license and asked the other fellow to show his. He was puzzled. He not only had no license but thought the obligation of carrying around such a thing an infraction of a man's rights. So it is, when you think of it; but habit had wiped out of my mind any such estimate of the license. In like manner we are becoming inured to the habit of carrying on our person all kinds of identifications and permissions, as required by the state, and never think of them as shackles on our freedom. The other day a man to whom I was speaking about this pulled out of his wallet eighteen pieces of paper necessary to his functioning as a human being.

Thirty years ago Americans argued that the proposed income tax would be an infringement of their liberty. Now that we have become accustomed to the levy—and how!—do we think of it in that way? Hardly; it is, in fact, an "instrument of democracy." Conscription is being puffed up into a form of freedom by the offspring of the very folks who came to America to avoid it. In its potentiality, if not yet in its methods, is the FBI any different from the Gestapo? Yet we don't see the similarity simply because we have incorporated this inquisitorial system into the American way of life. The Russians boast of their freedom, just as we will boast of our freedom when we habitualize our thinking to the world's greatest, most stupendous and supercolossal planned economy.

Let me recall the statement that freedom is what we become accustomed to—*if* we set aside any idea of freedom in the abstract. There's the rub. Some of us, afflicted with a passion for nonconformity, get ourselves an axiom of freedom—that it is a condition of living based upon inherent and inalienable rights—and insist on measuring every social institution and convention palmed off on us by that yardstick. And, though we may be impotent as far as changing the current of events, we will not permit our axiom to be swamped by them. Some of us protest out loud; more of us, under the duress of three meals a day, grumble in private. We think things out for ourselves, we do not let the prevailing ritual supplant our sense of self-respect—and that is what "saving" amounts to.

Peculiarly enough, though this attitude of self-edification smacks of asceticism, it is in fact the only way by which the "good society" can be brought about. If I do a good job on myself in the way of improving my fund of knowledge and my understanding, and of maintaining a sense of responsibility toward my judgment, the result might strike the fancy of a fellow man; if he is activated by the example to go to work on himself, my personal effort will have burgeoned into what we call social improvement. After all, do not our social institutions reflect the sum total of current intelligence? Can society be any better than its parts?

If We Quit Voting

N ew York in midsummer is measurably more miserable than any other place in this world, and should be comparable to the world for which all planners are headed. Why New Yorkers, otherwise sane, should choose to parboil their innards in a political campaign during this time of the year is a question that comes under the head of man's inscrutable propensity for self-punishment. And if a fellow elects to let the whole thing pass him by, some socially conscious energumen is bound to sweat him with a lecture on civic duty, like the citizeness who came at me.

For twenty-five years my dereliction has been known to my friends and more than one has undertaken to set me straight; out of these arguments came a solid defense for my nonvoting position. So that the lady in question was well parried with practiced retorts. I pointed out, with many instances, that though we have had candidates and platforms and parties and campaigns in abundance, we have had an equivalent plenitude of poverty and crime and war. The regularity with which the perennial promise of "good times" wound up in depression

"If We Quit Voting" appeared in analysis *(July 1945) and became part of chapter 4 of* Out of Step.

suggested the incompetence of politics in economic affairs. Maybe the good society we have been voting for lay some other way; why not try another fork in the road, the one pointing to individual self-improvement, particularly in acquiring a knowledge of economics? And so on.

There was one question put to me by my charming annoyer which I deftly sidestepped, for the day was sultry and the answer called for some mental effort. The question: "What would happen if we quit voting?"

If you are curious about the result of noneating you come upon the question of why we eat. So, the query put to me by the lady brings up the reason for voting. The theory of government by elected representatives is that these fellows are hired by the voting citizenry to take care of all matters relating to their common interests. However, it is different from ordinary employment in that the representative is not under specific orders, but is given blanket authority to do what he believes desirable for the public welfare in any and all circumstances, subject to constitutional limitations. In all matters relating to public affairs the will of the individual is transferred to the elected agent, whose responsibility is commensurate with the power thus invested in him.

It is this transference of power from voter to elected agents which is the crux of republicanism. The transference is well nigh absolute. Even the constitutional limitations are not so in fact since they can be circumvented by legal devices in the hands of the agents. Except for the tenuous process of impeachment, the mandate is irrevocable. For the abuse or misuse of the mandate the only recourse left to the principals, the people, is to oust the agents at the next election. But, when we oust the rascals do we not, as a matter of course, invite a new crowd? It all adds up to the fact that by voting them out of power, the people put the running of their community life into the hands of a separate group, upon whose wisdom and integrity the fate of the community rests.

All this would change if we quit voting. Such abstinence would be tantamount to this notice to politicians: since we as individuals have decided to look after our affairs, your services are no longer needed. Having assumed social power we must, as individuals, assume social responsibility; provided, of course, the politicians accept their discharge. The job of running the community would fall on each and all of us. We might hire an expert to tell us about the most improved firefighting apparatus, or a manager to look after cleaning the streets, or an engineer to build us a bridge; but the final decision, particularly in the matter of raising funds to defray costs, would rest with the town-hall meeting. The hired specialists would have no authority other than that necessary for the performance of their contractual duties; coercive power, which is the essence of political authority, would be exercised, if necessary, only by the committee of the whole.

There is some warrant for the belief that a better social order would ensue when the individual is responsible for it and, therefore, responsive to its needs. He no longer has the law or the lawmakers to cover his sins of omission; need of the neighbors' good opinion will be sufficient compulsion for jury duty and no loopholes in a draft law, no recourse to "political pull," will be possible when danger to his community calls him to arms. In his private affairs, the now sovereign individual will have to meet the dictum of the marketplace: produce or you do not eat; no law will help you. In his public behavior he must be decent or suffer the sentence of social ostracism, with no recourse to legal exoneration. From a law-abiding citizen he will be transmuted into a self-respecting man.

Would chaos result? No, there would be order, without law to disturb it. But, let us define chaos. Is it not disharmony resulting from social friction? When we trace social friction to its source do we not find that it seminates in a feeling of unwarranted hurt, or injustice? Then chaos is a social condition in which injustice obtains. Now, when one man may take, by law, what another man has put his labor into, we have injustice of the keenest kind, for the denial of a man's right to possess and enjoy what he produces is akin to a denial of life. Yet the power to confiscate property is the first business of politics. We see how this is so in the matter of taxation; but greater by far is the amount of property confiscated by monopolies, all of which are founded in law.

While this economic basis of injustice has been lost in our adjustment to it, the resulting friction is quite evident. Most of us are poor in spite of our constant effort and known ability to produce an abundance; the incongruity is aggravated by a feeling of hopelessness. But the keenest hurt arises from the thought that the wealth we see about us is somehow ours by right of labor, but is not ours by right of law. Resentment, intensified by bewilderment, stirs up a reckless urge to do something about it. We demand justice; we have friction. We have strikes and crimes and bankruptcy and mental unbalances. And we cheat our neighbors, and each seeks for himself a legal privilege to live by another's labor. And we have war. Is this a condition of harmony or of chaos?

In the frontier days of our country there was little law, but much order; for the affairs of the community were in the hands of the citizenry. Although fiction may give an opposite impression, it is a fact that there was less per capita crime to take care of then than there is now when law pervades every turn and minute of our lives. What gave the West its wild and woolly reputation was the glamorous drama of intense community life. Everybody was keenly interested in the hanging of a cattle rustler; it was not done in the calculated quiet of a prison, with the dispatch of a mechanical system. The railriding of a violator of town-hall dicta had to be the business of the town prosecutor, who was everybody. Though the citizen's private musket was seldom used for the protection of life and property, its presence promised swift and positive justice, from which no legal chicanery offered escape, and its loud report announced the dignity of decency. Every crime was committed against the public, not the law, and therefore the public made an ado about it. Mistakes were made, to be sure, for human judgment is ever fallible; but, until the politician came, there was no deliberate malfeasance or misfeasance; until laws came, there were no violations, and the code of human decency made for order.

So, if we should quit voting for parties and candidates, we would individually reassume responsibility for our acts and, therefore, responsibility for the common good. There would be no way of dodging the verdict of the marketplace; we would take back only in proportion to our contribution. Any attempt to profit at the expense of a neighbor or the community would be quickly spotted and as quickly squelched, for everybody would recognize a threat to himself in the slightest indulgence of injustice. Since nobody would have the power to enforce monopoly conditions none would obtain. Order would be maintained by the rules of existence, the natural laws of economics.

That is, if the politicians would permit themselves to be thus ousted from their positions of power and privilege. I doubt it. Remember that the proposal to quit voting is basically revolutionary; it amounts to a shifting of power from one group to another, which is the essence of revolution. As soon as the nonvoting movement got up steam the politicians would most assuredly start a counterrevolution. Measures to enforce voting would be instituted; fines would be imposed for violations, and prison sentences would be meted out to repeaters. It is a necessity for political power, no matter how gained, to have the moral support of public approval, and suffrage is the most efficient scheme for registering it; notice how Hitler, Mussolini, and Stalin insisted on having ballots cast. In any republican government, even ours, only a fraction of the populace votes for the successful candidate, but that fraction is quantitatively impressive; it is this appearance of overwhelming sanction which supports him in the exercise of political power. Without it he would be lost.

Propaganda, too, would bombard this passive resistance to statism; not only that put out by the politicians of all parties— the coalition would be as complete as it would be spontaneous—but also the more effective kind emanating from seemingly disinterested sources. All the monopolists, all the coupon-clipping foundations, all the tax-exempt eleemosynary institutions—in short, all the "respectables"— would join in a howling defense of the status quo. We would be told most emphatically that unless we keep on voting away our power to responsible persons, it would be grabbed by irresponsible ones; tyranny would result. That is probably true, seeing how since the beginning of time men have sought to acquire property without laboring for it. The answer lies, as it always has, in the judicious use of private artillery. On this point a story, apocryphal no doubt, is worth telling. When Napoleon's conquerors were considering what to do with him, a buck-skinned American allowed that a fellow of such parts might be handy in this new country and ought to be invited to come over. As for the possibility of a Napoleonic regime being started in America, the recent revolutionist dismissed it with the remark that the musket with which he shot rabbits could also kill tyrants. There is no substitute for human dignity.

But the argument is rather specious in the light of the fact that every election is a seizure of power. The balloting system has been defined as a battle between opposing forces, each armed with proposals for the public good, for a grant of power to put these proposals into practice. As far as it goes, this definition is correct; but when the successful contestant acquires the grant of power toward what end does he use it? Not theoretically but practically. Does he not, with an eye to the next campaign, and with the citizens' money, go in for purchasing support from pressure groups? Whether it is by catering to a monopoly interest whose campaign contribution is necessary to his purpose, or to a privilege-seeking labor group, or to a hungry army of unemployed or of veterans, the over-the-barrel method of seizing and maintaining political power is standard practice.

This is not, however, an indictment of our election system. It is rather a description of our adjustment to conquest. Going back to beginnings—although the process is still in vogue, as in Manchuria, or more recently in the Baltic states—when a band of freebooters developed an appetite for other people's property they went after it with vim and vigor. Repeated visitations of this nature left the victims breathless, if not lifeless, and propertyless to boot. So, as men do when they have no other choice, they made a compromise. They hired one gang of thieves to protect them from other gangs, and in time the price paid for such protection came to be known as taxation. The tax gatherers settled down in the conquered communities, possibly to make collections certain and regular, and as the years rolled on a blend of cultures and of bloods made of the two classes one nation. But the system of taxation remained

Why Don't You Propose Something Constructive?

after it had lost its original significance; lawyers and professors of economics, by deft circumlocution, turned tribute into "fiscal policy" and clothed it with social good. Nevertheless, the social effect of the system was to keep the citizenry divided into two economic groups: payers and receivers. Those who lived without producing became traditionalized as "servants of the people," and thus gained ideological support. They further entrenched themselves by acquiring sub-tax-collecting allies; that is, some of their group became landowners, whose collection of rent rested on the law-enforcement powers of the ruling clique, and others were granted subsidies, tariffs, franchises, patent rights, monopoly privileges of one sort or another. This division of spoils between those who wield power and those whose privileges depend on it is succinctly described in the expression, "the state within the state."

Thus, when we trace our political system to its origin we come to conquest. Tradition, law, and custom have obscured its true nature, but no metamorphosis has taken place; its claws and fangs are still sharp, its appetite as voracious as ever. In the light of history it is not a figure of speech to define politics as the art of seizing power; and its present purpose, as of old, is economic. There is no doubt that men of high purpose will always give of their talents for the common welfare, with no thought of recompense other than the goodwill of the community. But, so long as our taxation system remains, so long as the political means for acquiring economic goods is available, just so long will the spirit of conquest assert itself; for men always seek to satisfy their desires with the least effort. It is interesting to speculate on the kind of campaigns and the type of candidates we would have if taxation were abolished and if, also, the power to dispense privilege vanished. Who would run for office if there were "nothing in it"?

Why should a self-respecting citizen endorse an institution grounded in thievery? For that is what one does when one votes. If it be argued that we must let bygones be bygones, see what we can do toward cleaning up the institution so that it can be used for the maintenance of an orderly existence, the answer is that it cannot be done; we have been voting for one "good government" after another, and what have we got? Perhaps the silliest argument, and yet the one invariably advanced when this succession of failures is pointed out, is that "we must choose the lesser of two evils." Under what compulsion are we to make such a choice? Why not pass up both of them?

To effectuate the suggested revolution all that is necessary is to stay away from the polls. Unlike other revolutions, it calls for no organization, no violence, no war fund, no leader to sell it out. In the quiet of his conscience each citizen pledges himself, to himself, not to give moral support to an unmoral institution, and on election day he remains at home. That's all. I started my revolution twenty-five years ago and the country is none the worse for it.

What Individualism Is Not

The bottle is now labeled libertarianism. But its content is nothing new; it is what in the nineteenth century, and up to the time of Franklin Roosevelt, was called liberalism—the advocacy of limited government and a free economy. (If you think of it, you will see that there is a redundancy in this formula, for a government of limited powers would have little chance of interfering with the economy.) The liberals were robbed of their time-honored name by the unprincipled socialists and near socialists, whose avidity for prestige words knows no bounds. So, forced to look for another and distinctive label for their philosophy, they came up with libertarianism—good enough but somewhat difficult for the tongue.

They might have done better by adopting the older and more meaningful name of individualism, but they bypassed it because it too had been more than sullied by its opponents. The smear technique of winning an argument is as old as argument. The mud with which individualism has been bespattered still hides its true character, and every so often new gobs are thrown at it by "scholars" who simply don't like it. Some of the modern traducers even affect the conservative title.

Chodorov wrote this article for National Review *(June 20, 1956)*.

The mudslinging started long ago, but the more recent and best-known orgy occurred in the early part of the century when the heaven-by-way-of-government muckrakers attached to individualism a value-impregnated adjective—*rugged.* The word itself has no moral content; when applied to a mountain it is purely descriptive, when applied to an athlete it carries a favorable connotation. But, in the literary usage of the muckrakers, it designated what in plain language would be called skulduggery. It has no more to do with a philosophy than has any form of indecent behavior. Thus, the "rugged individualist" was the fellow who threatened to foreclose the mortgage on the old homestead if the fair damsel refused his hand in marriage; or he was the speculator who made use of the stock market to rob "widows and orphans"; or he was the fat and florid buccaneer who lavished diamonds on his ladylove. He was, in short, a fellow whose conscience presented no obstacle to his inclination to grab a dollar, and who recognized no code of ethics that might curb his appetites. If there is any difference between an ordinary thief and a rugged individualist, it is in the fact that the latter almost always keeps within the letter of the law, even if he has to rewrite the law to do so.

To the socialist, of course, intellectual integrity is excess baggage, even as morality is excess baggage to the rugged individualist. If the word *rugged* could confound the opposition, why not use it to the full? The fact that individualism, as a philosophy, looks upon the state with a jaundiced eye would hardly deter the socialist (to whom the state is the all in all) from equating individualism with the manipulation of the state in the interest of the rich. Rugged individualism was a propaganda phrase of the first order. It was most useful in bringing the soak-the-rich urgency to a boiling point.

The phrase gained currency at the time when the leveling

mania was fighting its way into the American tradition, before
the government, making full use of the new power it had acquired under the income tax law, took hold of the individual by
the scruff of the neck and made a mass-man out of him. It is
an odd fact that the socialist is quite in agreement with the
rugged individualist in advocating the use of political force to
achieve one's "good"; the difference between them is only in
determining the incidence, or the recipient, of government-
given "good." It is doubtful whether the robber barons (a synonym for rugged individualists) ever used the government, before the income tax, with anything like the vigor and success
of the socialists. At any rate, the stigma of ruggedness has
stuck, so that the collectivist "intellectuals," who ought to
know better, are unaware of the difference between thievery
and individualism.

ORIGINAL SMEAR WORDS

The besmirching of individualism, however, had a good start
before the modern era. The original defamers were not socialists but solid proponents of status, the upholders of special
privilege, the mercantilists of the nineteenth century. Their opposition stemmed in part from the fact that individualism leaned
heavily on the burgeoning doctrine of the free market, of laissez-faire economics, and as such presented a challenge to their
preferred position. So they dug into the age-old bag of semantics and came up with two smear words: *selfish* and *materialistic*. Just like the later socialists, they had no compunction
about twisting the truth to suit their argument.

Laissez-faire—that is to say, an economy free of political
interventions and subventions—holds that the instinct of self-
interest is the motive power of productive effort. Nothing is

produced except by human labor, and labor is something the human being is most parsimonious about; if he could satisfy his desires without effort, he would gladly dispense with it. That is why he invents labor-saving devices. But he is so constituted that every gratification gives rise to new desire, which he proceeds to satisfy by investing the labor he saved. He is insatiable. The log cabin that was palace enough in the wilderness seems quite inadequate as soon as the pioneer accumulates a surplus of necessaries, and then he begins to dream of curtains and pictures, inside plumbing, a school or a church, to say nothing of baseball or Beethoven. Self-interest overcomes his aversion to labor in his constant drive to improve his circumstances and widen his horizon. If the individual is not interfered with in the enjoyment of the products of his labor, his property, he will multiply his productive efforts and there will be a general abundance for the benefit of society as a whole.

It is in the free market that self-interest finds its finest expression; that is a cardinal point in individualism. If the market is regularly raided, by robbers or the government, and the safety of property is impaired, the individual loses interest in production, and the abundance of things men live by shrinks. Hence, it is for the good of society that self-interest in the economic sphere be allowed to operate without hindrance.

But self-interest is not selfishness. Self-interest will impel the manufacturer to improve upon his output so as to attract trade, while selfishness will prompt him to seek the special privileges and state favor that in the end destroy the very system of economic freedom on which he depends. The worker who tries to improve his lot by rendering better service could hardly be called selfish; the description rather fits the worker who demands that he be paid for not working. The subsidy seeker is selfish, and so is every citizen who uses the law to enrich himself at the expense of other citizens.

THE FREE MARKET

Then there is the charge of "materialism." Laissez-faire, of course, rests its case on abundance; if people want lots of things, the way to get them is through freedom of production and exchange. In that respect, it could be called "materialistic." But, the laissez-faire economist *as economist* does not question or evaluate men's desires; he has no opinion on the "ought" or "should" of their aspirations. Whether they prefer culture to gadgets, or put a higher value on ostentation than on spiritual matters, is not his concern; the free market, he insists, is mechanistic and amoral. If one's preference is leisure, for instance, it is through abundance that his desire can be best satisfied; for an abundance of things makes them cheaper, easier to get, and thus one is enabled to indulge a liking for vacations. And a concert is probably better enjoyed by a well-fed aesthete than by a hungry one. At any rate, the economist refuses to pass judgment on men's preferences; whatever they want, they will get more of it out of a free market than one commandeered by policemen.

But the critics of the nineteenth century blithely passed over this point, even as modern socialists ignore it. They insisted on attaching moral content to the free economy; it is a philosophy, they asserted, that puts a premium on things, rather than on cultural and spiritual values. Its emphasis on abundance is materialistic and the ultimate outcome of a free economy is a society devoid of appreciation for the finer things in life.

In point of fact—while the free market is itself a mechanism neutral to values expressing men's desires, whatever they may be—the free market theory rests on the tacit acceptance of a purely spiritual concept, namely: that man is endowed with the capacity of making choices, with free will. If it were not for this purely human trait, there would be no marketplace, and human life would be akin to that of the birds and the beasts. The economist of the laissez-faire school tries to skirt around this philosophical and theological point; yet if hard pressed he must admit that his entire argument is based on the axiom of free will, although he might call it something else. And that axiom certainly is not materialistic; any discussion of it leads ineluctably to a consideration of the soul.

By way of contrast, it is the socialist (whatever subspecies) who must begin his argument with a rejection of the idea of free will. His theory requires him to describe the individual as purely materialistic in composition. What is called free will, he must maintain, is a batch of reflexes to environmental conditioning. The choices a man makes, whether in the field of culture or material things, are determined by his training and the influences brought to bear on him. Hence, he cannot be held accountable for his behavior. The individual is putty out of which omnipotent government builds the good society, nothing else.

"HEDONISM"

Returning to the defamation of individualism, another value-laden word that was, and still is, hurled at it is *hedonism*. (At least one modern writer, who maintains that a Christian cannot be an individualist, seems to be championing this nineteenth-century criticism.) The label stems from the fact that a number of self-styled individualists and disciples of Adam Smith associated themselves with an ethical creed known as utilitarianism; the most famous are Jeremy Bentham, James Mill, and John Stuart Mill. The basic tenet of this creed is that man is constitutionally driven to avoid pain and to seek pleasure. Hence, in the nature of things, the only morally good conduct is that which favors this pursuit. But, a problem of definition arises, since what is pleasure for a philosopher might be pain for the moron. Bentham, founder of the school, who was more interested in legislation than in philosophy, solved the problem nicely by drawing up a coarse calculus of pleasure; and then he enunciated a principle of legislation based on it: that is morally good which promotes the greatest good for the greatest number.

Coming from an avowed opponent of privilege and an advocate of limited government, this do-gooding doctrine is a strange anomaly. If the moral measure of legislation is the greatest good for the greatest number, it follows that the good of the minority, even a minority of one, is immoral. That would hardly accord with the basic tenet of individualism that man is endowed with rights which the majority may not tamper with. This contradiction bothered Mill (whose essay *On Liberty* is high dogma in the individualist's creed) no end; his doctrine of freedom of thought and expression was hardly consistent with the majoritarianism of Bentham. In this philosophic conflict, his loyalty to his father (Bentham's closest associate) and to Bentham won out, and in the event he was logically driven to a qualified endorsement of socialism. Without intending to, he demonstrated the incompatibility of utilitarianism and individualism.

Neo-socialists are not all unaware of the fact that utilitarianism plays into their hands. Nevertheless, when discussion gives way to epithet-throwing, individualism is still denounced as "hedonism."

TENETS OF INDIVIDUALISM

If individualism is not what its detractors call it, what is it? That is a reasonable question to ask, but a more difficult one to answer, simply because as a pattern of thought it has engaged many minds over the ages, and has thus acquired a number of facets; philosophy knows no "party line." Yet, it is possible and permissible to summarize in a single paragraph the principal tenets of individualism, or those which its modern votaries are in some agreement upon.

Metaphysically, individualism holds that the person is unique, not a sample of the mass, owing his peculiar composition and his allegiance to his Creator, not his environment. Because of his origin and existence, he is endowed with inalienable rights, which it is the duty of all others to respect, even as it is his duty to respect theirs; among these rights are life, liberty, and property. Following from this premise, society has no warrant for invading these rights, even under the pretext of improving his circumstances; and government can render him no service other than that of protecting him against his fellow man in the enjoyment of these rights. In the field of economics (with which libertarians are rightly concerned because it is there that government begins its infringement), the government has no competence; and the best it can do is to maintain a condition of order, so that the individual may carry on his business with the assurance that he will keep what he produces. That is all.

Thought and the World of Action

A friend of mine—one with whom amity rests on understanding—writes me that "ideas have no commodity value today." He does not elaborate. Therefore, the meaning of this remark must be garnered from the context of his background and his present preoccupation.

When one who dwells in the realm of ideas is suddenly thrust into a maelstrom of action—as, for instance, a college professor turned politician—the resulting sense of accomplishment is quite exhilarating. Now he is "doing something." He is like a football player who after many rainy afternoons of blackboard instruction has finally dug his cleats into the sod.

There is a physical satisfaction which the ivory tower denied him. Things are moving; the ringing telephone portends importance; people are coming and going; orders are given and received; there are motion, noise, tense situations to meet, problems to solve—he is "doing something."

It is natural and necessary that he should give value, "commodity value," to the something he is doing. It is natural because self-sanction is compensatory. It is necessary because it makes for the efficiency that is reflected in the pay envelope.

Chodorov wrote this editorial for the January 1941 issue of The Freeman.

The man who does not enjoy his work places no value upon it, and hence loses in that self-esteem which is the balm of life; nor can he achieve the emoluments of success. Pride and profit lead to job rationalization.

But objective values, those that obtain in the marketplace of history, have a way of making the hustle-and-bustle values of temporary achievement appear picayune. And these objective values are entirely in the field of ideas.

The glory that was Greece, as we see it now, was not in the make-work programs of Pericles but in the ideas expressed in its art and its philosophy; the grandeur that was Rome may have seemed at the time to be the conquest of the known world, while now we think of it in terms of Cicero, Plutarch, Cato, Vergil, et al. It is the ideas of Voltaire that now have "commodity value," not the activity of the guillotine.

My friend might answer: "I am not interested, because I cannot influence the verdict of history; I am concerned only with those values which in my time and by my effort can gain currency."

This point of view is sound and cannot be dismissed offhand as expediency. We must do things now, first because we live now, and second because we must live. But even the things we do are important only insofar as they express ideas, and their importance is in direct proportion to the soundness of these ideas.

We must dig potatoes or make shoes or write briefs, to sustain life. But we have a choice. We can do these things only because of the profit involved or we can grow better potatoes, fashion therapeutic shoes or build justice into our briefs. Or, better yet, we can do these things for profit and invest our lives with the most satisfying "commodity value"—ideas.

The glorification of action for action's sake is a soporific. It lulls that intellectual curiosity which makes for real action, a change in the status quo of thought. For it satisfies the restless soul with a refuge from reality; it substitutes physical exertion for mental adventure; it replaces the difficult values of ideas with the quasi-value of movement.

To this my friend might retort: "In the long run, it is true, ideas influence thought and change social conditions; but there is the immediate problem of existence that must be met, and the short-term policy most important to the contemporary scene requires the doing of something now."

But if what can be done now must in its results invalidate basic principle is it even temporarily desirable? Is the palliative worthwhile if it makes the patient sicker and delays his recovery? Or kills him?

The yearning for palpable results is the mirage which unbalances the mind. It arises from an identification of one's corporeal and finite existence with all reality. It is the search for immortality here and now. It is compensation for the deflated ego. It is the sign of sophomoric immaturity, but it is by no means the insignia of youth. It is the idolatry of evanescent success.

Calisthenics have their proper function, and in the routine of existence it is necessary that action must implement ideas and record results. But emphasis upon action *per se,* or idealization of recordable results, is like identifying amorous conquests with love. It is a false evaluation. The only true values are ideas, which, permeating the depth of the human mind, work in their inscrutable way toward a better world of better men.

Why Teach Freedom?

A student writes: "I have read the pamphlets you sent me, also most of the books you recommended. I am more convinced than ever that the planned economy is a dangerous delusion and that man's greatest good can be achieved only through freedom. But I am troubled by the reaction of my professor when I try to talk to him along these lines. He is an honest thinker: I am sure of that. Also, I am sure that he has read more about the free economy than I have. Why is it that he rejects the premises I present to him and refuses to accept the facts? Can you explain this to me?"

I can't, not unless I call upon an hypothesis that is hardly provable. For many years I have struggled with the problem the student has put to me: Why are some people libertarians, why are others of equal learning and background socialists? It isn't a matter of education. Once I attended the closing session of a course given by the noted laissez-faire economist Ludwig von Mises, and listened to the reactions of his students. It was a gabfest. Some gave distinct evidence of rejecting all they had learned from him in fifteen previous lectures, even what they

This article appeared in The Freeman *(May 1955).*

had presumably read in his books. Others were enthusiastic exponents of his thesis. Why?

The bureaucratic socialist, of course, must be excluded from this speculation. In his case, socialism is a job, not necessarily a conviction. I knew a thoroughgoing libertarian who entered the bureaucratic service out of economic necessity; within six months he sang the collectivist tune.

In the same class with the bureaucrat is the professor whose job depends on his going along with the head of the department, or whose income is in part derived as a "consultant" on government projects. I have known one or two such who, in private conversation, had some strong reservations on the collectivism they taught in class. These, like the bureaucrats, are "boughten" socialists; their cases can be easily explained.

But how do you account for the socialistic attitude of those whose economic status ought to incline them to the opposite point of view? I know a very successful stockbroker who makes out a strong case for government manipulation of the economy; to him it is dogma, even though his comfortable living is derived from the free marketplace. The story of a book is a case in point. In *God and Man at Yale,* William F. Buckley, Jr., pointed out that the textbooks used in the freshman course in economics decried the free economy and extolled planning; the alumni bought his book, but also increased their contributions to Yale. I have found audiences heavily sprinkled with "upper-bracket" men quite cool to the proposition that the income tax amendment ought to be repealed on the ground that it violates the right of property, while audiences consisting mainly of wage earners and small businessmen ask to be organized for action. Not that all rich men are socialists, nor all poor men are libertarians, but that you cannot account for their attitudes along economic lines.

Neither education, background, nor income can explain either the socialist or the libertarian. Whenever you try any of these criteria you are faced with cases that refute your premise; you find that both types come from penthouses and slums, that they include Ph.D.'s and illiterates. You are driven to the conclusion that if there is a causative principle it must be found somewhere in the makeup of the person rather than in environmental influences. Psychology does not help, for it too seeks explanations for mental attitudes in conditioning and shies away from the realm of inherent traits or temperament. So, the best you can do is to describe the socialist—or the libertarian—as you have known him, and to leave the "why" of him alone; it is beyond understanding.

The characteristic that invariably identifies socialists is an urgency to improve other people. It is a passion that blinds them to the fact of immutable individuality and leads to faith in the therapy of force. It is utterly irrational; so much so that they find it necessary to cover up the impulse with an inordinate display of logic. When you examine their arguments you find them based on axioms which support their inherent drive. In short, they are so constituted that they cannot let other people alone.

Perhaps it is an inner need that impels the socialist to his ideology, for I have never met an advocate of government intervention who did not admit, inadvertently, his own capacity for commissariat functions. He always has a plan, to which others must submit, and his certainty that the plan will produce the contemplated results does not permit him to brook criticism. Always he is the fanatic. If you disagree with him it is not because you are in error; it is because you are sinful. You are not an ignoramus; you are a "class-conscious capitalist," or a "reactionary," or at least an "antisocial." Why is it that name-calling is stock argument with all socialists?

That this inclination toward social improvement through force is an innate, not an acquired, characteristic is proven by the attitude of many ex-socialists. I know a writer of repute who, though he has rid himself intellectually of all Marxism, of which he once was an articulate advocate, still insists that large fortunes ought to be regulated. Compulsion is in his innards. Former communists find it difficult to accept fully the faith of the libertarian in social improvement through individual improvement; some kind of political regulation need not lead to the Moscow excesses. It is not true that "once a socialist always a socialist"; but intellectual conversion does not automatically rule out the possibility of an atavism.

If, then, the socialistic attitude—and, by implication, that of the libertarian—stems from an ingredient of personality, why put so much stress on education? The libertarian is particularly concerned over the spread of socialistic doctrine in the schools and in the public press, and is most anxious to bring his own philosophy into opposition. On the face of it, this concern seems unwarranted, for an innate tendency toward freedom will not be changed by words into an acceptance of slavery.

Basically, this is true. But a character trait, like a seed, germinates best under proper cultivation, and the inclination toward freedom is strengthened by intellectual conviction; as in the case of the student who wrote me. There are many who, like this young man, are instinctively repelled by government intervention but who crave intellectual support for their inclination. It is to them that the proponent of libertarianism must address himself; the socialist is beyond redemption. That is to say, the libertarian teaches not to "make" libertarians, but to find them.

Likewise, the socialist teacher does not make converts; he merely confirms the socialistic inclination of his willing students. And there the intellectual battle between the two schools of thought might rest.

But socialism is not an intellectual pursuit, it is primarily a drive for political power; and if its proponents succeed in enthroning themselves, the case for libertarian thought will be most difficult. Hence, the reason for seeking out the natural libertarians through education is to prevent, by constant and intelligent reiteration of its tenets, the suppression of the philosophy of freedom and the driving of its advocates underground.

Part VI

Education and Freedom

My Friend's Education

A friend of mine did what all good friends do; he died. The loss caused the proper amount of grief, of course; but in this case the grief was polluted by an odd petulance. For some unknown reason I felt that he had abused his rights by dying at that time. For his going left me at loose ends. He had "done me wrong."

The friendship had been a highly profitable one for me. He was an intellectual warehouse from which I was always free to lift as much merchandise as I was capable of carrying; and much that I lifted and incorporated into my stock-in-trade was borrowed while we sipped a beer or munched a midnight rarebit. For he was a superb raconteur, always with the parable that exactly fitted the subject at hand, and for his illustrations he could draw on an intimate knowledge of a half-dozen literatures, ancient and modern, augmented with much intelligent travel. He had digested a lot of thoroughly nonutilitarian information, covering such fields as medieval architecture, manners of the Second Empire, music, the culinary art, the Bible (in the original), lovemaking in the tenth century, and the econ-

"My Friend's Education" was a tribute to Albert Jay Nock and his views on education. It appeared in The Freeman *(August 1954).*

omy of the Minoans, and if you knew how to draw him out (he preferred to listen) an evening with him would prove a bonanza. A companion of that sort is not easy to come by.

Well, the inevitable is the inevitable, and one turns to pleasant memories. And to cogitating. The thought that hung on with tenacity was that all the knowledge and understanding he had stored away in three-quarters of a century went down into the grave with his body, and that seemed to be a terrible loss. That "you can't take it with you" is a self-evident fact; but the "it" referred to in the aphorism is the fund of tangible things the average man usually piles up in a lifetime. My friend, however, was outside the average, in that he never gave a hoot for anything that could be listed in a will; he acquired only learning and that he surely took with him. And except for examples of it in the half-dozen books he published, the literary style he never tired of perfecting was gone forever. Being something of a utilitarian, I could not help asking, why put in all that time and effort at pursuits that produced so little that could be seen and catalogued? It seemed so un-American.

To which he would have answered, I am sure, "Didn't I have fun doing it? And what can a fellow get out of life more valuable than fun?"

And thereby hangs a theory of education which he exemplified. It runs something like this: education is the pursuit of knowledge that pays off in the enjoyment of it; if it does not yield that kind of profit, you quit the pursuit, and you keep at it only in proportion to returns. For instance, he once told me that he had got so much fun out of reading the Greek and Latin classics, in his college days, that he later took on Hebrew, and found its literature just as gratifying. On the other hand, if he found a book uninteresting, even one he had been hired to review, he would drop it; one book which had received accolades from eminent litterateurs he discarded after the first fifty pages with the remark, "I ain't got education enough for that kind of tripe."

THE TEST OF EDUCABILITY

According to this theory, some people are educable and some are not, and there is nothing one can do to change this natural arrangement. This does not mean that some people are "better" than others, for in respect to functional ability the noneducable are usually better endowed than the educable, and their contribution to material progress is certainly greater. Then again, the educable are so engrossed in self-betterment that they are of no use in the democratic business of improving others, and as reformers or politicians they are quite inept; in fact, they are a bit on the antisocial side, even though they can be wonderful companions. However, it is idle to pass value judgment on either of these personality groups; each is what it is and cannot be the other. As for determining who is educable and who is not, there is no other test than the purely subjective one of pleasure; the educable get satisfaction from the pursuit of learning, the others find the occupation distasteful.

It is an individualistic theory of education, resting its case on the premise of innate characteristics. My friend, obviously, was an individualist of the first water; he would have no truck with the notion that the individual is what his environment makes him. Environment, including college, can make it difficult for the educable to get an education, but it cannot prevent them from getting it. Just as a tree will work its way around impediments to reach the sun, so those bothered by a questing spirit will persist in reaching for "the best that has been said and thought in this world," and will absorb their share of it.

On the other hand, those born without the eternal "why" in their souls can live among books all their lives without being touched by learning.

The theory, most assuredly, rejects the democratic notion that all are equally and indefinitely educable. In point of fact, nobody really takes that notion seriously, least of all the hierarchy of professional teachers who pay it lip service.

In what is called "progressive education" the general objective is to produce what is called a social consciousness, with emphasis on both uniformity and conformity; but to reach that objective individual differences must be minimized; thus, it is inferred that all are equally educable only if those of greater intellectual capacity are written off, as if they did not exist.

COURSES GROW EASIER

Likewise, the democratic notion of education gets a lift in the colleges by the adjustment of courses to fit the lowest common denominator, which gets lower as more and more candidates for the commercially necessary degree are enrolled. It is certainly true that all are equally educable if you equate education with the ability to pull teeth, to use a slide rule, to memorize a legal code, or to order a meal in a foreign language; and you prove your case incontestably by fitting examinations to the examinee.

This is not to condemn our educational system; far from it. Given the premise of democracy, no other educational system would do. Certainly if the system were shaped to serve the needs of the educable, education would be making a concession to aristocratic notions, which democracy simply cannot do. The axiom of uniform perfectibility must be adhered to at all costs, even if this involves the redefinition of education. It would hardly be democratic to deny the badge of educability—the degree—to those whose intellectual capacity finds expression in tending cows; therefore, we must have agricultural colleges. And so that there will be no discrimination against the geniuses of the household, a school of domestic science must have the power to grant appropriately engraved parchments.

It is only if you are a stickler for the purity of words that you find fault with our system of education. For instance, my late friend maintained that what goes by the name of education in a democracy is in fact only training. The high schools, with their courses in carpentry and bookkeeping, have replaced the discarded apprenticeship system, while the law school is simply a glorified clerkship in a legal office. Even in the schools of philosophy, the guiding spirit is utilitarianism rather than speculation; in the popular pragmatic philosophy—if it is a philosophy—the only absolute recognized is "that whatever works is good," which is putting a premium on skill as against learning. However, since everybody above the grade of idiocy can be trained to do something, the democratic dictum that all people are equally educable is proved true by a simple device of semantics.

Not only does the democratic idiom give support to this equation of education with training, but so does another important facet of our mores—economism. From the time of birth, the American learns of the importance of getting on in the world, of acquiring wealth and social position, and it would be inconsistent with this ideal if his schooling did not take it into account. No American father should, in the circumstances, channel his offspring's development along any but utilitarian lines; were he to stress learning for the sake of learning he would be unfaithful to his parental duty. Should his own son or daughter prove educable, he must use his influence to try to overcome the handicap, so that his progeny may not suffer from social disabilities. And, as a citizen and taxpayer, he must bring the conventional point of view to bear upon the established educational facilities.

A SANCTUARY FOR INQUIRING MINDS

If the intellectually curious find such facilities unsatisfying, they have only themselves, or their misfortune, to blame. They must shift for themselves. Curiously enough, they always do, as a matter of necessity, even if the colleges make the going rough for them; not infrequently, they pass up both the college and the degree in favor of an education. As a consequence, they will probably find it difficult to get a job as an insurance sales-man, and about all they can claim for their educational spree is a lot of fun. That is all they ever get from it.

One wonders how many of these rare and unfortunate birds there are around. About the only way one could estimate their number would be by the establishment of a college designed for them, something like a sanctuary set up for almost extinct animal species. The special feature of such a college would be that one could get nothing from it except an education, and no one would think of going there for any other purpose. Not a single utilitarian course would pollute the curriculum. For in-stance, one might learn how to appreciate Molière and Racine, even though one might have difficulty in reading a French news-paper; economics would be taught as the science of how we make a living, not as a preparation for a job in the government; as for psychology, the textbooks would be Shakespeare and Tolstoy.

To make sure that none but the educable would enroll, this college would give no degrees or even certificates of attendance; it would not deign to peddle such papers. In fact, no record of attendance would be kept, nor would there be any examinations or other means of judging the educability of the students. Each student would have to figure that out for himself, if the matter bothered him, by the test of fun.

That, I believe, would be a practical application of the theory of education my late friend propounded and lived. By the way, he was the editor of the original *Freeman,* published between 1920 and 1924, and his name was Albert Jay Nock.

Why Free Schools
Are Not Free

D ixon is an obscure mountain village in New Mexico; population 1,200. Its obscurity is presently disturbed by a
problem of democracy: the divorcement of secular and religious
training in tax-supported schools. Reports have it that the Catholic citizenry, who seem to be politically in the ascendancy in
New Mexico, have got hold of the management of the Dixon
school system, introducing their catechism into the curriculum
and putting the teaching nuns on the payroll. The Protestant
minority vehemently denounce this as an abuse of democratic
principle, as well as a misuse of public funds, and have brought
the matter to law. Non-Catholic elements outside New Mexico
have come to their support, and thus the contention becomes
national in scope. Dixon is no longer a village; it is a new
battleground in the old war between ecclesiasticism and secu-
larism in education.

The issue will not be settled in the court of law, which can
come up with only a temporary compromise, for involved is
the larger question as to whether schooling is a proper function
of the state. If we admit that it is, then we must also admit that
the subject matter of education will be decided by those in

This was the lead article in the October 1948 issue of analysis.

control of the political machinery and will vary with the incidence of control. It is silly to think otherwise. The notion that a political institution can be divorced from politics is typical American jabberwocky.

Right now the group most concerned with getting control of tax-supported schools is the theologians. Catholics are particularly active in this effort—for reasons inherent in their faith—but that they have the support of other creeds was shown in the fight for "released time" in New York. Practically the entire clerical fraternity (except Jews, whose religious classes are conducted in the evening) joined in demanding that time be set aside for out-of-school religious education. Suppose the children prefer to devote this time to play, rather than the designated purpose; suppose they are encouraged to do so by their nonreligious parents, will not the clericals carry on? Will they not strive to put religious training into the regular curriculum? In the matter of "released time," and in the demand that public funds be used to convey children to parochial schools, the clericals have shown that they can throw their political weight around. How can they be prevented from asking that their teachers be permitted to give religious instruction in the school buildings? Or, perhaps, that these teachers be put on the public payrolls?

Let us extend the doctrine of "separation" to other than religious subjects. Large gobs of socialistic doctrine have seeped into our school textbooks and teachers of that persuasion are its protagonists. While socialism is not organized along church lines, the element of faith in it gives that ideology a religious tinge, and the attitude of socialists toward nonbelievers as sinful and wicked suggests a further similarity. Well, how did socialism creep into the school curriculum if not by the political power acquired by its devotees? The outlawing of the teaching of evolution by the anti-Darwinians is another case in point. Then again, because the constitutionalists were in the ascendancy in the beginning of our country, the Federalist point of view never got into our history books. How can it be otherwise? As long as schooling is a function of the state, the dominant political group will determine what and how the children will be trained. And for good reason.

The business of education is the transmission of ideas from those who have them to those who are lacking; that is, from elders to youngsters. But, all ideas acquire value, and those which carry the greatest weight with the elders are the ones which the pupils will be exposed to. Education, therefore, can never be free from the prejudices and preconceptions of elders; even if the teacher enjoys "academic freedom," he is not free from the values he has built up in his mind. Objectivity is impossible, save with a mind that is incapable of weighing facts. A transcendentalist will somehow drag in the concept of natural laws even in teaching physics, and the pragmatist will go out of his way to denounce it; a collectivist cannot help insinuating that Jefferson's natural rights are an archaism, or extolling the modernism of Hamilton's centralization idea. Can the free trader avoid berating protectionist history?

It is because of this value emphasis that private schools are established and endowed. The parent selects for his son a classical school or a military school because he puts a higher value on that kind of education; he believes his son is deserving of what he deems better, even if "better" is mere ostentation. One may question the judgment of the parent, but one does not question his right; it is his son and his money.

When we get into adult education the heterogeneity of values is most confusing. There are schools for the teaching of anarchism, the mystic religions, existentialism, decentralism, every shade of Marxism, the ideas of Mary Baker Eddy, of Henry George—schools without end, to say nothing of purely vocational schools. Every enthusiasm has its discipline, and so long as private opinion and private property are not outlawed there will be institutions designed to propagate it. Society is none the worse for this practice; in fact, it can be socially beneficial, so long as it remains a private pursuit, for the more values flying around in the cultural air, the less likelihood of its being fouled up with a dead uniformity.

The tax-supported school cannot permit such free flight to intellectual enthusiasm. By right of ownership every citizen feels that his values should be included in the curriculum, but by the same right others press their values and in the end somebody must be cheated. The monopolist objects because his line of business is disparaged in the economics course, the chauvinist denounces the history teacher for debunking national heroes, the classicist decries the emphasis on modernism, and—above all—the secularization made necessary by a diversity of creeds satisfies nobody except the irreligious. The tax-supported school is abomination to somebody, no matter what or how it teaches.

The state as teacher tries to keep to the middle road, which is a denial of all values and satisfies nobody. But, even as a compromiser the state is a failure, for it is compelled by political considerations to favor the values of the dominant elements in the community. The Texas school reader glamorizes the oil industry, trade unionism must be treated gingerly in industrial centers, and in the South "white supremacy" is intimated even by the fact of segregation. Furthermore, the attempt to find a compromise is abandoned and bias reigns supreme when the state grinds its own ax in the schoolroom. In mentioning our fiscal system, can the tax-paid teacher even hint at the immo-

rality of taxation? Can he void the glorification of political
scoundrels in the school books? And now that we have gone in
for state capitalism in a big way, how can he question the
correctness of TVA, public housing or the monopoly of the
mails?

The private school—the school in which you pay for what
you want—would be ideal if it were truly private. But, as in all
human affairs, the tentacles of the state reach out into this
sphere of education and create disturbance and iniquity. Escape
from political interference is impossible as long as men use
political means to advance their private purposes.

In pushing their claim for tax-paid transportation for parochial school pupils, the Catholics maintain that under our fiscal
system they were paying double for the education of their children; they taxed themselves for the kind of education they
deemed desirable and were levied upon for the maintenance of
secular schools. Though the transportation issue was finally
decided by the weight of the Catholic vote, not by reason, there
is an enticing plausibility in this argument; but, when you extend it you come to disturbing questions. Since the general
taxpayer provides books and lunches and equipment for the
public school pupil, as well as transportation, why not spread
this largess? Should not the private schoolteacher be put on the
public payroll? On the other hand, if the taxpayer contributes
anything to the maintenance of the private school, why should
he not have some say in the subject manner taught?

Furthermore, private schools forfeit their right to complete
privacy by asking for and getting tax favors; exemption of their
real estate from local levies for one thing. Not only is the
property they use for educational purposes untaxed, but in some
localities even the property they rent out to commercial institutions is similarly favored. The exemption amounts to a sub-

sidy. For the values of these properties, frequently located in city centers, are enhanced by the conveniences provided by the taxpayers; the amount of this subsidy is sometimes considerable, as can be ascertained when a school, or a church, disposes of its old site.

There are other tax favors which make the private school beholden to the state. Where sales taxes obtain, its purchases are frequently excused. If it carries on any commercial venture in connection with its educational business, such as publishing, that venture pays no tax profits. Then, of course, there is the big advantage of being able to advertise that under its "charter" contributions to its treasury are deductible in computing personal and corporation income taxes.

Thus, the private school sacrifices its integrity on the altar of special privilege. It cannot claim immunity for its values simply because it regularly sells out its immunity. Under the circumstances, "academic freedom"—vis-à-vis the state—is a specious assertion; no private school is likely to jeopardize its privileges by teaching what the state may deem "subversive," and should the state decide to make use of the school's facilities (including the faculty and the curriculum) for its own purposes, it would be entirely within its rights.

In the full sense of the word, a free school is one that has no truck with the state, via its taxing powers. The more subsidized it is, the less free it is. What is known as "free education" is the least free of all, for it is a state-owned institution; it is socialized education—just like socialized medicine or the socialized post office—and cannot possibly be separated from political control. As for being "free" in the sense of being without cost, that is one of those impostor terms we like to use to hide ugly facts from ourselves; our public education is fully paid for, with all its deficiencies and inadequacies. And it is paid for mainly by the poor, not the rich, because the poor in the aggregate constitute the largest segment of society and therefore pay the most in taxes. It would be an interesting, though useless, exercise to compute the number of private schools that could be maintained with the total amount exacted from us, locally and nationally, for politicalized education.

The root question raised by the Dixon affair is not the separation of the church from the school; it is the separation of the school from the state. The channeling of education along religious lines is a consequence of socialization. These days we associate the effort to introduce ecclesiasticism into the schoolroom with the Catholic church. But, the fact is that in the early history of our country the Protestant denominations fought bitterly against the secularization of all American institutions, including the school, and their lack of success was due mainly to their rivalries; wherever any sect was in the saddle, its particular catechism was obligatory education. Even in the lifetime of the present writer, the reading of the New Testament in the daily school assembly was objected to by the Jews, who were promptly rebuffed with the assertion that this is a "Christian country." It should be recalled that only the agnostic leanings of several constitutional fathers prevented the official designation of the new nation as a "Christian country"—which, by a strange twist of bigotry, meant an anti-Catholic country; there were few Jews and fewer Muhammadans in the colonies.

If we start with the premise that education is a proper function of the state, we must be prepared to accept the corollary: that the kind of education the state dispenses will be that which those in control think desirable. For the state is not an impersonal or impartial diety; it is a committee of persons, replete with desires, prejudices, values. To the Catholic the highest values are embraced in the sacraments of his church—enjoying divine sanction—and his conscience impels him to promote acceptance of these values. For a thousand years, therefore, he has been preeminently a teacher. When the opportunity falls into his hands, as it has in Dixon, to use political power to advance his cause, he would indeed be lacking in integrity if he failed to take advantage of it. Would it be any different if a Hindu, a Baptist, an atheist, or a communist fell heir to political power?

This wrangling over ecclesiasticism in education is a Tweedledee-Tweedledum argument. If we would reform our educational system basically, we must desocialize it. We must put it back where it belongs, in the hands of parents. Theirs is the responsibility for the breeding of children, and theirs is the responsibility for the upbringing. The first error of public schooling is the shifting of this responsibility, the transformation of the children of men into wards of the state. All the other evils follow from that.

Private Schools: The Solution to America's Educational Problem

Periodically and with annoying persistence, the public school bobs up as a social problem. Nobody leaves it alone; it leaves nobody alone. Right now the most prominent point of contention about it is the matter of federal subsidization. While legislation toward that end was sidetracked by a minor issue—whether parochial schools should participate in government largess—the political potential of subsidization will not let it die. The public school will be injected into the campaigns in the offing.

Teachers keep the public school in the headlines by their agitation for larger stipends. In this they are generally supported by parents, who are equally vehement in their opposition to the higher taxation that increased salaries call for. Lack of funds and opposition to taxation are also the points of debate over inadequate school facilities, overcrowded classrooms, lack of personnel.

Meanwhile, the curriculum is under attack. The infiltration of collectivist concepts into our textbooks is a matter of wide concern. Parents and even public officials are inquiring whether

This was originally published in pamphlet form by the National Council for American Education (no date).

the schools are being used as an instrument of socialist indoctrination. How far has the teaching fraternity gone down the line? Loyalty tests come into conflict with the doctrine of academic freedom and the debate pro and con becomes acrimonious.

A pedagogical controversy rages over what is called "progressive education." Many, both professionals and lay students, maintain that this innovation is not education at all and point to its product with derision. There is much viewing with alarm.

Recently, an Illinois couple challenged the compulsory attendance law, and the supreme court of that state decided that parents who have the necessary qualifications may teach their children at home. To what extent will voluntary withdrawal from the school system go? It is a certainty that further deterioration of the schools will prompt many parents to give their personal attention to the three Rs.

Thus, the battle over the public school rages on all fronts. One never hears a solid, unequivocal defense of it, for even its loyal advocates are strong for some kind of reform; on the other hand, there are not a few who argue with considerable cogency that the public school is basically unsound and the only cure for it is abolition.

And yet, if one stands off a way from the heat of the argument and calmly reflects on the problem of education as a whole, a compromise suggests itself that comes near to being a solution. There is nothing wrong with the public school that could not be cured by putting it into active competition with the private school. This is not to say that the private school is without fault, for no institution can possibly provide the capacity for learning that every mother ascribes to her offspring, and when the results fall below her expectations the institution will certainly be blamed. But, if parents could exercise a choice between private and public school, if they had the means to make the choice, the entire controversy over public schooling would collapse. For the responsibility would then be on the parent alone; he would have nobody to blame for a wrong selection.

The immediate reaction to this suggested solution is that it is economically impossible. Only the rich can afford private schooling, it will be said, and recourse to it means that the children of the poor will be deprived of this advantage. However, it must be remembered that public schooling must be paid for; it is not a gift from heaven. And since the poor are in the aggregate the largest contributors to the tax fund, it is they who pay the largest share of the educational bill. It should be possible to derive a method by which they could pay for their schools directly, rather than through the taxing powers of the government. This can be done; but first we must be convinced that our public school problem cannot be solved in any other way.

THE NATURE OF LEARNING

Whatever else education is, whatever its ultimate purpose may be, in substance it is the transmission of ideas. In the case of children, the ideas must come from adults. Even if the child is not submitted to any formal education, his natural curiosity about the new experiences with which he is confronted leads to interrogation of those who presumably have had some acquaintance with the phenomena. That is in the nature of things. The child might be able to dig out the facts by laborious observation, but his instinct is to shortcut the process by asking questions.

It is in this very necessity of learning that the troubles of our school system begin. For, we who are called upon to transmit the knowledge we have acquired are in disagreement as to the validity of that knowledge. Even in matters on which no particular importance is put, like fishing, the uncle and the father may differ violently in their instruction. To religious parents the teaching of the catechism comes first in the curriculum; others would call this the transmission of error.

The teachers, the parents, find it most difficult to free themselves from the values they put on the knowledge they are called upon to transmit. We might all agree, to take a simple example, that the child should learn to read, because reading is the prerequisite for further learning. But, should it learn to read from the classics, the newspapers, or the Bible? Will the boy profit more from an understanding of Milton or from a study of business letters? It is most important, say some parents and teachers, that the child confine his education to subjects that will aid him in the making of a living. They contend that effort in any other direction is wasteful, perhaps harmful. Other teachers and parents take the cultural point of view.

At this particular time, many of us are disturbed over the emphasis in education on social rather than on individual values. In teaching American history, for instance, one can lay stress on the doctrine of natural rights or one can dismiss it as an eighteenth-century fairy tale. There is a tendency in professional pedagogy to take the latter point of view, or to twist the doctrine into a meaning it never had before. Civics can be taught as the art of public management, or as a demonstration of the necessity of submerging one's individuality for the common good. Even biology can be channeled ideologically; the teacher can point out that just as the organs of the living body are interrelated and interdependent, so the individual is not an integer in himself, but only a necessary part of the body politic.

Not only the textbooks for grade schools and high schools, but even the comic strips to which the tots are exposed lend themselves to the transmission of "social values."

One of the factors that makes the educational problem so difficult is this disparity in the values we put on ideas. For example, one mother is an aesthete, the father is of a practical turn, and the professional teacher harbors a "social conscience." What set of values shall be put before the pupil? Shall we first agree on a common set? But that, if it were possible, is undesirable. The striving for a better life, the search for truth, is a matter of selection, and selection presupposes freedom of judgment. That which we call progress results from man's capacity to weigh evidence and make decisions. When that capacity is stultified by repression, civilization declines; when one cannot choose, one cannot aspire. The animal, as far as we know, is incapable of making evaluations and his world is, therefore, delimited. A uniform and rigid set of values would make education a simple process, but the education would be extremely simple.

Well, if the child must learn from adults, and if the adults are not in agreement on what ought to be taught, or how, the public school must resort to the political expediency of compromise. It is odd how, in discussing the public school, we are wont to overlook its inherent political character, the fact that it is tax-supported and subject to political considerations. There is no way of ridding politics of politics. The best the public school can do as a transmitter of values is to favor those that are held by the most numerous, the most aggressive, or the most dominant element in the community. That is not only a necessity, but also in accordance with the democratic process.

While we are on this topic of political schooling, we might consider, parenthetically, the probable effect of federal subsidization. Certainly nothing inimical to the interest of the party in power would pass as sound education, while the historical doctrines of home rule and states rights would have to be reinterpreted. Would the subsidized teacher, if he were so convinced, stress the undesirability of other forms of federal subsidization? The values taught would emanate by direction, suggestion, or tacit understanding from Washington. It could not be otherwise.

However, the political principle of majority rule does not work well in educational matters, simply because of our great concern with the welfare of our children. In this country we have not yet come around to relieving ourselves of the obligations of parenthood; our children are still ours, not the state's. We feel this obligation keenly, and are as determined to protect their minds from hurt as we are to protect their bodies from harm. If the public schools are inculcating ideas we think wrong, or even if we think the education inadequate, we do not blithely submit to majority rule, as we do in matters that concern adults only. We may accept the decision of the ballot box, or the directives of officialdom, because we are helpless, but we nevertheless resent the plight of our children. That is why controversy over public education takes on a peculiar bitterness.

The only way out of this impasse is to throw the responsibility for the education of their children on the parents. Those who find the public school inadequate must be permitted a choice. The teaching of the children at home is one choice. But that way presents difficulties. There is the probable incompetence of the parents as teachers, the compulsory education laws in many states, and, most important, the effect on the child of withdrawing him from the companionship of his friends. That leaves us with a second alternative, that of the private school, the school that offers for a price the kind of education the parent wants; and it leaves us with a problem of meeting the price.

THE PRICE OF LEARNING

There is no such thing as free schooling; it must be paid for and, taking the school system as a whole, its cost is defrayed by the toil of those who are under the delusion of "free" education. In the cities, where the schools are most numerous, the budget is met primarily by levies on real estate. If the dwellings are owned by the occupants, most of whom are merchants and artisans, it is they who pay the bill; if they are occupied by tenants, the taxes are incorporated into the monthly rent. The "rich"—a word of no definite meaning—pay their share as consumers, but their consumption as a class is infinitesimal compared to that of the rest of the population, and their share is correspondingly small.

Whatever kind of education the children get is paid for by the parents. If the parents do not like what they are involuntarily buying, the only thing for them to do is demand that their share of the bill be remitted to them so that they can patronize schools to their liking. They should be permitted to make a choice.

Most of the cost of public schools is met by local taxes— state, county, city, or school district. If all the parents were property owners, the problem of remission for school tuition would be simple; but a great difficulty arises where the taxation is indirect, as in the case of the tenant, or where sales taxes are imposed. The obstacle could probably be overcome, but it would require a study of the various fiscal systems in the states and political subdivisions. Those states that levy on the incomes of their citizens could readily solve the problem of allowing a deduction for tuition fees paid to private schools; thus, they not only would right a basic wrong, but would also relieve the state and local budgets of the perennial and troublesome school problem.

However, since federal income taxation is the largest single direct burden put upon the household, and since comparatively few of us are now free of it, the simplest way of solving our school problem is by a federal exemption for tuition. This proposal should commend itself particularly to the present administration, which has expressed interest in the improvement of our educational establishment. Instead of subsidization, with a consequent increase in taxation, it could more easily improve our school system by putting it on a competitive basis. Incidentally, the federal government would thus remove the widely held suspicion that its interest is not in the betterment of the child's mind through education but in the control of it through indoctrination.

There are not enough private schools in the country to take care of the influx of pupils which would result from such exemption. Even now, the private schools in New York City find it difficult to accommodate all the applicants for admission; it is interesting to note, by the way, that many of their pupils are children of public school teachers. The increased demand resulting from such exemption as here proposed would bring into being an untold number of these selective schools. Every pedagogue who takes pride in his profession would be tempted to start on his own, to ply his skill free from institutional restrictions. Every school of thought would offer its wares to the public. Every pedagogical theory would have a chance of proving itself. Every denomination would expand its parochial activities. There would be, so to speak, a private school on every city block.

BETTER LEARNING

The public school would then be forced to offer a product of competitive value. It should be in a better position to do so. If only a quarter of the present public school attendance should be lost, the school could do an infinitely better job. The over-crowded classroom would disappear and the teacher might show her skill as such, rather than waste her energy in mob discipline. The lure of the private school would certainly draw off many of the more competent in the profession, but the public budget would be relieved of its present strain and the authorities could pay for and demand higher standards. An-cient, unsanitary, and dangerous structures now pressed into service could be abandoned and the land returned to the tax roll. The cost of transportation would be considerably reduced, for one of the competitive features of the private school would undoubtedly be nearness to the home. There would be impor-tant collateral savings, such as less equipment, and fewer text-books and lunches to provide.

The spur to education would be phenomenal. A single teacher could maintain herself with an enrollment of a dozen children, giving each of them the personal attention that is often the difference between successful education and failure. A high school staff of four good instructors could do wonders with a hundred boys and girls. Every teacher would bend his efforts toward building up a reputation for efficiency, not only to attract enrollment but also to justify higher fees. Pride in the profession would replace its present status as a unionized trade.

There would be, to be sure, schools in which socialistic ideology permeated the curriculum, but these would be sup-ported by parents of that persuasion, just as denominational schools would draw upon their members for patronage. The taxpayer would not be forced, as he is now, to maintain objectionable schools or teachers. He could take the pride of his life right out of that environment and march him across the street to one more conducive to a proper upbringing. He would always be able to find just what he wants, for competition would see to it. There would be schools in which music or art play the leading part; others would stress the classics or mathematics or history or manual training; or various combinations. One can imagine young mothers discussing with experienced matrons the relative merits of this or that school, this or that pedagogue, all in the interest of Junior.

MORALS AND FREEDOM

The improvement in educational methods and standards following from the proposed competitive system is secondary to the moral consequences we can expect. The sense of responsibility for the welfare of the child they brought into the world would be returned to the parents. They could no longer shift their personal obligation to an amorphous thing called society; that is, they could not do so without losing the respect of their offspring. The teacher would likewise attain a position of esteem by the necessity of properly discharging her duties. She would be a teacher, not a political timeserver. Her first concern would be with the children in her charge, not with the terms of tenure; no law, no union could cover up incompetence or negligence.

Second, the proposed reform would remove the injustice of compelling payment of unwanted and unused facilities. The argument of the Catholics on this point is well worth considering; it applies equally to every parent who pays a tuition bill. They complain that they are subjected to "double taxation"—

once for the schools they use and again for those they do not. The injustice is obvious. The rejoinder that the public school is at their disposal is silly; they do not deem it satisfactory, and who is endowed with the right to compel a contrary opinion? Is the majority favored with omniscience? But, the unfairness is not righted by making a return to the Catholics of some slight service for their tax money, like furnishing transportation for children attending parochial schools; that is patchwork. The moral thing to do is to remove the imposition.

Finally, the exemption proposal should help restore to America the concept of freedom on which it was founded and built. The public school has been pictured as the guarantee of an informed citizenry, which in turn is the necessary condition for a free society. This plausibility has obscured the fact that the public school is a political institution, and as such can be used for ends quite the opposite of freedom. For example, Hitler, Mussolini, and Stalin did not abolish the public school, but, rather, favored it as a necessary integral of their regimes; and the word *freedom* was not erased from their textbooks. Does the word carry the same weight in present usage that it had before World War I? At that time, as an instance, freedom and conscription were opposite ideas; are they now? Freedom in those days implied an obligation of the citizen to his government, while today it has acquired quite the opposite connotation; one is free only in proportion to the amount of social security, unemployment doles, subsidies, and parity supports the tax fund can furnish him. The public school has not been the entire cause of this perversion, but it has helped greatly. The high school graduate today, even if he has heard of them, has little understanding of the theory of checks and balances or of the doctrine of states rights; to him the idea that a weak and divided government is a condition of freedom would be rather strange.

To be sure, the private school will not automatically restore to the concept of freedom the values of self-reliance and responsibility. There are too many influences working the other way. But, those parents who hold to the philosophy of individualism will most certainly patronize the schools that teach it, and the teachers who lean that way will cherish the opportunity to stress it. Thus an influence will be fostered that will counteract the trend in thought; an intelligent opposition to the indoctrination by the public school must eventually make itself felt. Indeed, if the proposed tuition exemption should reach the legislative stage, who would oppose it but those who are hellbent for a regime of socialism?

Part VII

Taxation Is Robbery

The Revolution of 1913

T he replacement of one ruling regime by another does not in itself measure up to a revolution; that can be accomplished by a gang fight or an election. A revolution is an effective change in relationship between rulers and ruled, a shifting of the incidence of power from society to the state, or vice versa. The American Revolution was an effective one not because it got rid of the British crown, but because it set up a weaker state, vis-à-vis society.

The Constitution was not necessary to the revolution. The new relationship between rulers and ruled was summed up in the Articles of Confederacy, and the country could have managed without another legal document. But we cannot argue with a fact: the Constitution of 1789 charted the course of the new state-society relationship as nearly as a political document could, and thus became the profit-and-loss statement of the preceding rebellion. The going ethos was individualistic; in his pursuit of happiness the early American felt quite satisfied to go it alone, accepting restraint only insofar as restraint was necessary for the security of property and the maintenance of

This article appeared in analysis *(November 1950).*

peace. He would tolerate coercion to restrain coercion, and no more. His experience with the British crown taught him to distrust political intervention, and his skepticism necessitated delimitation of the powers of the proposed establishment. Otherwise, he would have nothing to do with the Constitution.

We pervert the fact when we speak of the Constitution as a guarantee of rights; such an idea did not occur to the framers, nor even to those who opposed ratification. A Bill of Rights was incorporated into the document as a concession to the prevailing skepticism; but the Bill did not establish the prerogatives of the individual and the new government did not guarantee them; it simply agreed to respect them. They inhered, by common consent, in the individual as a matter of existence or as a gift from God, and the Bill was merely a memorandum to that effect. It was a warning signal that the authority of government must not transgress these prerogatives. As James Madison put it in one of his letters, the Bill of Rights was superfluous and unnecessary, and though he did not object to its inclusion, he was apprehensive lest a specific Bill of Rights should invite circumvention and thus defeat the purpose. After all, government simply has no business with rights, except to leave them inviolate.

The principal preoccupation of the framers of the Constitution was with restraints on authority, and those who opposed it argued the insufficiency of these restraints. Much has been said about the "checks and balances" incorporated in the Constitution, but entirely too little emphasis is put on the temper of the times that made these provisions necessary. In the light of the present abdication of social power in favor of political power, the early American attitude toward government is most striking. True, there were some who favored a strong centralized government, and some went so far as to advocate monarchy; but it is doubtful whether even these envisioned a concentration of power such as our present government wields. It was simply unthinkable. The revolution was in the hearts of men.

Not the least of the checks put on the new government was the limitation of its taxing powers. It was understood, of course, that authority is always in proportion to revenue, and if the latter could be held down, the former would take care of itself. About the only taxing power generally conceded to the proposed federal government was that of levying on imports; the "infant industry" argument carried weight, particularly as it implied retribution against the recent enemy. Hamilton argued that customs revenues would be insufficient and begged for internal excise taxes; his argument on this point, in *The Federalist*, is a remarkable piece of special pleading. If the government were not permitted to tax production, he said, it would have to ask for direct taxes. The principal direct tax, that on land values, he peremptorily dismissed on the ground that it would do hurt to the small holders who constituted the bulk of the population; this appeal to mass prejudice conveniently ignored the effect of land value taxation on the large estates in being, and on the prospects of the land speculators who were not without influence in the Convention. The other direct tax, that on incomes, he declared both unjust and impractical; in an agricultural economy, where trade on a barter basis is considerable, a levy on incomes would not yield enough to offset the unpleasantness of collection. His plea for excise taxes prevailed.

And there the matter of federal taxation rested until, as a war measure, the Lincoln administration put through a tax on incomes. The constitutionality of this measure was questioned, and the matter might have been brought to adjudication if the tax had not been dropped, in 1872. Again the constitutionality of income taxation engaged the legal talents of Congress during the latter part of the nineteenth century. The argument was tortuous; yet there can be no question about the intent of the framers of the Constitution. Putting aside the written evidence, it is inconceivable that these leaders of a rebellion that was sparked by resentment over taxation far less oppressive would have countenanced a levy on incomes. That was not what the Americans fought for.

NO MONEY, NO POWER

The federal government rubbed along on what it could get out of customs duties and excise taxes until the enactment of the Sixteenth Amendment in 1913. It was a relatively weak government. It did not transgress the rights of the people because it could not. The balance of power was with society, as envisioned by the revolutionists, and the profits of their struggle endured in the immunities enjoyed by the citizenry: the immunities of property, person, and mind.

In respect to the right of property, the people were protected from encroachment by the strict limits put on the federal power of taxation. And because it therefore lacked the wherewithal, the government could not engage in ventures tending to invade the immunities of person and of mind. Thus, Lincoln's attempt at military conscription was unsuccessful because he did not have an army to ferret out reluctant draftees; when World War I rolled around, that lack had been overcome, thanks to the Sixteenth Amendment, and now encroachment is so effective that even peacetime conscription presents no difficulty; the person of every American may be impounded.

As for the immunity of mind, that was undermined by the

subtle process of subvention, when the funds became available. With public and private educational institutions beholden to the state for their existence, it was inevitable that the doctrine of benevolent statism should have insinuated itself into textbook and classroom; and as employment in the burgeoning bureaucracy presented opportunities, both as to emoluments and self-glorification, the minds of educators and educated became receptive to the idealization of the state. The doctrine of natural rights was gradually washed out of political science and social philosophy, and in its place we have the doctrine of permissive rights. In all the disciplines dealing with human relations, including, of course, the law, the primacy of the mass, rather than the individual, has achieved axiomatic position. It is a new American ethos, induced by state beneficence. Even the tax-exemption privilege granted eleemosynary institutions is not without its influence; because of it, as well as permissible deductions from income, contributions to school and church became more liberal before limits were put upon contributions; so that, perhaps unconsciously, even the teachers of Christianity have come around to minimizing the dignity of the individual and the glorification of directed behavior. Though it cannot be said that this inclination toward collectivism was deliberately planned, the state has not failed to use the funds at its command to propagandize itself into public favor.

Thus, the immunities written into the compact of 1789 have been eradicated by the proceeds of the Sixteenth Amendment. This one measure effected a change in the relationship between society and its ruling regime as thoroughly as if it had been done by invasion and conquest. The revolution of 1913 undid the profits of the revolution of 1789.

Our adjustment to the new relationship blinds us to the fact; perhaps an exercise in speculation will help to clarify it. Let us imagine an impossible bargain entered into between the American colonials and George III: in exchange for the removal of all their disabilities and indignities he had put upon them, as enumerated in the Declaration, they offered him the power to tax their incomes. Assuming that he understood the proposition—which is as unlikely as their making it, since income taxation was only vaguely apprehended in those days—he would most assuredly have accepted it. Why not? A prior lien on all their production would have been an attractive price for the gewgaws of liberty they wanted. There would have been no revolution. The dominance of the British crown would have been assured, and the immunities of property, person, and mind enjoyed by Americans between 1789 and 1913 would never have been known. The American attitude toward the state would always have been what it is now; that is, one of dependence and subservience.

It requires no great imagination to draw up a bill of particulars against the present American state comparable to the indictment of the British crown in the Declaration, and one could well argue that there is more cause for revolt today than there was in 1776. The will, however, is absent.

POLITICAL PERVERSITY

Among the casualties of the revolution of 1913 is the doctrine of federalism. It is a casualty of major importance. From 1789 until the Civil War, the tradition of coequal authority between local and federal governments held firm, and even after that war (which settled only the question of secession), the states maintained their autonomy by virtue of their economic independence. The country was a Union, not a nation; it was only when the federal government obtained power over the citizens' property that our constitutional structure was mutated. The events leading up to it are well worth reviewing.

It all began when the passion for leveling was let loose by a too literal interpretation of the doctrine of equality. The revolt against feudal absolutism was sparked by the truth that "all men are created equal," and envy was quick to turn this truth into a license for spoliation; the early American was no freer of covetousness than any other man. Recognizing this, the Founding Fathers sought to prevent the use of the powers of government for a program of confiscation; that, indeed, was the primary purpose of the checks and balances. However, during periods of economic distress, these safeguards of property rights regularly became the target of demagoguery; "hard times" were invariably blamed on the cupidity of the few. After the depression of 1873 the passion for leveling was whipped into a froth and there was a general demand for reforms, most of them aiming to break down the immunity of property safeguarded by the Constitution.

One of the reforms called for during the latter part of the nineteenth century had a substratum of economic sense. It was a demand for tariff reductions. The South (which had tried secession as a means of righting the injustice of the protectionist system) was now joined with the West in this demand. Its position was sound. The prices the South obtained for its raw products were set in the competitive markets of the world, while the prices it paid for manufactured goods were loaded with tariffs. The consequent disaffection found expression in the Granger-Populist movement.

This was grist for the mills of the Democratic party, idle and gathering dust for many years. The party was historically committed to free trade, even though its integrity had been more than tarnished by protectionism, and Grover Cleveland, its candidate in the campaign of 1892, grabbed at the ready-made issue presented by the agricultural malcontents. His sagacity went further. Contending that the loss of tariff revenues would go hard with the federal treasury, he proposed to make up the deficiency with an income tax. This was a direct appeal to the passion for leveling, for in those days it was taken for granted that an income tax would be levied on the wealthy only. Thus, a measure of justice was packaged with an appeal to envy into a successful campaign platform.

The income tax law introduced by the Cleveland administration (and declared unconstitutional in 1894) was indeed attached to a low-tariff bill. And up to the enactment of the Sixteenth Amendment, the political fiction was maintained that an income tax was needed to offset lower customer returns. This was pure hogwash; the state never relinquishes one form of revenue for another, for it is inherently incapable of restraining its lust for power. The highest tariff walls in the history of the country sprang up after income taxation was constitutionalized.

Ironically enough, the hope of those who favor free trade, or even lower tariffs, was forever done away with by the income tax. The state now has no economic interest in importations, no reason for encouraging them. Before the Sixteenth Amendment, nearly half of all the revenues of the federal treasury came from customs duties; today that source provides less than two percent. Were it not for the large revenues from income taxation, the state would be compelled by its own needs to pursue a tariff-for-revenue-only policy, rather than a protectionist policy. The current program of economic isolation—including quotas, so-called quarantine restrictions, and the devaluation of our money in respect to foreign moneys—would simply be impossible. Foreign trade would be as important to the treasury as it is to the general economy.

A tariff-for-revenue policy, furthermore, would have made impossible the current urgency for a managed economy, for no state can go in for that sort of thing if the country's borders are open to the goods of other nations. Fixed or regulated prices cannot stand up against foreign competition, and an arbitrary scale of wages is likewise undermined. A hermetically sealed economy is the prerequisite of a managed economy. Our venture into socialism known as the New Deal would never have been undertaken if the barriers to foreign trade had not first been set up, and such barriers could not have been erected if the fiscal affairs of the government were dependent on tariffs; the income tax obviated that dependency.

THE UNION IS DISSOLVED

Protectionism breeds protectionism. The relief expected by the agricultural communities did not follow on the Sixteenth Amendment; their difficulties were rather increased. The further entrenchment of protectionism gave rise to the argument that if the manufacturers are to be protected from foreign competition, why not the farmers? Thus came "parity" prices and the whole program of taxing consumers in favor of agriculturists. Naturally, the disequilibrium in the economy was felt by other groups, who in turn clamored for relief through special privilege for themselves. Government by pressure groups is inherent in democracy, but it is held within limits by the amount of munificence the government can dispense. The income tax extended these limits to nearly the full productive capacity of the country. The power of confiscation this law conferred on the government led inevitably to the taxing of Peter to quiet Paul, and back again, meanwhile gathering to the political machinery the luxury of unlimited coercion over both.

All of this naturally turned the attention of the citizen from home government to the national establishment; their loyalty followed their property. But, the final disintegration of the Union was effected by the rise of another pressure group, that of the home politicians. From the very beginning of the Union, congressmen were in the business of purchasing political preferment with whatever special privileges and grants they could wangle from the central authority; "pork barrel" legislation did not begin with the Sixteenth Amendment. But with the enlargement of the barrel, their preoccupation with it overshadowed any interest they have had in principles of government or in national affairs as such. Before income taxation, the best the government could offer the local politician in the way of bribery were land grants, franchises, a few posts in the limited bureaucracy and "rivers and harbors" bills. The price was not high enough to buy up the integrity of the people's representatives completely; a truly patriotic congressman was not a rarity.

The ink was hardly dry on the Sixteenth Amendment before the heretofore picayune grant-in-aid program began to blossom; in 1914 came the Smith-Lever Act establishing the Agricultural Extension Service with, in those days, the rather considerable initial appropriation of $480,000; this was followed in rapid order by others; it would take a book of proportions merely to list the legislation passed since 1913 to favor political ambitions. It is a truism to say that the congressman is now only a liaison officer between his constituents and the Treasury Department. In fairness, one should not point to this consequence of the Sixteenth Amendment as evidence of the moral decline of the politician; it is rather proof of a dwindling social integrity. That the politician unashamedly boasts of the prosperity his "influence" has brought to his community, by way of airfields, bridges, dams, and smokestacks, only reflects the general attitude. And the general attitude, visibly expressed in the endless safari to Washington in behalf of "worthy" causes, is in turn the result of the transfer of economic power from society to the state.

The swag principle of government is favored by the natural distribution of population and the resultant concentration of wealth in the more populous areas. There is no way out of it; some sections of the country offer greater productive opportunities than others, and there the aggregate of wealth must be greater. As a result of this economic phenomenon, seven states in the Union yield more to the income tax fund than they get out of it, and forty-one show a net profit. Covetousness is encouraged. Somehow, a Mississippian does not see any immorality in forcing a Pennsylvanian to support his local economy. His pride might prevent him from accepting a gratuity from a neighbor, but he suffers no such inhibition when it comes to a "foreigner." Thus, it has come to pass that the more numerous "poor" states have constituted themselves a congressional bloc (organized only by their common cupidity), intent on getting all they can from the seven opulent states. That is the bald fact; the justification for it is the doctrine of "national interest."

But, the *quid pro quo,* whether a Nebraska governor gets a new road or post office for his state, or the senator from Arizona brings home a chunk of patronage, is the abdication of local social power in favor of the greater monopolization of coercion by the central establishment. The price of favors is sovereignty. Just as the citizen was turned into a subject by the confiscation of his property, so does the local politician transfer his allegiance from his community to the source of munificence. A Calhoun, struggling to keep inviolate the customs of his state, has no place in our *mores;* the people would not elect him. Nor could a governor of Rhode Island hold office today if he presumed to defy, as did several of his predecessors, the authority of Washington. State lines are practically obliterated, the states reduced to parish status, their politicians nationalized. The independent home government emerging from the revolution of 1789 has been destroyed by the revolution of 1913. The Union is dissolved.

Socialism via Taxation

W henever it declares itself on the subject of taxation, socialism shows how well it knows its stuff. The Pharisees
of that order have pointed out how the bourgeois system of
"forced dues and charges"—as the *Encyclopedia Britannica*
describes taxes—can well bring about the abolition of private
property. It is a device for both siphoning capital out of citizens'
pockets into the coffers of the state and discouraging the accumulation of capital. In that they are eminently correct, even
though, characteristically, they avoid mentioning the greater
peculation of wages. But, since the end justifies the means,
they are strong for taxes, the bigger the better.

The scribes of what we call capitalism, neither as knowing
nor as honest, have gone about camouflaging taxation with
theories, canons, sanctimonious justifications, and, of course,
a library of laws, until its mask has become its true face. When
you unmask it, by means of reason and historical investigation,
you see that taxation is highwaymanry made respectable by
custom, thievery made moral by law; there isn't a decent thing

This article first appeared in analysis *in three parts (February, March, and April
1946). It was the basis for the* Human Events *pamphlet Chodorov authored a year
later, "Taxation Is Robbery."*

to be said for it, as to origin, principle, or its effects on the social order. Man's adjustment to this iniquity has permitted its force to gain momentum like an unopposed crime wave; and the resulting social devastation is what the socialists have long predicted and prayed for.

The fact of taxation was known long before it was so named. If the thing was referred to by any particular word, it must have been some prehistoric counterpart of *swag*. The Danes who made periodic collecting visits to their neighbors called it *Dannegeld*. However, a name and a theory are unimportant to the unsophisticated brigand who takes what he likes; both become important only after the browbeaten victim learns how to buy peace at a price, and the brigand finds it nice to put himself on a par with the merchant. The path of skulduggery is made easier with a coating of morality, which is aptly applied to an established custom, by the lawyer and the professor of economics. And so, the business of taking what does not belong to you has been well obfuscated by a "philosophy" of taxation.

Our adjustment to taxation is so complete that these statements will undoubtedly be put down as brash, incontinent, crackpot. One could call upon modern practices to prove the point, for the ancient art of getting something for nothing has not been lost, nor have we forgotten the habit of making peace with iniquity. The "protection" tariff levied on businessmen by racketeers is, in substance, taxation, although it cannot be so dignified because it is not recognized in law; not yet, anyhow. On the other hand, the recently legalized (and moralized) checkoff system by which the laborer is compelled to pay the job monopolist for the privilege of making a living is definitely a case in point. But, it is a recognized principle of logic that analogies prove nothing; so, we must apply ourselves to an analysis of the theory and practice of taxation to prove that it is in fact the kind of thing above described.

PERMISSION-TO-LIVE PRICE

First, as to method of collection, taxation has been divided into two kinds, direct and indirect. Indirect taxes are so called because they reach the state by way of private collectors, while direct taxes arrive without bypass. The former levies are attached to goods and services before they reach the consumer, while the latter, with the exception of stamp taxes, are demands made upon previous accumulations of wealth.

It will be seen that indirect taxation is a permission-to-live price. You cannot find in the marketplace a single satisfaction to which a number of taxes are not attached, added to the price, and you are under compulsion either to pay them or go without; since going without amounts to depriving yourself of the meaning of life, or even of life itself, you pay. The inevitability of this charge on existence is expressed in the popular dichotomy, "death and taxes." And it is this very characteristic that commends indirect taxation to the state, so that when you examine the load carried by the goods you live by you are astounded by the disproportion in the price between the cost of production and the charge for permission to live. Somebody has computed the number of different taxes carried by a loaf of bread and has come to the figure 125, but the computer admits the probability of unascertainable taxes. Whiskey is perhaps the most notorious example of the way products have been transmuted from satisfactions into tax gatherers. The manufacturing cost of a gallon of whiskey, for which you pay around twenty dollars, is less than a half-dollar; the spread is partly taken up by the cost of distribution, but at least ninety percent of the money passed over the counter goes to maintain city, county, state, and national officials.

The hue and cry over the cost of living would make more sense if it were aimed at taxation, the largest single item in the cost. And humanitarians who are concerned with this matter would do well to consider this: the incidence of indirect taxation falls most heavily on goods of the widest use, so as to ensure the greatest return, and as the poor are the largest segment of society and therefore the greatest consumers, it is on those least able to support the state that the burden is put.

TAKING WHILE YOU'RE NOT LOOKING

It is not only the size of the yield, or its certainty, which gives indirect taxation preeminence in the state's scheme of appropriation. Its most commendable quality is that of being surreptitious. It is taking while the victim is not looking. Those who strain themselves to give taxation a moral character are under obligation to explain the state's preoccupation with the hiding of taxes in the price of goods. Is there not a confession of guilt in that? In recent years, in its search for additional sources of revenue, the state has been tinkering with a sales tax, an outright and unequivocal permission-to-live price; wiser solons recognize in this measure a political danger and have therefore vigorously opposed it. Why? If the state serves a good purpose, the producers will hardly object to paying its keep.

Merely as a matter of method, not with deliberate intent, indirect taxation yields a profit of proportions to the private collectors, for which reason they support the state in making such levies. To the original payer of the tax it becomes a book-keeping cost, and as such it must be added to all the other costs of operation which go into price making. As each processor and distributor computes his profits as a percentage of the total costs of operation, the original tax is pyramided from hand to hand, and what the consumer pays for the product is considerably in excess of the amount delivered to the state. The most notorious of indirect taxes are custom tariffs. Follow an importation of raw material, say silk, from importer to cleaner, to spinner, to weaver, to finisher, to manufacturer, to wholesaler, to retailer, each one adding his markup to the price paid his predecessor, and you will see that in the price paid by milady for the petticoat there is at least double the toll collected at the customs office. It is because of these profits that merchants and manufacturers cannot see the wrong in customs duties.

Support for this indirect method of robbing the worker comes from still another source. The greater the tax load of an industry, the greater the investment necessary for engaging in it, giving large accumulations of capital a distinct competitive advantage. Any farmer can make whiskey, and many of them do; but the investment in revenue stamps and the various license fees that must be paid in advance make the opening of a distillery and the organizing of distributive agencies a business only for the affluent. It is the state which has turned the individually owned and congenial grog shop into a palatial bar under mortgage to the brewery or distillery which advanced the license fees. The manufacture of cigarettes has likewise been concentrated into the hands of a few giant corporations by the tax system; three-quarters of the price of a package of cigarettes is an outlay in taxes which the manufacturer must be prepared to meet. It would be strange indeed if these powerful interests were to voice any opposition to indirect taxation, which they never do, and the inarticulate, uninformed, and unorganized consumer is forced to pay the higher prices resulting from limited competition.

SOAKING THE POOR RICH

Direct taxes differ from indirect taxes not only in the manner of collection but also in the more important fact that the former cannot be passed on. Those who pay them cannot demand reimbursement from others. In the main, the incidence of direct taxation falls on accumulations rather than on goods in the process of exchange. Since under our monopoly system only a few can accumulate any considerable amount of wealth, this method of appropriation appeals to popular envy; it makes its way with a soak-the-rich label. But the label turns out to be a false one, since the principle involved permits the application of direct taxes to the most modest incomes. There are more poor than rich, and therefore their income in the aggregate is the largest mine to be tapped. So that every soak-the-rich tax must become in time a soak-the-poor tax.

The clear-cut direct taxes are those levied on incomes, inheritances, gifts, land values; included also are road tolls, licenses, and, since in effect they are taxes, punitive fines. As for incomes, what started as a modest imposition on those who would hardly feel it, has been widened until it includes taxation on wages at the source. Employers are now required to deduct and turn over to the authorities a percentage of the worker's wage; the so-called social-security taxes are in fact levies of the same kind. The sugarcoated fiction of a gratuity to the taxed wage earner is maintained by requiring the employer to make an equal contribution to the security fund, but since this contribution is added to his cost of doing business and therefore to his prices, it will be seen that the wage earner pays this part too when he buys the product. A further dishonesty of the social-security tax is that the revenues thus obtained are used to meet the general expenses of the state, while the old-age pensions and unemployment benefits, for which the tax is ostensibly levied, are met by new taxes on current production.

Direct taxation is the last resort of the state, being applied only when indirect taxation has been stretched to the political breaking point, and when the state has attained the necessary strength. In ordinary times the opulent, to whom direct taxation is a threat, are able successfully to oppose it; for the opulent are also articulate, resourceful, and powerful. Yet, when war or mass poverty endangers the social and political structure under which these elements of society prosper, their opposition to direct taxation slackens; the mass fear which in such times weakens social power gives strength to the political arm, which then ruthlessly reaches out into every pocket in the country. Once the "emergency" is passed, social power must reassert itself to gain any amelioration in taxation, but its cause is a difficult one because the precedent and the method remain. The history of every country in the world is a record of progressive increase in taxation, culminating, as it must, in a complete breakdown in the national economy.

Taxes, of all kinds, discourage production. It is a silly sophism, and thoroughly indecent, to maintain that the state spends what it collects and that therefore there is no lowering of purchasing power; thieves also spend their loot, with more abandon than the rightful owners would have spent it, and one could therefore make out a case for the social value of thievery. Neither thieves nor officials produce a marketable good to offset what they take; they contribute nothing to the purchasing power because they contribute nothing to the general fund of wealth. Every increase in the cost of living slows down the wheels of industry, while every levy on savings discourages the accumulation of capital. Why work when there is nothing in it? Men do not go into business to support politicians.

YOU HAVE NO RIGHT TO PROPERTY

A word on the income tax is in order—a book would be more appropriate. In principle this tax, as the founders of the Constitution realized, is more vicious than any other, for it is a direct attack on the sanctity of private property. By its very surreption indirect taxation is a backhanded recognition of the right of the individual to his savings, and the argument for all other taxes is the need for revenue; but the income tax establishes the prior right of the state to the property of its subjects. If you follow through on the principle involved you come to the conclusion that the individual's right to property is a temporary and revocable stewardship. The Jeffersonian ideal of inalienable rights is liquidated, and substituted for it is the Marxist concept of state supremacy. It is by this tax measure, rather than by violent revolution, or an appeal to reason, or popular education, or any ineluctable historic force, that the reality of socialism is forced on us. Notice how the centralization advocated by Alexander Hamilton is accomplished by this fiscal measure, and that the contemplated union of independent commonwealths is effectively dissolved; not only are these states reduced to parish status, but the individual is no longer a citizen of his state but belongs to the nation.

A basic immorality becomes the center of a vortex of immoralities. When the state invades the right of the individual to the products of his labors, it appropriates an authority which is contrary to the nature of things and therefore establishes an unethical pattern of behavior, for itself and for those upon whom the authority is exerted. Thus, the income tax has made the state a partner in the proceeds of crime; the law cannot distinguish between incomes derived from production and incomes derived from robbery; its concern is with income and not with its source. Likewise this denial of the right of property arouses a resentment which, under the circumstances, finds expression in dishonesty and perjury. Men who in their personal relations would hardly think of such methods, or who would be socially ostracized for practicing them, are proud of, and are complimented for, evasion of the income tax law. No other measure in the history of our country has caused a comparable disregard of principle in public affairs, or has had such a deteriorating effect on the morals of the people.

Taxation has surrounded itself with doctrines of justification; it had to; no miscreant can carry on without a supporting philosophy. Until recent times this pilfering of private property sought to gain the approval of its victims by protesting the need for maintaining social services. The growing encroachment of the state upon property rights necessarily brought about a lowering of the general economy, resulting in disaffection, and now taxation is advocated as a means of alleviating this condition; we are now being taxed into betterment. Whether for one reason or the other, the yardstick for all levies is the ability-to-pay formula, suggesting a leveling-off process and quite appealing to our instinct of envy. Let us look into these two postulates of taxation and the supposedly ethical yardstick.

TAXATION FOR SOCIAL SERVICES

Taxation for social services hints at an equitable trade. It suggests a *quid pro quo,* a give-and-take, a relationship of justice. But, the essential condition of trade, that it be carried on willingly, is entirely absent from taxation; the very use of compulsion which taxation must resort to removes it from the field of commerce, puts it squarely in the field of politics. Taxes cannot be compared to dues paid to a voluntary organization, for such services as one expects to obtain from membership, because the choice of withdrawing does not exist. In refusing to trade one may deny oneself of a profit, but the only alternative to taxes is jail.

In respect to social services a community may be compared to a large office building in which the occupants, following widely differing businesses, cannot carry on without the aid of common services, such as elevator transportation, heat, cleaning, window washing, and so on. Each tenant might provide these conveniences for himself, as indeed is done in smaller buildings, or when one tenant occupies the entire space. The more tenants in the building the more important do these overall specializations become to each one, and at a pro rata fee far less than the cost of individual self-service the operators undertake to supply them; the fee is included in the room rent. Each of the tenants is enabled to carry on his business more effectively because he is relieved of his share of the overall duties.

Just so are the citizens of a community better able to carry on their several occupations because the streets are maintained, the fire department is on guard, the police department provides protection to life and property. Like all analogies, this one is not quite a synonym because the tenant may avoid the fee by moving to a building which does not provide the services, may build his own house, may go out of business; the only way to avoid taxation is to die.

When a society is organizing, as in a frontier town, the need for these services is met by volunteer labor. The road is kept open by contributions of time and effort, there is a volunteer fire department, the respected elder performs the services of a judge. As the town grows these extracurricular jobs become too onerous and too complicated for volunteers, whose private businesses suffer because of the increasing demands of social services, and the necessity of hiring specialists appears. At this point, also, compulsory taxation appears, and the question is, why must the residents be compelled to pay for being relieved of work which they formerly performed willingly? Why is coercion a correlative of taxation?

WHY TAXATION NEEDS COMPULSION

The answer may be the obvious one that men are inclined toward getting something for nothing. Then again, it may be the realization that while these social services do provide certain conveniences, these merely spell more chances to work but no more returns per unit of labor. The barber, for instance, does earn more than he did when population was sparse because he has more customers, but his increased earnings arise from a greater exertion of effort and not from the social services. The clothier cannot charge as much as he did per suit when he sold only one suit a week, because he now has competitors, but he does have a larger net profit because he sells more suits. The printer has more jobs but he gets no more per hour. That is to say, the population increase offers more opportunity to produce, and it is to this greater effort that the increase in earnings must be credited. The per-hour wage does not go up because of increased population or the social services introduced.

The natural inclination is to hold on to one's wages, because the natural inclination is to associate wages with oneself, as an inalienable right. If I have a right to myself I have a right to what I produce, as against all men, even if they are organized and possess political power. The greater concentration of population does in fact enable me to produce more, to work more intensely; but to take from me part of my product seems to be a charge for the opportunity to live, and that strikes me as unfair, unjust. The natural inclination against taxation arises then from an innate sense of its injustice. The practice of injustice necessitates the use of force.

Trace an injustice to its cause and you will find another injustice. The burgeoning community which necessitates better streets, a sanitation department, traffic policemen, a park for the children, and so on, brings about an economic betterment which, peculiarly enough, does not accrue to the population as a whole. Where the bank building now stands there was once a pigsty, and what was once the site of a barn now supports the general store. The bank and the general store represent more intense productivity, opportunities to render wider services to the community. Competition between bankers and storekeepers for the use of these sites has greatly enhanced their value. This value arises not from the services rendered by these entrepreneurs but from the presence of the population they serve, while, as we have seen, the presence of this population necessitates the social services enjoyed by the community.

It would seem logical that this value—which we call land rent—should go to defray the expenses of these common services. However, under our prevailing land-tenure system this economic increment accrues to the erstwhile farmer who holds title to the sites, or maybe to the banker who holds a mortgage on them. The economic betterment which the community as a whole creates is diverted to individuals who return nothing for it to the general fund of wealth. This is the injustice which fosters the injustice of taxation.

It is the landowner, then, who in truth owns the social services for which the producers of the community are forced to pay. And he owns them in the full sense of the word, for he collects the rent which follows from them, and sells them when he disposes of his holding. He makes no bones about it; when he puts his plot on the market, he proclaims the advantages of the subway station, the neighborhood school, the efficient fire and police protection given it, and he computes his price accordingly; the buyer, likewise, acquires title to the social services which center in that location. It's all open and aboveboard. What is not advertised is that these social services have been paid for by compulsory "dues and charges" levied on the producing part of the public. These folk receive for their pains the vacuous pleasure of writing home to their country cousins about the marvelous underground railway system, the beautiful boulevards, the fabulous zoo and the other wonders of the great city; also, they have the opportunity of working more intensely. And that is all they get for their tax bill.

TAXATION AS A CURE-ALL

We come now to the modern doctrine of taxation—that its justification is the social purpose to which the revenue is put. It is interesting to note that this doctrine emerges from a general condition of poverty, and hence of social unrest, and that the advocates advance it as a cure-all. It is quiescent during the short interludes of relative prosperity which the country enjoys. It is the humanitarian's prescription for the social malady of poverty amidst plenty, the doctrinaire's method of leveling economic inequalities, the charitarian's first-aid treatment of apparent injustice. But, like all proposals which spring from the goodness of heart, taxation for special purposes is an easy top-surface treatment of a deep-rooted illness, and as such is likely to do more harm than good.

In the first place, this doctrine denies the right of the individual to his property. That is basic. Having tacitly or openly fixed on this premise, it jumps to the conclusion that the needs of society are the end of production, and offers the mechanism of taxation as the means for its diffusion. In the fact that it concerns itself not with the control of production, or with the means of acquiring property, but only with distribution, it is, strictly speaking, not socialistic, and its proponents are usually quick to deny that charge. Their purpose, they assert, is reform, not revolution; even like boys whose innocent bonfire inadvertently puts the forest ablaze.

The doctrine does not distinguish between property acquired through privilege and property acquired through production. It cannot, must not, do that, for if it did it would question the validity of taxation as a whole. When we examine privileges we find that they are economic advantages granted by the political power, and political power is born in and thrives on taxation. If taxation were abolished, for instance, the cost of maintaining the necessary social services of a community would fall on rent—there is no third source—and the privilege of collecting rent would vanish. If taxation were abolished the sinecures of public office would vanish, and these constitute a privilege which in the aggregate bear heavily on production. If taxation were abolished, our so-called protective system would go out and with it would go the privilege of collecting higher prices from producers. Taxation for social purposes has no intent of abolishing existing privilege, but really creates new privileges for bureaucrats who will carry out the plan. Therefore, it doesn't dare to make a distinction between the two kinds of property.

Furthermore, the discouragement of production which must follow in the wake of this distributive scheme further aggravates the condition it hopes to correct. If Tom, Dick, and Harry are all engaged in producing goods and services, the taking from one of them, even if what is taken is given to the others, must lower the economy of the three. Tom's opulence, in this case, is because he has rendered services to Dick and Harry which they found desirable. He may be more industrious, or gifted with superior capabilities, and as a result they have favored him with their trade; although he has acquired an abundance, more than they have, he has not done so at their expense; he has because they have. If the political power deprives him of his possessions, he must cease to patronize Dick and Harry, and they are to the extent of the tax levied on him without employment. So that the dole handed out to Dick and Harry actually impoverishes them. The economy of the community is improved not by the distribution of what has already been produced but by an increase in the abundance of things men live by. We live on current production. Any measure, therefore, which discourages, restricts, or interferes with production must lower the general economy, and taxation for social purposes is distinctly such a measure.

TAXATION BREEDS POWER

Putting aside the economics of the matter, the political implications are even more damaging to the soundness of the idea. Never must it be forgotten that taxes are *compulsory* "dues and charges." That being so, every increase in the limits of taxation automatically extends the limits of compulsion and, consequently, decreases the power of resistance. If the end to be achieved is the "social good," the power to take can conceivably extend to total production, for who shall say where the "social good" terminates? At present the "social good" embraces free schooling, free hospitalization and medical services, unemployment insurance, old-age pensions, farm subsidies, aid to "infant industries," low-rent housing, free employment service, contributions to the merchant marine, projects for advancement of the arts, and the distribution of expensive literature on how to get well, keep well, and do well. We have seen how, as the problems of poverty increase, the "social good" has spilled over from one private matter to another, and now the definition of this indeterminate term seems to include every human interest and activity. The democratic right to be wrong, uninformed, misguided, or even stupid is no restraint upon the imagination of those who undertake to interpret this goal; and whither this goal goes, there goes the power to enforce compliance.

The omnipotence to which taxation for social purposes leads rests on an assumption of human omniscience. The infallibility of committees, science, graphs, charts, and tables is accepted *a priori,* and any questioning of the dicta of experts is frowned upon as presumptuous heresy. Society as a whole is divided into those who know and those who are incapable of knowing; upon the first devolves the duty of leading the unfortunate. There may be something in the theory of superior people, in the nature of things, but nature's failure to put upon them distinctive indicia is a handicap which can be overcome only by the assumption of political power. That power the self-anointed are never reluctant to assume.

Taxation's final claim to rectitude is its ability-to-pay formula, and this turns out to be a bit of too much protesting. It is in fact a cruelly deceptive shibboleth. In the levies on consumption, from which the state derives its largest revenues, it is impossible to apply the formula. Whether your income is a thousand dollars a year or a thousand dollars a day, the tax on the loaf of bread is the same; ability to pay plays no part. Because of the taxes he pays on necessaries, the poor man may have to deprive himself of some marginal satisfaction, say a pipe of tobacco, while the rich man, who pays the same taxes on necessaries, will hardly feel impelled to give up his cigar. After all, the rich man consumes more than the poor man only in the matter of luxuries; he probably eats less than the laborer, and no man can wear more than one suit at a time; therefore, the permission-to-live price bothers him far less than it does his less fortunate fellow man.

The formula is applicable only in levying taxes on incomes before they are spent, and here again its claim to fairness is unfounded. Every tax on wages, no matter how small, affects the worker's pattern of living, while the heavy levy on the rich man, depending on his income, may affect only his indulgences. Wage income, moreover, is easily ascertainable, and avoidance of any part of the tax, legally or illegally, is negligible, while income from the operation of a business or from investments can be lost in the intricacies of accountancy, honestly or dishonestly, and hence ability to pay loses its egalitarian meaning. The claim to equity, which is implied in the formula, would be valid only if all above a predetermined, uniform standard of living were confiscated by the state. But then, of course, the equity of confiscation would have to be established.

When we look to the intent behind ability to pay we see that it is an unconscious confession of immorality. What is this but the highwayman's code: take where the taking is good? Neither the highwayman nor the tax collector gives any thought to the source of the victim's wealth, only to the quantity. The state is not above taking what it can from the income of known or suspected thieves, murderers, or prostitutes, and its vigilance in this regard is so well established that the breakers of other laws find it wise not to break the income tax law. Nevertheless, ability to pay finds popular support—and this must be accounted the reason for its promulgation—because it assuages the sense of injustice aroused by the inequities of our monopoly economy. It is an appeal to the envy of the incompetent as well as to the disaffection of the mass consigned by our system of privileges to involuntary poverty. It satisfies the passions of avarice and of revenge. It embraces the promise of retributive justice, the leveling-off ideal. It is Robin Hood.

TAKING WHAT THE STATE CREATES

Supporting the formula is the argument that incomes are relative to the opportunities afforded by the state, and that the amount taxed is merely payment for these opportunities. Again the *quid pro quo*. This is only partially true, and in a sense which is not intended by the advocates of this fiscal formula. Where income is derived from a privilege—and every privilege rests on the power of the state to support it—it is eminently fair that the state confiscate the proceeds, although it would be fairer if the state did not create the privilege in the first place. The monopoly rent of natural resources, for instance, is income for which no service to society is rendered, and is collectible only because the state makes it possible; a 100 percent tax on rent would therefore be equitable. The profits garnered by "protected" industries because of the embargo on foreign competition would be fair game for taxation. A tax on all businesses which receive subsidies, to the full amount of these subsidies, would make sense, although the granting of subsidies would still require explanation. Bounties, bonuses, doles, the "black market" profits made possible by political restrictions, the profits on government contracts—all income which would disappear if the state withdrew its support from that particular business or occupation ought properly to be taxed. The state should take what it is responsible for.

But that is not what is meant by those who promulgate ability to pay. They insist that the state is a contributing factor in production, and that its services ought properly to be paid for; the measure of the value of these services is the income of its citizens, and a graduated tax on these incomes is only due compensation. If earnings reflect the services of the state, then it follows that larger earnings result from more services, and the logical conclusion is that the state is a better servant of the rich than of the poor. That may be so, but it is doubtful that the tax experts wish to convey that information; what they want us to believe is that the state helps the individual to better his circumstances. That idea gives rise to some provocative questions. For the tax he pays, does the farmer enjoy more favorable growing weather? The merchant a more active market? Is the skill of the mechanic improved by anything the state does with that part of his production which is taken from him? How can the state quicken the imagination of the creative genius or add to the wisdom of the philosopher? Where the state receives a cut from gambling, is the luck of the winner bettered? Are the earnings of the prostitute increased because her trade is legalized and taxed? Just what part does the state play in production that would warrant its demand for a rake-off?

All this argument, however, is a concession to the obfuscation with which custom, law, and sophistry have covered up the true character of taxation. There cannot be a good tax, or a just one; therefore, every tax rests its case on political power. And the power behind every levy fattens on its collections, while the power of the individual is commensurately weakened. The ultimate of the progressive process of taxation is the absorption of all production by the state—which is the ideal of socialism.

Part VIII

An Individualist's Heritage

Thomas Jefferson, Rebel!

It was some years after I had burned my fingers with a Roman candle before I learned why Americans made particular fools of themselves on the Fourth of July. It was not until I looked into the life and letters of Thomas Jefferson that the full import of his Declaration of Independence dawned on me. Which is as it should be. Great thoughts are not isolated accidents, but, rather, the product of reflection and personality, and to be fully appreciated they must be considered within this context. The historic document left us by Jefferson is best understood when it is measured against his philosophy of government, as revealed in his many letters; nor should we overlook the environment which bore down on that philosophy.

When we consider the Declaration in this light we see that it is not at all the charter of a new nation. It is a rationalization of rebellion. The indictment of the British crown was but a springboard from which Jefferson launched a political principle: that government, far from being an end in itself, is but an instrument invented by man to aid him in bettering his circumstances, and when that instrument fails to function properly it

This article appeared in analysis *(June 1945). It was originally intended to be a chapter in* Out of Step, *but was left out for space reasons.*

is high time to kick it out. And, which is most important, he meant *any* government, not only the particular one which at that time engaged his attention. If you have any doubt of it, reread the opening sentence of the Declaration; it will pull you up, this Fourth of July, when every politician in the world is fixing so to integrate political authority with our way of living that there will be no way of prying it loose. The current "course of human events" is far more ominous, as regards freedom, than that which justified Jefferson in calling for a change, even at the cost of a revolution; if his theory of government is still valid, as we seem to imply by our annual obeisance to it, every American should be eyeing the place where the musket ought to be.

That this doctrine of resistance to government was not a chance idea, but inherent in his political philosophy, is attested by the reiteration of it in a number of Jefferson's private letters and public statements. To Mrs. John Adams he wrote in 1786, "The spirit of resistance to government is so valuable on certain occasions that I wish it to be always kept alive." Aristocratic Yale College, which had conferred an honorary degree on him, got for its pains this piece of wisdom: "If the happiness of the mass of people can be secured at the expense of a little tempest now and then, or even of a little blood, it will be a precious purchase." He was in Paris when Shays' Rebellion against the burdens of debt and taxation (yes, taxation) took place; and even though the thunder of a big-league revolution was breaking about him, his comment on the outbreak at home was true to form: "God forbid we should ever be twenty years without such a rebellion. The people cannot be all and always well informed. The part which is wrong will be discontented in proportion to the facts they misconceive. If they remain quiet under such misconceptions, it is a lethargy, the forerunner of death to the public liberty."

Very few of the signers of the Declaration were at one with Jefferson in his philosophy of government; most of them were for kicking out the arrogant personnel imposed by George III, but had no intention of abolishing the British system of government by and for the "rich and well-born"; while a few had no nobler purpose than to grind their own axes. But Jefferson lived at a time when the doctrine of natural rights was on the upswing. For a political thinker to reject or even question this starting point of social institutions was to invite doubt as to his intellectual soundness, just as any one who today points to the state as a disease of society is regarded as something of a freak. Morover, the abundance of free land in this new world gave natural rights a solid meaning; one could escape intolerable conditions within the colony by merely moving out beyond the limits of its exercisable power, and one could always find subsistence. Under such conditions faith of the individual in himself flourished easily, and it was not difficult to root that faith in "naturalness." The climate was good for the Jeffersonian philosophy of government.

Times have changed. There is no free land to which one can apply oneself when factory wages fall below the level of mere subsistence; there is no frontier escape from the long arm of the law. Thus economically frustrated and politically hemmed in, the individual tends to lose faith in himself and is not above selling his soul for a mess of pottage. He who is hungry for food has no stomach for natural rights. At this point political science conveniently changes its postulates. Now that the poverty-ridden public is more concerned with "security" than with natural rights, philandering philosophers are quick to cast doubt on the virtue of the Jeffersonian charmer; and as their forebears fell to praising "divine right of kings" when that courtesan was riding high, wide, and handsome, so our current stock of "best brains" is all for the seductive charm and voluptuous promise of state regulation, and to hell with principle!

Somehow, notwithstanding, the lure of natural rights is persistent; she has her admirers always, and their ardor is of the kind that brooks no obstacles, even to the point of martyrdom. Were it not for the ebullience of these swains, serenading most vigorously when human dignity hits bottom, there would be no revolutions and the history of man would indeed be a drab story of hopeless decadence. But, though at times she seems forsaken—as at present—the lovers of liberty will always put in an appearance.

During the war of 1917–18 there were a number who for their espousal of the Jeffersonian ideal were put in jail. Memory brings up the glamorous name of Eugene V. Debs, but there were thousands of unknowns who for insisting on the right not to kill or be killed were unceremoniously flogged and incarcerated, while the number of World War I anarchists who boldly declared what the war was all about and were therefore locked up, peremptorily and illegally, will never be known. While many of them, as Jefferson foretold, suffered from "misconceptions," nevertheless they did not "remain quiet," and thereby they kept alive the "spirit of public liberty."

In like manner, the conscientious objectors of the second war are rendering an inestimable public service. In an age in which the doctrine of natural rights has all but gone under, these boys have questioned, refused, objected, and in so doing have just about kept her head above water. The majority of them, unfortunately, are without a basic philosophy; they just "hate war."

Cunningly, the state has indulged their pet passion by simply removing them from society, but has scrupulously avoided acts which might be interpreted as punishment for holding to principle; so that, having avoided the horror and danger of war, these boys have gradually sunk into personal adjustment with the state. Their quarrel with the state is no longer on a point of principle, but over the minor discomforts of camp life, loss of wages, financial suffering of their relatives. A comparative few—like those who walked out of the camps and into prisons, and those so-called incorrigibles consigned to the late "Alcatraz" at Germfask, Michigan—resisted the "passive resistance" by which the state sought to subdue their ardor, and by so doing gave notice to the world that natural rights is not without admirers. But, alas! they are few; among them is no name of such prominence as to force the subservient public press to call attention to the principle they stand for; and, except for the glorious self-respect which they maintained by it, their fight for the Jeffersonian doctrine is without visible victory.

The war is drawing to a close. Soon the lickspittles who switched philosophies on December 7, 1941, will be perjuring themselves anew; on a mountain of Bibles they will swear fealty to peace. Then there will be a flood of "disillusionment" literature, beside which that which came after 1918 will be a puny trickle. The selfsame professionals who for the past three years have been preaching the sermon of destruction and murder and hate will now shamelessly tell us how the war was mismanaged (as if sound management is ever applicable to a crazy enterprise); how the period of slaughter was improved upon by fortune hunters (as if that opportunity did not always influence the rationalization of war); how moral values went down in the holocaust (as if moral values ever have a place in any adventure of the amoral state); how liberty was seduced by our politicians while we were fighting its battle in Asia and Europe (as if this were an unfortunate accident and not a necessary consequence); and so on.

But all these protestations and fulminations will be sound and fury, signifying nothing. It will be pleasant and popular, and perhaps profitable, to attack where there is no resistance; a peacetime pacifist, an exposer of past iniquities, or a defamer of dead politicians courts neither a prison sentence nor social ostracism. He effects no opposition. Let him rant. He is not a rebel in the Jeffersonian sense, but must be put down as a quixotic attacker of nothing in particular; for he advocates no principle dangerous to the status quo.

The "spirit of resistance to government" which in the Jeffersonian political philosophy is the taproot of liberty finds its justification in an unprovable axiom: the inalienable rights of the individual. These inhere in every man by the fact of existence; any infraction of them by a single citizen or a group of citizens, organized or unorganized, is immoral. It is to prevent such immoral behavior, or at least to discourage it, that governments are instituted among men. That is the ethical basis for political authority. In the final analysis it amounts to nothing more than a covenant between citizen and policeman, whereby the latter is hired for the sole purpose of protecting the former's life and property; or, as political science puts it, to maintain a social climate in which the individual may carry on his business of pursuing happiness. Nothing more. When the individuals who constitute government utilize the power vested in it for those purposes, even those which in their opinion make for "the greatest good for the greatest number," they have broken the covenant and should be sheared of their power. That is the principle, the moral tenet, upon which Jefferson justified "the spirit of resistance to government."

Jefferson did not pursue the thought; but in postulating the principle he started the train of investigation which later came up with a clear distinction between government and state. The one is a social instrument, the other an unsocial perversion of it; the one is healthy, the other pathological. It is when those in power engage in projects which jeopardize the life or property of the individual, or utilize that power so that either they or a favored group benefits at the expense of the producing public, that government is transformed into state. Perhaps Jefferson vaguely sensed this distinction when he commented, in a letter to Madison, on the highly organized and orderly society among Indians, getting along on customs and public opinion, and seemingly without any of the coercive powers associated with government. He wondered whether this condition might not be the best; but he dismissed that thought as "inconsistent with any great degree of population."

Jefferson was short on economics; the absence of chaos which he found among the free Indians traced not to their lack of government but to the fact that whatever political authority existed was devoid of the power of taxation. It is in fact this power which transforms the social government into the anti-social state, and must in the end bring about a softening of the moral fiber of a people. The process of deterioration is quite simple. As more of the individual's production is absorbed by the state, the less he has for his own enjoyment, and the greater effort he must put out to maintain himself or to better his circumstances. A man's worth to himself is in indirect ratio to the toil entailed in his pursuit of happiness; the dignity of the individual disintegrates under the hammering of want and the fear of it. On the other hand, the power of the state waxes in proportion to the wealth it absorbs through taxation. And as economic power is thus transferred from the individual to the state, the individual is pressed into bargaining for some of what was properly his by right of production; in the bargaining process he offers up his inalienable rights for a handout. The handout might be unemployment insurance or a place on the public payroll or a subsidy, but in any case the nonproductive state gathers economic strength and political power, while the productive individual becomes a supplicant. We have seen the ultimate of this moral disintegration in Germany, Russia, Italy, Japan, where the power to tax made a shambles of all property rights, and for further evidence we might look into the history of lost civilizations. The power to tax is the power to destroy human dignity.

Never before in the history of the country was Jefferson's admonition more pertinent than now. Never before has the state battened on so large a proportion of the wealth produced by its subjects. What is even more ominous is the growing public acceptance of the doctrine that state taxation may be made an instrument for social good; for which we can thank that brood of anti–natural rights theorists hatched out of the Marxist cesspool. So thorough has been the work of these missionaries of state paganism that they have got people to put a moral purpose on being robbed. It is this mental adjustment to the confiscatory inclination of the state, this rationalization of an immoral use of power, that bodes no good; for it is evidence of "a lethargy, the forerunner of death to liberty."

George Mason of Virginia

These days it is the "right to work." Yet the fervor put into this newfangled American ideal falls flat when we reflect that toil is on a par with disease in desirability. Men want things, not work. So that, when we shake down this right to work, the residue turns out to be the "right to a living and we don't give a damn how we get it."

What, specifically, are the advocates of this doctrine pumping for? Is it not a mess of gratuities? Is it not unemployment insurance, make-wage jobs, pensions, free doctoring, free schooling even up to the postgraduate courses? For such largess these idealists are quick to settle out of court. The right to work thus appears to be every individual's claim, inherent in citizenship, on the production of everybody else. The claim is made on government, of course, and therefore amounts to a demand to partake of the tax fund. Thus the privilege of being an American becomes the privilege of pushing one's snout into the public trough.

It was not always so. Before the fear of want became the national psychosis the word *rights* had an entirely different

"George Mason of Virginia" appeared as the lead article in the September 1945 issue of analysis.

connotation. There was nothing mundane or sordid about it; rather, it gave expression to a high moral value. And it was peculiarly American, for nowhere else in the world had there ever been an attempt to establish a polity based on this ethical principle. To be sure, the question of rights—or natural rights, as it was called—had been the subject matter of philosophic speculation for several centuries before America became a political entity, and it had also been the battle cry of a few rebellious undertakings in Europe; but never and nowhere was its content equivalent to that which it attained in the freak republic carved out of the western wilderness. Here it became a formula for the guidance of organized life, a standard by which to measure the correctness of political institutions. It was a principle, not a handout.

But what are rights? How did the idea originate? When we look to the background of rights, we see how the right to work is indicative of decadence in the American character. We have gone back in our political thinking—back to the theory that the state is some superior sort of person.

The earliest notion of a right came from the boon granted a slave by his master. It was the conqueror's voluntary restriction on the exercise of his power over the vanquished. The purpose of such self-imposed restraint was to further the economic purpose of conquest, for it was evident that the unlimited harassment of the slave would reduce his productive capacity and thus lessen the loot. The slave was advised how far the master would go and made his adjustment accordingly; the conqueror profited by the resulting orderly *modus vivendi*. In time these limitations became traditionalized, even put into legal form, and the conquered endowed them with the value of prerogatives, privileges, and immunities. The inhibitions of privilege became rights. So much so that when unscrupulous members of the conquering class overstepped the bounds, the slave class could invoke their rights and demand that restraint be put upon the offenders; it was not uncommon for the rulers to enforce these rights with severe punishment of their own people.[1]

The Romans, of all the ancients, were most adept at this procedure. It paid them to guarantee to their subjugated peoples noninterference in all matters relating to religious customs and social habits, limiting their overlordship to the maintenance of order and the collection of stipulated tribute. The story of the trial of Jesus illustrates the scrupulousness with which Pontius Pilate recognized the "rights" of the Jews and the manner in which the latter invoked them.

But the Romans always remained a people apart and the rights they established were concessions which might be conveniently withdrawn. Furthermore, whenever they left a territory, the rights disappeared with them. It was only where conquerors settled down and became integrated with the conquered, thus forming a new nation, that the doctrine of rights acquired a fixed place in the *mores* of the people. The best known of such integrations is the English nation, and since our modern concept of rights is a direct lineal descendant of the English concept, we might profitably look into the latter.

It was not long after William the Conqueror established himself on the British isle that demands were made on his suzerainty, not by the natives but by his own nobility. These demands amounted to nothing more than the privilege of retaining for

[1] The American army now in Japan has agreed to respect the "prerogatives" of the emperor. These rules of behavior, if the army stays there long enough, will come to be looked upon by the Japanese as their "rights"; infractions by American soldiers or politicians will bring complaints to the higher command or even to Washington. It now appears that the Russians will not move out of the territories they occupy and take their "rights" with them, but will settle down with and completely enslave the inhabitants.

themselves a greater share of the proceeds of exploitation. The culmination of this rivalry between king and barons was the affair at Runnymede. Tradition has made the Magna Carta the cornerstone of the British structure of rights; and so it is, but the structure and the cornerstone are not what romance has read into them, that is to say, a charter of human freedom; for all that happened at Runnymede was a clipping off of the king's power of exploitation in favor of the barons. Henceforth, John agreed, the sovereignty over their vassals which his kingship invested in him was to be shared with his tenants-in-chief, and in the exercise of these privileges they were to enjoy immunity; and he conceded, not as an article of justice but as a guarantee of noninterference, the trial by a jury of peers. Now, the point to be kept in mind was that the barons did not question the king's sovereignty, for to do so would have undermined the polity which supported their own prerogatives. The validity of his signature to the compact could not be doubted without throwing doubt on their own position. And so, Magna Carta established the underlying principle of British "rights," that they are patents and indulgences wrested from the higher political power.

The same holds with the Bill of Rights, of 1688. It came, be it noted, as a petition to the king, for the parliament was well versed in precedent and could not but acknowledge the necessity of the king's seal on the contract. Again we find a class— the rising industrialists—demanding privileges and immunities, and employing their coercive position to enforce these demands; for William and Mary were in need of war funds and the petition was presented as a *quid pro quo* for a tax levy. And, as in the case of the Magna Carta, the rights which were thus woven into the fabric of English law were mere pieces of power captured from the acknowledged source of power by a group temporarily strong enough to rival it. That is the history and the theory of British rights. Throughout the years this clipping-off process has all but divested the kingship of its original prerogatives, but the tradition of a sovereign and transcendent state in which all political authority resides, and from which all privileges and immunities are derived, is still the basis of British polity. For the total of the contracts between this state and the long line of successful pressure groups forms that pattern of precedents known as the British constitution. It is a tacit compromise with conquest, not a stated philosophy of government.

And so we come to America.

We cannot know just when or how the concept of the primacy of the individual—as distinguished from the claims of his clan—took root in the human mind; most likely it was always there. Some are pleased to give credit for its discovery to the prophets of Israel, others find in the parables and the life of the Nazarene the finest, if not the first, expression of the idea. There are historians who trace to the Protestant Reformation the individual's revolt against his political debasement. Regardless of its original expression, for at least two centuries before the American Revolution political philosophy had been phrasing such ideas as—that the unit of social life is the individual, that political institutions derive their justification from his purposes, that the moral basis of political authority is the necessity of existence. They bolstered this thought with the hypothesis of a natural law, and pointed to the prevalence of friction and unhappiness as evidence that this law had been ignored and violated. The high goal of human endeavor could be achieved only in a condition of harmony or justice, and this condition, they maintained, can exist only when political institutions chart their course by the natural law.

But the speculations of Rousseau and Montesquieu and Locke and the physiocrats seemed destined to remain lost between the covers of their books. Then came the American Revolution, and out of the virgin soil of the spawning nation sprang an intrepid band of philosophic adventurers who made bold to give the ideal of freedom a working chance. Among these the foremost, because he held most closely to the visionary blueprint, was George Mason of Virginia.

Americans know but too little of this great American, and, what is most regretful, less about the definitive value he gave to Americanism. Now that we are on the high road of abandoning that value, substituting for it the opposite one, the one which the "well-born" strove so persistently and unscrupulously (and with some success) to incorporate into the basic law of the new nation, we would be well served by a full acquaintance with the work of Mason. A review of his arguments before the Constitutional Congress and the Virginia Convention for ratification would be mighty helpful in any discussions of current events. For Mason foresaw the dangers the new nation was heading for because its foundations did not rest foursquare on the law of justice, and now that these dangers have met up with us it might save us from further trouble if we gave thought to his reasoning. It is as sound today as it was then, and more pertinent. But in the space allotted to this article, all that is possible is an attempt to show how Mason tried to give the new nation a political soul.

On May 17, 1776, the state of Virginia having declared for independence, its delegates assembled at Williamsburg for the purpose of drawing up a constitution. It fell to the lot of George Mason who, although no lawyer, had already achieved some reputation as a political thinker, to frame a bill of rights as a guide in framing the constitution; the declaration he produced

was destined to become in effect part of each of the forty-eight
state constitutions and is embraced in the first Ten Amendments
to the federal Constitution. On the first and second articles all
the others rest:

> 1. That all men are created equally free and independent and have
> certain inalienable rights, which they cannot by any compact deprive
> or divest their posterity, among which are the enjoyment of life and
> liberty, with the means of acquiring property, and pursuing and ob-
> taining happiness and safety.
> 2. That all power is by God and nature vested in and consequently
> derived from the people; that magistrates are their trustees and serv-
> ants, and at all times amenable to them.

If we accept these two propositions as axioms of government, then any bill of rights based on them becomes a mere
memorandum—a lest-we-forget reminder for every political
situation. For here we have a philosophy to guide us, not a
compendium of precedents; a light for the future not the past.
The rights, be it noted, are not the subject of legislative action,
which can only conform with or run contrary to them, for they
existed before lawmakers were and will continue as long as
human life persists; they inhere in the individual by the fact of
existence and need no other confirmation; they are not to be
gotten, hat in hand, by a supplicant citizenry. Indeed, it is to
implement these rights that men institute government, appoint-
ing magistrates whose business it must be to carry on communal
affairs according to these tenets.

The vision of Mason in proclaiming this moral basis for
political authority is matched by his courage, for at the time all
the known governments in the world were built on the conquest
principle by which they came into being. Even among his con-
temporaries there were comparatively few who held with him
in this departure from the established order, and it was only the

ardor of these few which prevented the establishment of a self-contained power instrument in the new nation. At the Philadelphia Convention he struggled vainly to hold the delegates to this new American ideal, and when the Constitution which emerged failed to live up to that ideal he not only refused to sign it but returned to Virginia resolved to fight its ratification by his home state. Though there again he lost in the fight against the centralizers, the "well-born" who relished political power in the European manner, the cogency of his argument had made a strong impression on the times, and at last the bill of rights which he had prescribed for the health of the new nation was ultimately, though grudgingly and only in part, incorporated into its Constitution.

Mason was a slave owner, but he opposed slavery; he was an aristocrat, by any standard, yet he rejected government by aristocrats; he advocated a single term of seven or eight years for the presidency lest an ambitious man seek to perpetuate himself in that office; he feared a standing army in peacetime, seeing how this instrument of force was the backbone of autocratic government, and declared a volunteer militia all the military a free nation should have; he anticipated Jefferson and Washington in opposing foreign alliances; he opposed federal power to regulate elections because he saw in this a centralizing force; he was a wealthy man, but he fought features of the federal judiciary which he knew would favor the wealthy litigant; he thought that tariff bills and all commercial measures should require a two-thirds vote of both branches of Congress; in the general-welfare clause of the Constitution he recognized the danger of undefined authority; taxation he feared because of its political potential and he espoused weak government because its corollary is a strong people. But in taking these positions on particular measures Mason had no choice. One can always foretell the direction of thought which starts with a philosophy; the unpredictable is the expedient. Mason's contribution to America is not what he advocated or opposed, but the character he tried to give its political philosophy.

Factually, the doctrine of natural rights hasn't a leg to stand on. This is so by very definition. Nature has not made a right visible, nor does she notify us in unmistakable manner when we have hit on one. The niggardliness of nature in this instance is matched by her reluctance to identify other abstractions which we trace to her, like justice and freedom. To get to the bottom of the question: What exactly is nature? Who is the accredited liaison officer between nature and man?

On the basis of this lack of sensual evidence, the latter-day logicians who hog the front row of philosophic fashion peremptorily throw the doctrine out the window of reason. According to them, natural rights are an absurd assumption. They are an assumption, all right, but whether absurd is another question. When we reject this assumption we come logically to conclusions which in themselves are absurd, and because of these absurd conclusions we are forced to restore the unprovable hypothesis to its place as a starting point for our thinking. Thus, if we deny that in the nature of things a man has an exclusive right to the product of his labor—because we are not on speaking terms with "the nature of things"—then we actually deny him the right to life, and we are on the way to asserting that the master has a right to the property and life of the slave. But, where did the master get that right? From his good right arm, since, it is admitted, he also has no "pull" with nature. So then, by denying the hypothesis of natural rights we are forced to the conclusion that a right is a relationship between man and man, resting on power and shifting with the incidence and intensity of that power. And where does that conclusion lead us to? To the absurdity that the only way for men to live together in harmony is for each one to maintain an arsenal as big as any likely combination of arsenals his neighbors might bring to bear on him.

Confronted with such logical though nonsensical conclusions, the show-me pragmatists—some of them—have come up with an *as if* escape. That is, even if the doctrine of natural rights is an unprovable assumption, they say, it is a necessity of experience that we accept it as a functional idea, and we must act and reason *as if* natural rights were factually demonstrable. They are willing to go along with the doctrine so long as they are not asked to take it as a fact. It would be poor sportsmanship to deny them this face-saving device.

But the harm of this pragmatic approach to political problems has been done. It is difficult to say whether the philosophy was the cause of it, or was merely an expedient accommodation to a *fait accompli;* but the fact of the matter is that opposition to the doctrine of rights, as exemplified by Mason, has been successful in liquidating the only norm by which freedom can be measured. The Constitution which Hamiltonian centralists forced upon the new country, against the advice of Mason, Henry, Gerry, and the other pleaders for government to serve, not to master, the people, has done its work; so that today the rights of an American, like those of an Englishman, are the privileges he can force a reluctant government to disgorge. Whereas our country began as a more or less voluntary association of freedom, while British polity was born in conquest, because our basic law permitted the concentration of power, our doctrine of natural rights has become a dead letter and we are operating on the British system. We have been conquered by our original error.

What is standard practice today in the relations between the

American government and the American people? When a group of us are determined to obtain certain privileges—which we euphemistically call rights—we organize ourselves and in various ways notify our representatives how many votes we control, and they had better be sensible and give us what we want. So long as they submit to our demands we have no objection to their acquiring additional power over us, by the imposition of more taxes or the passage of laws which restrict our freedom of action; we relish being subservient to benevolent despotism. And, are our representatives guided by basic principles in the handling of public affairs? Hardly. Their business is primarily to "keep their ears to the ground"—to ascertain which pressure group has the most to deliver and to make settlement accordingly. That is the conquest principle.

Mistakes multiply themselves. If the federal Constitution had been built in the spirit of Mason's recommendations, it is quite likely that many of the economic errors which have since come home to plague us would have been avoided; certain it is that the institution of slavery would have been scotched, the Civil War prevented, and our stupid wall of protection would not have been built. When you study the Virginia Bill of Rights with an eye to economics, you see how a faithful adherence to its dictates could not but have suggested measures which would have avoided the economy of scarcity from which we suffer, and to overcome which we vainly pile power upon power on our government. For, in the final analysis, we get the kind of government our stomachs want.

Whether the situation can be righted at this late date is doubtful. As a people we have no knowledge of freedom and therefore no taste for it. So low has our concept of freedom fallen that we interpret it as the right to work. The old Greeks knew enough to let Fate have its way. So be it. But for some of us, the incorrigibly unadjusted, there are music and poetry and spiritual uplift in the advice given by George Mason, in his will, to his sons:

> I recommend it to my sons from my own experience in life to prefer the happiness of independence and a private station to the troubles and vexation of public business, but if either their own business or the necessity of the times should engage them in public affairs, I charge them on a father's blessing never to let the motives of private interests or ambition induce them to betray, nor the terrors of poverty and disgrace or the fear of danger or of death deter them from asserting the liberty of their country and endeavoring to transmit to their posterity those sacred rights to which themselves were born.

Henry David Thoreau

T he secretary of the Thoreau Society reports increasing interest in the long-forgotten "ne'er-do-well." It takes a long
time for word-of-mouth advertising to get around, but because
that kind of publicity attaches itself only to first-class merchandise, its effectiveness is irresistible. Recognition of Thoreau's contribution to the philosophy of individualism could
not be put off forever. Several books and articles have, of
course, cropped up to meet the market created by this new
interest in Thoreau, but unfortunately these "lives" and commentaries have come during an era when the dominating
thought vogues are psychology and collectivism; so that these
studies are somewhat overladen with psychoanalysis and social
theory.

Therefore, if you want to know Thoreau you had better pass
up the diagnosticians and get down to reading Thoreau. You
will find him an open book—quite willing to tell you frankly,
and interestingly, what he thought and why he lived as he did.
He is quite companionable. Begin, then, with his essays: *Civil*

*Thoreau was one of Chodorov's great favorites, as one can see from this article
printed twice in* analysis *(November 1945 and February 1949). It also appeared
as chapter 20 of* Out of Step.

Disobedience, Slavery in Massachusetts, John Brown, Life Without Principle; if you want more, and you will, go in for *Walden*—but you will have to read it slowly to get the full value of it—and then put in an evening or two with the revealing extracts from his journals, or diaries as we call them.

Maybe you too will decide that Thoreau was "maladjusted." But you might withhold judgment until you define this pathological mouthful. Before the war the boy who ran away from home and joined the army was "maladjusted"; during the war the boy who refused to join the army on principle was similarly labeled. The word, therefore, as used, simply means that the person so described is either incapable or unwilling to submit to the herd cult. It connotes some emotional mental weakness, and carries a bit of condescension and of pity with it; that the ability and willingness to stand the crowd off may indicate that exceptional self-reliance is overlooked. Sometimes one cannot help suspecting that the "adjusted," those who are quick to fit themselves into any thought pattern prepared by the neighbors, find the term *maladjusted* a convenient covering up of some weakness of their own. Maybe the word is plain name-calling, pulled up out of the gutter by "science." The suppressed rebel in us resents the courage of those who rebel openly.

In this connection I am reminded of a story told by Artemus Ward about Billson, his partner in show business: "Billson," says I, "you hain't got a well-balanced mind." "Yes, I have, old hossfly," he says (he was a low cuss). "Yes, I have. I've a mind that balances in any direction the public rekwires, and that's what I calls a well-balanced mind." Thoreau did not have that kind of a mind; which makes him, it seems, quite a tidbit for psychologists. Their scalpels might more usefully dig into the minds of conforming mediocrities; it would be socially beneficial to discover the consistency of mass putty.

A biography of Thoreau worth reading, because it concerns itself with revealing the man from his own point of view and not with the biographer's estimate of him, was done by a Frenchman, Leon Bazalgette. "The gods," says Bazalgette, "have made a Henry who is all of a piece, and they have placed him on the earth among objects and souls that are different and queer." There you have it. What do we mean by "queer"? If all but one of us were color-blind, that one would indeed seem queer to us; but how would our inability to distinguish colors appear to the gifted one? And so, as this country bumpkin went through Harvard in his stout green suit, while the fine young gentlemen were uniformed in traditional black, the incongruity which caused them to smile was as nothing to the oddity, as he saw it, of voluntarily squeezing one's personality into a convention. Even in his teens he displays that "militant devotion to various axioms that he identifies with himself." He could not be cast into a mold; he was not made of that stuff. Harvard had facilities which he could use to improve himself. It was a means; the end was a better Thoreau. It was not for the "old joke of a diploma" that he read enormously, far beyond the requirements of his curriculum, though outside of it. At nineteen he wrote: "Learning is art's creature, but it is not essential to the perfect man: it cannot educate."

When we reflect on a Thoreau, we must always consider the sanity of the world in juxtaposition to his. Take his first experience as a schoolmaster. In his pedagogy he finds no place for the whipping rod; for this heresy the headmaster calls him to account; being an honest man he must deliver what is expected of him for his wages; therefore, he lines up at random a half-dozen pupils and thoroughly flogs them. But, he must be honest with his axioms, too; therefore he resigns. He could not afford to let Thoreau drift into false values. Was he or the recognized rule of pedagogy queer?

A professor of economics once told me he was convinced that the last word on the subject was pronounced by Henry George. "Do you teach him?" I asked. "No, he is not in the curriculum, and if I tried to teach Henry George it would be worth my job." Thoreau could not understand that kind of thinking; if flogging were part of the curriculum he would cut himself off from it. He valued Thoreau more than his job.

We talk a lot about freedom these days. When you get to the bottom of this talk you realize that, first, very few know what freedom is and, second, still fewer want it. The fact is that what we call freedom is an increase in wages (or doles), more profits (or subsidies), or a bottomless abundance of privileges. For such things we—particularly the affluent among us—are ready to lay freedom on the line. The essence of freedom, which is an inflexible respect for oneself, is being bartered every day for mere trifles.

Thoreau was not in that business. Once the dwindling fortunes of his father's pencil factory needed looking into. Henry undertook the job and made the best pencil in America. He made only one; that was enough. As an honest workman he satisfied himself; as a good son he put his father on the way to a competence. Why should he sell himself for pencils? Profits were not among the axioms which he identified with H. D. Thoreau. Luxuries came too high if the price was freedom. Imagine our "captains of industry" passing up a profit or a privilege for a chance to be men.

Freedom is an individual experience. If you have it, its objective expression will find many forms; but if you don't have it, you will get along all right, like any four-footed animal or "sound" citizen, and you may even go to heaven; but you can never be free. Chattel slavery was the issue in Thoreau's time, just as state slavery is now. A lot of people talked about the iniquity of the institution. What did Thoreau *do?* He refused to pay the poll tax on the ground that it would be used by the commonwealth of Massachusetts to capture and return fugitive slaves. Now, when you refuse to pay taxes you are really a dangerous man, for you undermine the structure by which some men live on the labor of others; therefore you must be clapped into jail until you see the error of your ways and make your "adjustment." Of his one night spent behind bars Thoreau writes:

> I did not for a moment feel confined, and the walls seemed a great waste of stone and mortar . . . I could not but smile to see how industriously they locked the door on my meditations, which followed them out again without let or hindrance. As they could not reach me, they resolved to punish my body; just as boys, if they cannot come against some person against whom they have a spite, will abuse his dog. I saw that the state was half-witted, that it was as timid as a lone woman with her silver spoons. . . . I lost all my remaining respect for it, and pitied it.

Such a man can never be enslaved.

It need hardly be said that Thoreau had no truck with institutions, organizations, or "movements." When freedom submits to a formula it rids itself of responsibility, the responsibility to one's own axioms. To check one's thought and behavior against the dictates of one's conscience may prove unflattering; to chart one's course by such a checkup requires a powerful will; it is to avoid such revelation and responsibility that people are prone to hide behind rituals, constitutions, and bylaws. But flight from individual responsibility amounts to an abandonment of freedom. You are not free when you refuse to make choices in your own name. You enslave yourself when you take refuge from the consequences of your decisions in a committee, a nation, or any collective fiction. To Thoreau such "escapism" was unthinkable, queer. So, he writes: "as a snowdrift is formed where there is a lull in the wind, so, one would say, where there is a lull of truth, an institution grows up." For him there never was a lull of truth.

The value you put on freedom is, like all objective value, the price you are willing to pay for it. Thoreau's price came very high, and the difference between him and other people is to be found not in the lingo of psychology but in the greater worth he put on self-esteem, which is the essence of freedom. He rejected the mob because mingling with it demanded a sacrifice of that self-esteem at the altars of convention and hypocrisy. That he was not unsocial is evidenced by his friendship with people of similar timber and by his devotion to his family; whether it was with Emerson or the woodcutter, with Channing or an Indian guide, his social contacts had to be on an above-board basis, unencumbered with trivialities; any other terms did not interest him. If being social at any cost to self-esteem is the mark of balance, then Thoreau was decidedly queer. But the testimony points rather to his having a higher sense of values than the ordinary run of men. He was determined to be free of rubbish. Once he was asked to sign a pledge, to which the names of the "best" people in Concord were attached, that he would treat all people as brothers. He declined to do so until he found out how other people would treat him. He was not going to be sociable for the sake of sociability; he demanded as much as he gave. He would neither accept nor bestow condescension.

But the real price he paid for freedom was not in ridding himself of the strictures of society, but in curtailing his desires. He conquered his appetite in order to be free; he was not going to be a slave to things. His venture into the pencil business shows that he had the makings of a successful industrialist. With a brother he operated a school that was the envy and chagrin of rival schoolmasters, not only because of its success but more so because of some advanced ideas of pedagogy which the brothers introduced. As a surveyor he was in demand and highly respected, both for his accuracy (he made his own instruments) and for his integrity. Those who hired him out for any kind of a job, whether farm work or painting a fence, were sure to get their money's worth because Thoreau would not cheat himself by doing a poor job.

He might have made money also as a lecturer and a writer had he been willing to compromise his standards, for he was proficient in both fields. But he was not willing to give up what the making of money costs: freedom. For that reason he refused regular occupation of any kind—although he was never idle— and got himself the reputation of being a ne'er-do-well. From his own point of view he was doing far better than his detractors, for while they got only respectability for their pains, he had self-respect.

The rock upon which every attempt to rid man of his shackles is ultimately wrecked is man's unwillingness to pay the price of freedom—the price which Thoreau cheerfully paid. Every "cause" must crash on it. For when the theorizing is done, the books are all written, the debates have been resolved into a formula for action, there remains always this immovable obstacle: "One must live." By this dodge the lip-servicers simply admit that the worth they put on the ideal is less than that they put on their accustomed way of living or the prospect of improving it. The ideal was something nice to talk about, to use as a tonic for one's sluggish intellectual liver, but when it comes to giving up for it, that's another matter. It is more pleasant to make one's peace with the going order of things, right or wrong. And if your conscience is pricked by someone who insists that you pay the price, you simply kick him out of the way; and you salve your conscience by telling it the "time is not ripe" or "wait until I make my pile."

Thoreau said that if he saw a reformer coming his way he would run for his life. He had no need for reform. The man who identifies axioms with himself wants no preacher to show him how, while the preacher will have no influence with those who are constitutionally incapable of axioms. If the reformer justifies his calling on the ground that through education the lacking moral values may be instilled, the answer is that all experience denies that possibility. Education can present choices; it cannot make decisions. No pedagogical system has ever succeeded in eliciting values which do not exist in the person.

Improving on Jefferson, Thoreau says: "That government is best which governs not at all"; then he wisely adds: "And when men are prepared for it, that will be the kind of government which they will have." Will they ever be prepared for it?

The Articulate Individualist

"**N**obody gives a damn *what* you write; it's *how* you write that counts." So said a friend to Albert Jay Nock; when he repeated the *bon mot,* you detected in his expression the pride of the craftsman and the disappointment of a man misunderstood.

It is only when you reread *Our Enemy the State* and *Thomas Jefferson* and his *Memoirs*—when you take his style in stride and are no longer dazzled by its perfection—that you catch the flavor of his thought and you plumb its substance. He was not a voluminous writer. He had the rare gift of editing his ideas, so that he wrote only when he had something to say and he said it with dispatch. When you use the right word you are under no obligation to explain because the right word explains itself; elucidation for the benefit of people who cannot read is cheap and futile at best. This standard of literary exactitude sets a fast pace for the ordinary reader to follow, especially when his concentration is being diverted from the thought by the style, and a second reading is necessary to catch up.

This was the lead article in an eight-page memorial issue of analysis *dedicated to Albert Jay Nock (August 1946). Chodorov was forty-nine when he first met Nock, but Nock stood next to Henry George as an intellectual mentor. Also see Chodorov's chapter on Nock in* Out of Step.

Nock had a very definite philosophy. He had plenty to say. Though he wrote on many subjects, from political science to marriage, from literary criticism to manners, a distinctive pattern of philosophic thought pervades all his books and essays. It is what we would name, for lack of a surer word, the philosophy of individualism. But, it is not a doctrine or theory; it is a quality of the man himself, elusive and somewhat mystical, but nevertheless rational and communicable. It is possible only to sketch in this limited space the outlines of his philosophy.

Individualism, as a social philosophy, starts with the axiom that in the nature of things only the individual exists. Even the world about him is a matter of conjecture, since its existence is subject to his consciousness. When two individuals cooperate for their mutual advantage neither assigns his consciousness to the other; it simply cannot be done. As individuals, each of us is born, lives, and dies—alone.

Therefore, that which we call society has no reality. In point of fact, the word *society* is merely a convenient abstraction, designating a number of cooperating individuals, and the character which the ensuing milieu acquires in our minds is simply the reflection of the characteristics of its constituent parts. If the individuals are given to heavy drinking we have a drunken society; a free society consists of individuals who are under no restraint by others; a slave society is one in which a few are masters whose bidding the others must do. The individual is the only reality. That being so, the good society of which men have dreamed since the beginning of time is a matter of good men. There cannot be any social improvement except by way of individual improvement, and any formula which tries to shortcut the process is fatuous. On whether the human is capable of indefinite self-improvement—there cannot be any other kind—Nock has grave doubts. Nevertheless, he is all for giving men a chance at it, not only to see what they will do for themselves, but more so because as an individualist he is under obligation not to interfere.

The only obligation of the individual to his neighbor is to let him alone in all matters except when the neighbor interferes with his equal right to life and property. Therefore, while rebellion against repression is in order, the reformer with a "mission" is quite out of place. Nor has the reformer much chance of success. If he has something to say he ought to say it to those who will listen, but when he insists that those who do not listen are sinful as well as in error, he oversteps bounds. Besides, if people will not listen it may be because they are not prepared for what is being offered and the reformer is presumptuous in trying to force acceptance of what has no value to them. You can "put people in the way of learning," but you cannot educate them; that is a private operation. If the people are fools, they have a right to be and you have no right to disturb them against their will.

It may be asked, then, why Nock speaks in such high praise of Henry George, who was very definitely a reformer with a "mission." Those who are familiar with what Nock has to say on this point will recall that he protests a lifelong dissociation from the George "movement," and that he deplores George's reduction of his philosophy to a political nostrum. But, as in your reading you must learn to pick the good out of a book and throw the rest away—a favorite expression of his—so you must gather knowledge wherever you find it and not judge it by its presentation. Henry George enabled him to evaluate the state.

The individualist has one enemy: the state. As a scholar it was incumbent on Nock to look into the nature and equipment of this enemy, so as to show it up for what it is. He finds that this political institution originates in robbery and thrives on it.

But, what is the technique by which it carries on its business? In the first place, the state's predatory income is taxation; in the second, it gains comfort and aid from those to whom it dishes out privilege, at the expense of producers; in the third place, the principal privilege which it supports, by force, is the one which in the long run absorbs the productive power of the working population, that is, the privilege of demanding a fee for the use of the earth. Well, when Henry George advocates the abolition of taxes, he is hitting the state at its vitals. And when he further demonstrates how community collection of rent will abolish the basic privilege, thus destroying the exploitative power of monopoly, he gives you the main ingredient of that economic freedom without which political freedom is a mirage.

Without this understanding of the economic implementation of the state, the argument against it is one-sided. It is because of that lack that theoretical anarchism drifted into communism, the most vicious form of statism; and individualism which ignores the basic economic principles of Henry George is too likely to become that "rugged" kind which is nothing but legalized buccaneering. So Nock takes his economics from the philosopher, because without it he cannot round out his argument against the state, and passes up the reformer.

But what does the individualist propose to "do about it"? Nothing; that is, if by "doing" is meant commotion, organization, political action. That kind of "doing" is unwarranted by his basic premise. The ingredients of our social order determine its character, and if these ingredients are unprepared for freedom, incapable of understanding what it is, what can one do about it? There is strong reason to believe that such incompetence is widespread; in fact, that competence in this regard is very scarce. In spite of the aphorism that "all men are born equal," nature very specifically abhors uniformity. It is obvious that there are some men who, regardless of their backgrounds and environments, are more plentifully endowed with intellectual curiosity than others; that the proportion of this unexplainable "intellectual elite" to the number who are content to grub along is small; and that its cultural standards cannot be generally applied.

What hope is there for a stateless society? If by an accident of nature this "remnant" does run up as a proportion of the population, it may make its influence felt. Maybe a complete collapse of our civilization, brought about by the crushing weight of statism, will throw the "intellectual elite" into the ascendancy, as a last resort, and some good will come of it. In the meantime, the only thing anyone can "do" is to go to work on the one unit he can improve, the only one he has a right to tackle—himself.

Whether this is a negative and pessimistic point of view is beside the point. Does it accord with historical fact? Does it check with experience? Only by this test can its soundness be evaluated.

But, it is very definitely not the point of view of a misanthrope. Far from it. Any self-improvement which the individual does effect is a gain not only for himself but also for those with whom he comes into contact. Say he makes of himself a better keeper of bees, a more reliable banker, a more finished actor, does he not add to the fund of satisfaction by which men live? Every man becomes his brother's keeper by way of self-improvement, and it is the only way.

"I believe," Nock used to say, "that we are put on this earth to have some fun." He had lots of it; he found it in himself, where each of us must find it. Neither gadgets nor money nor acclaim interested him. A good book, congenial friends, a lofty discussion, a helping hand to a worthwhile person, how else can one find happiness? Speaking of the New Deal, he would say, "The one thing Franklin cannot take from me is my memories." He did a good job with his life.

Part IX

The International Scene

Reds Are Natives

If we had sent an army into Indochina (Vice President Nixon once suggested that we should), its immediate objective would have been to kill Indochinese, so as to intimidate those we did not kill. Of course, the dead would have died because they were communists, and the intimidated would have been intimidated for the same reason. But regardless of their ideology, our chosen targets would have been natives. There is no way of getting away from that fact. The same would have been true if we had intervened militarily in the Guatemalan affair, and it is a certainty that we mowed down many thousands of natives in Korea.

The point is self-proving. When two nations make war, whatever their reasons, the purpose of each is to subdue the nationals of the other. The only point at issue is the validity of the reason advanced by each side trying to subjugate the other.

The historic reason for slaughtering natives is conquest: to grab land so as to be able to collect taxes from those who inhabit and use it. Currently, however, the reason advanced by many Americans is that the natives carry an ideological germ that threatens our way of life. We must destroy them and their culture before it destroys ours.

This was one of Chodorov's editorials in the August 1954 issue of The Freeman.

Granted the premise, the question is, will the desired end be achieved by the slaughter of communist natives all over the world? There is no historic support for that belief. The Norman conquerors of England did not impose their culture on the natives they did not kill, but rather made their adjustment to what they found, and the traditional culture of the Jews managed to outlive the paganism of the Roman legions. The evidence of history is that ideas are impervious to weapons.

That our culture—the body of ideas, habits, and traditions indigenous to America—is under severe attack there is no doubt. But can we save it by killing off or subjugating the communist natives of other lands? And by the way, if that is the effective cure of communism, why not try it on our own natives infected with the disease? We harbor quite a few of them in our midst, and, far from slaughtering them, we grant them the protection of the American culture they aim to destroy, and even put them in positions of public trust.

Communism is not a person, it is an idea. True, communism without communists is an imaginative notion, just as sin without sinners simply cannot be. But you cannot get rid of the idea that has possessed the communist by killing him, because the idea may have spread and you cannot destroy every carrier of it. It is better, therefore, to attack the idea than to attack the natives.

Without going into a discussion of the idea of communism as a whole, let us get to its essence, and what we find is simply the notion that the individual would be better off if he were deprived of the right to own property; since property must be owned, the method of communism is to vest all property right in those who wield political power, the state. That, then, is the idea that we who believe in the American tradition should try to kill, and let all natives live.

Isolationism

When World War I broke out in 1914, the *Chicago Tribune* announced with considerable pride that it was sending a parcel of reporters to Europe to "cover" the battles and the capitals of the warring nations. This was something new in American journalism. What had constituted foreign news previously were reports of what royal families were doing, affairs in which peeresses were involved, or a "passion" murder. Most of these stories were taken bodily from the European press. In fact, my wife, before she was married, was engaged in getting up a European "letter" for a news agency with the aid of a pair of scissors and a paste pot. The *New York Times,* with some pretensions to internationalism even in those days, ran on an inside page a column entitled "Transatlantic Cable Dispatches to the New York Times"; it usually occupied about a half-page and consisted of stories that could well have been lifted from European papers.

The American press did not go to the expense of sending correspondents to Europe because there was little public interest in European affairs, and as for Africa, Asia, and even Latin

This first appeared as chapter 11 of Out of Step.

America, these were places one learned about in school geography. The country was isolationist. The people, judging from the front pages of the city newspapers, were interested in what went on with the neighbors, in local politics, crop conditions, and the weather. When Congress was in session, which was for a few months in the year, some of the debates were accorded prominence, but not too much; type for a three-column headline had not yet been invented.

The war, when we were finally drawn into it, was something of an adventure for most Americans. Three generations of Americans had come and gone since the country had experienced a full-fledged war; the Indian wars and a couple of "punitive" expeditions into Mexico and Central America were of interest only to the professional army, and the contest with Spain was in the nature of an opera bouffe. The war in Europe was the real thing, brought into every home by means of the draft and involving a new instrument of war, the bond. Woodrow Wilson glamorized the undertaking by dubbing it the "war to end all wars" and the "war to make the world safe for democracy"; the latter phrase had all the earmarks of "manifest destiny," of the duty of imposing our brand of democracy on the benighted peoples of Europe, and thus appealed to our missionary zeal. Yet, the general feeling was that once we had licked the kaiser, we could return to our wonted ways, which, in sum, meant isolationism.

After the war, as usual, disillusionment set in. It was soon realized that the conquest of Germany did not mean the end of wars, but was probably the prelude to yet another one, and that our brand of democracy did not sit well with other peoples. The opposition in the Senate to Wilson's League of Nations reflected the attitude of the people who had had enough of involvement in the tangled mess of European diplomacy and wanted out. For twenty years thereafter pacifism was the ruling passion of the country; in novels, on the stage, in magazine articles, and in college lecture halls the theme that war was inexcusable was repeated. The spirit of pacifism was reinforced by a resurgence of American isolationism, the feeling that nothing good could come to us from interfering in European internal matters, and that we would be better off minding our own business. It was this inbred isolationism which confronted Franklin Roosevelt when he set out to get us into World War II, and from which he was fortuitously delivered by Pearl Harbor.

Since then, isolationism has been turned (by our politicians, our bureaucracy and its henchmen, the professorial idealists) into a bad word.

And yet, isolationism is inherent in the human makeup. It is in the nature of the human being to be interested first in himself, and second in his neighbors. His primary concern is with his bread-and butter problems, to begin with, and then in the other things that living implies: his health, his pleasures, the education of his children, wiping out the mortgage on the old homestead, and getting along with his neighbors. If he has the time and inclination for it, he takes a hand in local charities and local politics. If something happens in his state capital that arouses his ire or his imagination, he may talk to his neighbors about the necessity of reform; that is, if the reform happens to engage his interests. Taxation always interests him. But events and movements that occur far away from his immediate circumstances or that affect him only tangentially (like inflation or debates in the UN) either pass him by completely or, if he reads about them in the newspapers, concern him only academically. A Minnesotan may take notice of a headline event in Florida, as a conversation piece, but he is vitally interested in what has happened in his community: a fire, a divorce case, or the new road that will pass through. How many people know the name of their congressman or take the slightest interest in how he votes on given issues?

It has become standard procedure for sociologists and politicians to take opinion polls and to deduce behavior patterns from such data. Yet, it is a fact that the subject matters of these polls do not touch on matters in which the questionees are vitally interested, but are topics in which the pollsters have a concern. Putting aside the possibility of so framing the questions as to elicit replies the pollsters want, the fact is that the pride of the questionees can well influence their answers. Thus, a housewife who has been asked for her opinion on South African apartheid, for instance, will feel flattered that she has been singled out for the honor and will feel impelled to give some answer, usually a predigested opinion taken from a newspaper editorial; she will not say honestly that she knows nothing about apartheid and cares less. On the other hand, if she were asked about the baking of an apple pie, she would come up with an intelligent answer; but the sociologists are not interested in knowing how to bake an apple pie.

The scientist immersed in the laboratory will weigh carefully any question put to him regarding the subject matter of his science and will probably not come up with a yes-or-no answer; but, he is positive that the nation ought to recognize the Chinese communist regime, because he heard another scientist say so. The baseball fan who knows the batting average of every member of his team, on the other hand, will denounce the recognition of the regime because he has heard that the "Reds" are no good. The student whose grades are just about passing will speak out boldly on the UN, reflecting the opinion of his professor on that organization. Everybody has opinions on international subjects, because the newspapers have opinions on them, and the readers like to be "in the swim." That is to say, interventionism is a fad stimulated by the public press, and like a fad, had no real substance behind it. If a poll were to be taken on the subject of our going to war, the probability is that very few would vote for the proposition; yet, war is the ultimate of interventionism, and the opposition to it is proof enough that we are isolationist in our sympathies. A poll on the subject of isolationism—something like "Do you believe we ought to keep out of the politics of other nations and ought to let them work out their problems without our interference?"—might bring out some interesting conclusions; but the politicians and the energumens of interventionism would prefer not to conduct such a poll. Our "foreign-aid" program has never been subjected to a plebiscite.

Isolationism is not a political policy, it is a natural attitude of a people. It is adjustment to the prevailing culture within a country, and a feeling of security within that adjustment. The traditions, the political and social institutions, and the moral values that obtain seem good, the people do not wish them to be disturbed by peoples with other backgrounds and, what is more, they do not feel any call to impose their own customs and values on strangers. This does not mean that they will not voluntarily borrow from other cultures or that they will surround themselves with parochial walls. Long before interventionism became a fixed policy of the government, American students went to Europe to complete their education and immigrants introduced their exotic foods to the American table. But these were voluntary adoptions, even as we welcomed German and Italian operas and applauded the British lecturers who came here to decry our lack of manners. We certainly enjoyed the bananas and coffee imported from Latin American countries, and, while we might deplore their habit of setting up dictatorships, we felt no obligation to inject ourselves into their political affairs; that was their business, not ours.

This was the general attitude of the American people before the experiment in interventionism known as World War I. Before that event, Woodrow Wilson had taken leave of his senses in backing one revolutionary leader against another in Mexico, and had even sent the marines to support his choice; his excuse for opposing Huerta was that that leader had not been "democratically" elected, overlooking the fact that eighty percent of the Mexicans were simply incapable of making a choice, or of caring about it. From that interventionary exploit we garnered a mistrust of American intentions vis-à-vis Mexico which haunts us to this day. But, Wilson's urgency to introduce "democracy" in Mexico was purely a personal idiosyncrasy, shared by his political entourage but not by the American people. We cared little about which brigand, Huerta or Carranza, got to the top, and were stirred up only by the fact that a number of American boys were killed in Wilson's invasion.

When World War II got going in Europe and it became evident that Roosevelt was intent on getting us into it, a group of Americans organized the America First Committee for the purpose of arousing the native spirit of isolationism to the point of frustrating his intent. They were for keeping the nation neutral. For various reasons (particularly Pearl Harbor) their plan failed, even though at the beginning they gained the adherence of many Americans. One flaw in their program was a tendency toward protectionism; the anti-involvement became identified with "Buy American" slogans and with high tariffs; that is, with economic, rather than political, isolationism. Economic isolationism—tariffs, quotas, embargoes, and general governmental interference with international trade—is an irritant that can well lead to war, or political interventionism. To build a trade wall around a country is to invite reprisals, which in turn make for misunderstanding and mistrust. Besides, free trade carries with it an appreciation of the cultures of the trading countries, and a feeling of goodwill among the peoples engaged. Free trade is natural, protectionism is political.

The America First Committee's opposition to our entry into the war was based on political and economic considerations. It is a well-known fact that during a war the state acquires powers which it does not relinquish when hostilities are over. When the enemy is at the city gates, or the illusion that he is coming can be put into people's minds, the tendency is to turn over to the captain all the powers he deems necessary to keep the enemy away. Liberty is downgraded in favor of protection. But, when the enemy is driven away, the state finds reason enough to hold onto its acquired powers. Thus, conscription, which Roosevelt reintroduced at the beginning of the war, has become the permanent policy of the government, and militarism, which is the opposite of freedom, has been incorporated into our mores. Whether or not this eventuality was in Roosevelt's mind is not germane; it is inherent in the character of the state. Taxes imposed ostensibly "for the duration" have become permanent, the bureaucracy built up during the war has not been dismantled, and interventions in the economy necessary for the prosecution of war are now held to be necessary for the welfare of the people. This, plus the fact that we are now engaged in preparing for World War III, was the net result of our entry into World War II. Whichever side won, the American people were the losers.

Aside from this necessary political consequence of our involvement, there was the further fact that our economy would suffer. More important than the direct effect of increased taxation was the indirect effect of inflation resulting from the sale of government bonds. Political duplicity and dishonesty reached the heights when these bonds were advertised as anti-inflationary. The prospective buyers were assured that their purchases would (a) help win the war, (b) make them a profit, and (c) avoid inflation; a strange appeal to their patriotism, their cupidity, and their ignorance. It is true that the "savings" bonds, which could not be sold or borrowed upon, would delay their inflationary effect. But, when the government redeemed them, at the will of the holders or at maturity, and was unable to resell these bonds to "savers," it would have to resort to borrowing from financial institutions, which would of course demand negotiable securities; these become inflationary. This result could have been anticipated by anyone with a grain of sense; but during the war this grain was missing and the bonds sold. They sold in spite of an article called "Don't Buy Bonds," which I published at the time. And the fiscal irresponsibility which the Roosevelt administration practiced before we got into the war was accelerated; it hasn't abated yet.

As isolationism is a natural attitude of the people, so interventionism is a conceit of the political leader. There does not seem to be area enough in the world to satiate his desire to exercise his power or, at least, his influence. Just as the mayor of a town hopes to become governor of his state, a congressman, or even president, so does the president or the king of a country deem it his duty to look beyond the immediate job of running his country. Necessity limits the interventionary inclination of the head of a small country, unless, indeed, he finds a neighboring small country incapable of resisting his advances. But, given a nation opulent enough to maintain a sizable military establishment and an adequate bureaucracy, his sights are lifted beyond the borders. To be sure, his interest is always the enlightenment or the betterment of the people over whom he seeks to extend his dominion or influence, never to exploit them. Thus, Alexander the Great offered the benefits of Hellenic civilization to the peoples of Asia, the Roman legions carried *Pax Romano* at the tip of their spears, and Napoleon imposed French "liberté, fraternité, egalité" on the peoples of Europe, whether they wanted it or not. Hitler tried to extend the influence of Aryanism and the late British Empire was built on the premise that a taste of English civilization would do the natives good.

"Foreign policy" is the euphemism which covers up this inclination toward interventionism. About the only foreign policy consistent with the natural isolationism of a people would be one designed to prevent interference of a foreign power in the internal affairs of the country; that is, protection from invasion. But that is too limited in scope to satisfy the cravings of the government of a powerful country. Theodore Roosevelt's foreign policy was avowedly designed to spread among other peoples the benefits of American civilization—even at the end of a Big Stick. Without an income tax, he could do very little beyond the display of naval might to execute this purpose, and the job was undertaken by Woodrow Wilson. It is interesting to note that Wilson was by persuasion an antimilitarist and an isolationist; yet the exigencies of office induced him to lead the country into war and into the missionary purpose of spreading American democracy far and wide. He failed, partly because the peoples of the world were not willing to adopt the American tradition and partly because he could not break down American resistance to interventionism. It remained for Franklin D. Roosevelt, aided and abetted by the Great Depression and a great war, to do that. And now that a monstrous bureaucracy with a vested interest in interventionism is in control of our "foreign policy," the nation is committed to a program of interference in the affairs of every country in the world.

Something new has been added to the technique of exporting our culture; instead of sending it abroad at the point of a bayonet, we (or rather our bureaucrats) are attempting to bribe the "underdeveloped" peoples into accepting it. But these peoples, accustomed as they are to their own traditions, their own customs, and their own institutions, seem to be unappreciative of our efforts, and the net result of our "foreign-aid" program (aside from supporting a free spending bureaucracy) is to support the politicians of the recipient countries in a manner of living to which they are not accustomed. The current rationalization of this international dispensation of alms is that it is necessary to prevent the spread of communism. But, communism is a way of life imposed on a people by their politicians, and if these, for their own purposes, choose communism, our "aid" simply enables them to make that choice. Meanwhile, the peoples of the world remain impervious to our brand of civilization; their loyalty to their own traditions is unimpaired by our largess; they remain isolationist. Adding insult to injury, they resent our intrusion into their manner of living, call us "imperialists," and impolitely ask our agents to go home.

In short, they ask us to return to that isolationism which for over a hundred years prospered the nation and gained for us the respect and admiration of the world.

A Byzantine Empire
of the West?

If you've an historic periscope in your equipment, now is the time to put it up. For, over the political horizon comes a view not seen these sixteen centuries: the sunset of a world empire. The Spanish Empire, the Austrian potpourri, the German pretension—many such affairs have collapsed and hardly raised dust. But what we're witnessing now is a crackup comparable to nothing that's happened since the Roman affair. In a few years, most likely after the very next war, surely within the century, what was the British Empire will be little more than the United Kingdom. Maybe the ultimate will be another Merrie England, and the islanders will be the better off for lack of imperialistic burdens. That is a consummation devoutly to be wished.

Something over two centuries ago this body of involuntary adhesions began forming. Thanks to British enterprise and British valor, tax-and-rent contributions from wherever the sun did not set bolstered the "national" economy. A wise division with native collaborators facilitated the arrangements, and the sub-

Chodorov published this article in analysis *(April 1947). It was one of his most widely read articles. Rep. Howard Buffet was so impressed that he put it in the* Congressional Record *of April 29, 1947.*

jected peoples made their peace with it because—well, one must live. The producers rubbed along somehow, in spite of the load, and things might have continued in the same way indefinitely were it not for that inevitable concomitant of imperialism, war. Short wars with weak peoples may bring a profit, but when it comes to a life-and-death struggle with a fellow your own size, you have all outgo and no possible return. Several such wars are bound to be disastrous to an empire, for the compounding costs drain production to the point where little is left for existence, let alone for further expansion. It then becomes difficult to maintain the constabulary which shores up the structure. When an empire cannot raise enough cash to "carry out its commitments," and must call upon a big brother for help, it is a dead herring. No, the socialists are not to blame for the collapse of the British Empire, as the Tories claim; even after World War I the fiscal difficulties at Number Ten Downing Street came to what the doctors call a "critical condition," and the mission of the present government is simply to administer the last rites. *Pax vobiscum.*

THE WORK OF MEN

This empire-building business has been going on for a long time, though only once in a while does it grow up to world-wide proportions, and always when an empire gave up the ghost its place was taken by some fledgling, and frequently several rivals sprouted at once. The Byzantine Empire followed hard on the heels of Rome. Though it did quite well for a time, it never made the grade of its predecessor; stirring in the sands of Africa and Asia Minor were imperialistic ambitions which stunted the growth of Constantinople, while a little later the father of Charlemagne sowed the seeds of competition from the West.

It would seem from the constant recurrence of empires that there is something inevitable about the business, that it belongs "in the natural order." Even now, while the British Empire is hardly laid away, the outlines of a new imperialistic picture are clearly discernible. In the West a lusty heir apparent is flexing his muscles, while the ponderous bear in the East is bellowing his ferocious lust. It looks like another Armageddon is coming down the line.

If we were sure that empires are the product of natural forces, like societies or cabbages, it would be foolish to stand up against their coming. But, when we examine the nature of empires, what their purpose is, and how they are formed, we realize that God hasn't a thing to do with them. They are purely man-made. In spite of their acquired pomposity, they are in fact pretty mean, sordid, and brittle affairs.

If folks knew exactly what an empire is, and resolutely refused to have anything to do with the business, its advocates would have to turn to decent pursuits for a living. The need of popular support is proven by the cheerleader technique of imperialism. The current slogan "Stop Communism!" is a case in point. In the early years of our country somebody put us on the path of plunder with a call to "manifest destiny," just as the British Tommy was long impelled by the "white man's burden" to commit murder or suicide, and Napoleon's grand army marched into the Russian refrigerator shouting "Liberty, Equality, Fraternity!" Even that forthright empire builder Alexander the Great said something about carrying Greek culture to his "barbarian" victims, and we can be sure that in the kitbag of Genghis Khan was a phrase like "to make the world safe for democracy." This is standard equipment in imperialism.

LAND, LABOR, AND EMPIRE

What is an empire? It is a lot of people who are under compulsion to hand over a good part of what they produce to a handful of people who employ the soldiery that does the compelling. There never was an empire of a different character; so, we are justified in calling this an overall definition. Noteworthy and instructive is the fact that all empires are built out of land and people, the two factors of production, showing that imperialists are pretty good economists. Barren and semibarren areas may be included in the framework simply because they are "strategic"—meaning that they afford access to the people under exploitation. The British lifeline was the path traversed by the tax-collecting soldiery.

Speaking of a tax-collecting soldiery, we come to the heart of this something-for-nothing scheme. In olden times, when empire builders were at least picturesque, the business was done with simplicity and directness. There were silks and rare spices in the East to be had, diamonds to be picked up in Africa, gold asking to be taken in America, backward peoples everywhere needing civilization so that they might be the better exploited. For which noble purpose the ancient counterpart of the marines was sent. When the marines had the situation "well in hand"—signifying that the natives had resigned themselves to their fate—the higher-ups instituted the reliable double-barreled scheme of regularized loot; first, they levied a tax on production; next, they fixed up titles to land necessary for production and charged the workers rent for the use of it. Eventually the taxes and the titles were recorded in leather-bound volumes, which, having been blessed with resounding words by solemn professors, achieved reverential status. Black-robed gentlemen infused "justice" into the adjustment and traditional acquiescence dubbed it "law and order."

The process was facilitated in the olden days by common acceptance of a predatory "upper class." Nobody questioned the purposes or the prerogatives of these demigods. Primitive honesty also condoned the picking up of a little loot by the common soldier, so that he too had an economic interest in empire building. However, such square-toed methods had to be abandoned with the advent of the printing press, which encouraged the habit of reading, which in turn aroused querulousness. Naturally, the people took to reading moralisms which flattered their egos—namely, the phrases of democracy—and lest this should stimulate any predisposition against plunder, the proper kind of reading had to be provided. Thus, propaganda was added to the arsenal of empire building.

CAME THE CARTEL

The ingenuity of man is coterminous with his cupidity. Out of the claptrap of law came the confusion-confounding device of corporate ownership. Thereby a man-made person, utterly soulless and therefore without moral identity, nevertheless serves to absorb the personal responsibility of moral beings. That this contraption prospers by virtue of an imperialistic venture must be sheer accident; for, surely, one cannot associate the stockholding widow with the exploitation of some worker in Iran or India. Nor can the directors be individually charged with moral turpitude, since they act only in a collective capacity and everybody knows that a collectivity is without moral responsibility. In Russia the cartel, or trust, has attained beatification by way of "common ownership," thus absolving all and sundry, especially the commissars, from conscious complicity in the exploitation of Finnish miners or Polish peasants. If "everybody" is an imperialist, nobody is.

Which brings us to the imminent American succession to Britain's imperialistic position. Who is behind the plan? Is there any such plan? After all, the only definite proposal is that financial aid be given the governments of Greece and Turkey in their fight against the scourge of communism. Although the exact words have not yet been used, we have been told "again and again" that the money will not be followed by armies, not even to do a little collecting on the loans. Polite usage bans even the suggestion of imperialism. Nobody thinks of it.

When what was later recognized as American imperialism first stepped off the continent into the Caribbean, the prime purpose was to "help our little brown brothers," the secondary one was to "remember the Maine." That our sugar interests profited, that some of our bank stocks likewise prospered, must be put down to sheer coincidence; no evidence of premeditated complicity is adducible. And so, if we go through with this empire-succession business, it is quite possible that certain oil and mining stocks will "hit new highs," certain communications systems will improve their financial position, certain investment trusts will pay out bigger dividends. But that there is any conspirational connection between such a result and the loans to Greece and Turkey will always be an unprovable conjecture. Such is the genius of the cartel.

Not only does the impersonal corporation serve the purpose of conquest while absolving particular persons of culpability, but it also facilitates an established imperialistic process. In olden times, whenever a roving swashbuckler made life precarious for a tribe or a prince, it was good practice for that tribe or prince to court the protective custody of a strong-armed neighbor. Such things are not being done in these days of international protocol. The British, for instance, could hardly be expected to apply for a secondary position in the big American Union; not only is national pride against it, but the cartel system makes such a crudity unnecessary. Through the orderly process of the securities markets, American participation in the profitable oil, rubber, tin, and other concessions will be allowed to infiltrate, so that the cartels may become sufficiently American in character to warrant the protective arm of a government capable of standing up against Russian aggression. Through stock transfers and interchange of directorships the transition from one flag to another is done without offense to national sensibilities or tradition. In some respects, this migration of capital is comparable to the transfer of wealth from tottering Rome to the burgeoning Byzantine Empire, in the third and fourth centuries; the modern cartel obviates the use of a moving van.

FUNCTIONAL FEAR

And so, as American "interests" enter new "spheres of influence," as our economy becomes adjusted to the rents, royalties, and taxes provided by peoples enjoying our benevolent exploitation, the American empire will take its place in the historic up-and-down parade. That will require the maintenance of a considerable law-and-order enforcement agency. Empires are made and maintained by armies; armies of conquest are followed by armies of occupation which by self-propulsion become armies of further expansion. From an opposite direction comes the "aggressive" army of a competitive empire and a mutually "defensive" war ensues. But neither logic nor the rules of evidence can point to the cartel as a cause, or even a contributory cause, of the conflict. All we can say is that the profits of imperialism, which in ancient times accrued to a well-defined social group, now flow to the coffers of the amorphous legal contraption.

Putting aside purpose, the methods of empire building require the active cooperation of the nationals who must foot the bill, in blood and dollars. In this country, unlike Russia, where the Communist party has attained that status, the doctrine of an omniscient upper class is without force, and the necessary cooperation must be gained by suasion. The ways of getting people to do that which they are disinclined to do comes under the general head of propaganda, of which the most effective is that which arouses fear. Currently, fear of communism, fear that it will engulf Europe, fear that it will eventually penetrate this country and destroy the cherished American "way of life," is seeping into our consciousness as if by the force of truth; and, as a consequence, belief in an inherent bestiality of communists is growing. Those we fear we hate, and those we hate automatically fall into a lower category of humans. This churning process is quite familiar to anyone who can remember back ten years.

If we will, we can still save ourselves the cost of empire building. We have only to square off against this propaganda, and to supplement rationality with a determination that, come what may, we will not lend ourselves, as individuals, to this new outrage against human dignity. We will not cooperate. We will urge noncooperation upon our neighbors. We will resist, by counterpropaganda, every attempt to lead us to madness. Above all, when the time comes, we will refuse to fight, choosing the self-respect of the prison camp to the ignominy of the battlefield. It is far nobler to clean a latrine than to kill a man for profit.

COMBATING COMMUNISM

Very well, then, let us begin by scrutinizing the spreading fear propaganda. If we don't help Greece and Turkey, we are told, European culture must give way to this horrible communism. But the fact which that scare head obscures, and which is sustained by a mounting mass of evidence, is this: *communism is already the religion of Europe.* It is the desperation of hopeless poverty which makes converts to communism, and to this desperation our national policy has made its contribution. By preventing the people from producing, by destroying the tools of production, by condoning wholesale robbery, and by rooting up populations, our politicians and our generals are the unwitting missionaries of communism. If we would kill that strange cult, we must abandon the policy which creates the conditions on which it thrives. Bayonets, or dollars to pay for bayonets, will only aggravate these conditions. The only antidote to communism is to let the people of Europe produce and exchange. If communism thrives on scarcity, plenty will destroy it. Hence a policy which leads to unlimited production is the one which we should pursue if we would do what loans to Greece and Turkey are ostensibly intended for. Such a policy would include the removal of our own trade restrictions so that Europeans may be able to buy our surpluses with theirs. Above all, we must take our armies off their backs. The way to stop communism, to put it briefly, is to let the people alone.

If it is argued that such a hands-off policy does not take into account the ruthless and malevolent Russian military machine, that our departure from the scene would leave the people its helpless prey, let us admit the possibility of that consequence and consider the outcome. Suppose Russia imposes on the peoples of Europe the slavery conditions prevailing within her borders. Without arguing the point that these conditions have so reduced her own economy that the robbery of subject peoples has become a policy of necessity, we must admit as a matter of experience that slaves are poor producers, and we can predict the collapse of communism in Europe from lack of production. There is the added fact that, unlike the Russians, Western Europe did experience a measure of freedom, the memory of which will engender subversive activity, further slowing up the productive machinery. In short, the slave economy will bring about primitive conditions (such as Morgenthau envisioned), and the vulture state will die from lack of sustenance. It is poor prospect for the next generation of Europeans, to be sure, but is it any worse than another war? Something might survive a spell of communism, while the result of another war, no matter which side wins, will be annihilation.

When we speak of communism spreading we have in mind, as a matter of habit, the Russian state as well as the ideology. We see Moscow as the capital of a continent, controlling the lives of hundreds of millions by means of a crafty secret police and a hobble-nailed army. In every hamlet, province, and national capital there will be, so the horror-story goes, cunning commissars whose ultimate allegiance will be to the Kremlin. The tale is well constructed, and credence for it is gained by the implication of a subnormal Russian character. We have not as yet been told that the Slav is a Mongolian of inherently low degree; that will come, as it did in 1941, when the campaign reaches the murderous stage. But the insinuation is already strong in news stories, editorials and radio commentaries, and is necessary to the fabricated fear complex.

Yet, when we analyze the horror story, we see how silly it all is. The more the Russian state spreads itself the weaker it must become; the further the central commissars are from their agents, the more tenuous the tie; and the impact of foreign languages, customs, and traditions must undermine the cohesion necessary to centralized power. Russians are people. Like every other people, they want freedom, to live, to love, and to laugh. That is true even of Russian secret agents and Russian soldiers. Give them a little leeway, a little distance from the knout, a small opportunity to hide and run away, and they will indulge desires common to all mankind. The centrifugal force of expansion has a way of weakening political power at the perimeter.

LET THEM COME

Will a retreat from empire building bring the colossus to our homeland? (Shades of the Hitlerian hobgoblin!) Let us admit that danger. Since war is the state's escape from a collapsed internal economy, an intercontinental venture might suggest itself to the commissars. Well, then, would we not be better able to meet the challenge because we had been conserving our resources, building up our stockpile of military power? It is an established fact of modern warfare that victory is shaped in the nation's factories, not on the battlefields; hence our concentration on production while the Russian bear was hungering on the bare bones of its victims would put us in better position to deal it a deathblow. On the other hand, the cost of hacking out new areas of exploitation in the world will tell against us when the inevitable clash, with Russia nearer to her base, takes place.

The strength to ward off any such danger will come not mainly from our production lines, nor even from our military establishment; it will come from the general antipathy toward communism which prosperity engenders. The lesson our imperialists seem unable to learn is that this strange malady of the mind is rooted in despair. Poverty, heavy taxes, unemployment, little to eat, and the uncertainty of eating—these are the environmental conditions which nurture that mental deformity. It should be plain, then, that the expenditure of wealth in imperialistic ventures must create home conditions very favorable to the purposes of the commissars. Russia's ally will be in our streets.

Thus, even if we accept at face value the worst forebodings our empire builders dish up, reason tells against carrying the fight to the communist's lair. There is, however, an even more vital argument in favor of minding our home affairs. If we go along with this poking into the business of Europe, what will happen to the liberty we have left in America? Already there is a "Red" witchhunt afoot, and experience tells us that when the exigencies of the situation require it the definition of *Red* will include every person who raises his voice against the going order. Mass hysteria will conveniently support such a definition. So that, in the shadow of the impending "emergency," the outlines of a crowded concentration camp can already be detected.

If war comes—and when did imperialism not bring it?—the worst of what we call communism will come with it. The essential dogma of this creed is that the individual exists only for the purposes of the state. In that respect it must be identified with all other forms of statism, from pharaohism to nazism. Now, when the existence of the state is at stake, even the fiction of individual liberty cannot be tolerated. This is particularly true under the totalitarianism necessitated by modern warfare. Therefore, when our imperialism comes to grips with the empire of the commissars, the very thing we are presumably fighting to preserve will go by the board. Automatically, our liberties will vanish into—communism.

This is what your historic periscope should show you. But since history is what people make it, the smashup which the lens suggests is not inevitable. What men can do, men can undo. We—you and I—can help to prevent it, if we will but assume the responsibility and accept the consequences. Even a losing fight for liberty is worthwhile, for there is always the profit of self-respect to be had.[1]

---

[1] A peaceful alternative:
1. Economic internationalism—The elimination of friction by allowing the free flow of goods and services from where there is a surplus to where there is a need. The resulting interdependence breeds mutual respect. Since cultures follow in the wake of goods, free trade leads to understanding and appreciation, and a break in relations becomes unthinkable.
2. Nonintervention—How a people choose to order their lives is their own concern, and meddling by an outsider, even "for their own good," arouses resentment. Since the internal affairs of any nation are never beyond reproach, invasion of the privacy of another is as presumptuous as it is mischievous. Political isolationism—minding one's own business—is an essential of peace.

Free Trade for
Preparedness

In the matter of preparedness, the war emphasized two facts. First, that a large standing army is neither a deterrent of nor protection against aggression; second, that offensive and defensive equipment designed on the basis of past experience becomes obsolete almost as soon as the fighting begins. The massive French and Russian armies, even with Allied accretions, could not protect the borders of these nations, nor did their elaborate fortifications prove as impregnable as the builders thought; while the initial mechanical advantage of the Germans was liquidated by the inventive genius of a nation uninhibited by a blueprint. The arms which won the war were designed and built as the battle raged.

Since no formula for international peace has as yet been devised, preparedness will continue to be the concern of politicians, and the larger and more affluent the nation the more the emphasis put upon it. Which means that as long as the United States retains its present position in the world, insurance against war will be a constant national concern. We should, therefore, learn well the two lessons of the war and apply this knowledge to our benefit.

"Free Trade for Preparedness" was written for analysis *(November 1946).*

If we follow through on these two lessons we come to the conclusion that the most effective instrument of preparedness is thoroughgoing peacetime free trade. How does this follow? Let us take one important industry and see how the breaking down of our trade barrriers would improve our capacity for making war. The automotive industry is perhaps the best example, because it impinges on virtually our entire economy in the first place, and, in the second place, because it has proven itself a necessary arm of the military establishment during war. Its factories and its engineers and its know-how came in mighty handy when the going was toughest; out of this incubator came the ships, the airplanes, the guns, and the rolling stock, to say nothing of technical knowledge on the field of battle, which won the war. Furthermore, everything we grow or make in one way or another finds its way into the automobile, and if free trade can build this industry into a more potential war machine, it can likewise strengthen our entire economy.

NO COMPETITION IN SIGHT

Even before the war American automobiles and trucks found foreign competition negligible. What nation can offer any now? Germany is finished, England is done in, Japan will have little to export for many years, Russia is still, in spite of its bombastic claims, a backward nation. In automobiles—and in practically everything else which can be made with machinery—the markets of the world are ours for the asking. If we made it possible for the world to pay for them, American cars would soon cover every strip of concrete, every dirt road which connects any two towns anywhere on this globe. As one consequence, Detroit would be entirely inadequate and we would have a dozen such monstrous automotive centers situated in various parts of the country, assuring us of a protective decentralization; as another, the world demand would stimulate competition to a point where no American could not afford a car, while the related lines, from steel making to road building, from agriculture to mining, would have to keep pace, increasing our military potential in every direction. Overlooking, for the moment, the increased demand for labor, with its attendant increase in wages, and thinking only of preparedness, what nation would be foolhardy enough to attack such an arsenal, spread out over millions of square miles? The greater danger might be in the temptation to use such strength and security in a military venture of our own.

The great *if* in this proposition is our willingness to permit foreign customers to pay for their automobiles. We have not shown any such willingness in the past, and, since the advent of the New Deal, our "protection" psychology has developed into a form of insanity. By money inflation, by import quotas, by "ceilings" we have made it most difficult for the foreigner to buy our products because all these devices simply reduce his capacity to pay. Need it be pointed out that the only way to pay for goods and services is with goods and services? That money pays no part to trade except as a measurement of value? Even as in transactions between nationals every purchase is ultimately liquidated with another purchase, every sale calls for another sale, so must international transactions be likewise balanced. Minnesota cannot sell flour to New York unless it buys New York clothing in return, and Detroit cannot sell automobiles to Argentina unless it is willing to accept payment in either Argentine beef or in some commodity from a third country which has acquired our claim on Argentine beef. That is primary. And yet, our mad primitive isolationism has blinded us to this basic fact of all business. Like the schizophrenic who seeks escape from reality in dreams, we have taken to the fancy that we can export without importing, by the trick of lending the foreigner our dollars with which to buy our goods; when we get our own dollars back we feel enriched until we ask the foreigner to liquidate the debt, and then we find that our own tariffs prevent him from so doing. When he defaults, as we force him to do, we write off the loss by some trick in accountancy (like lend-lease), and we start the silly thing all over again.

HOW TO STOP INFLATION

If there ever was a valid argument against free trade, there is not the semblance of one today. As a result of the war the productive capacity of any possible competition is nonexistent. Nobody has anything to "dump" on us. Are we afraid of Russia's slave labor. Or the Chinese coolie? In a desperate effort to build up its export business, England is actually starving its population; can a starved laborer compete with a well-fed one? Why should we keep out Australian wool or lamb chops when there is such a shortage of both in this country? We fear inflation and yet we bar entry of the stocks which will hold prices down. We have a shortage of copper wire and a tariff on copper. Printers and publishers are crying for paper while a ceiling on wood pulp is diverting Sweden's surplus of this product to other shores. The beeves of Central and South America are going elsewhere because of a hoof-and-mouth fiction, and American housewives stand on line at our butchershops. So it goes.

If, as has been said, the nations of the world are too impoverished to buy what we can offer, then it follows that they are too impoverished to pay back the dollar loans we are making them. We make these loans on the assumption that when they get back to production they will become sellers of their respective surpluses, and out of the proceeds of these sales (to other countries) will come the funds for repayment. Well, then, if we can trust them with our dollars, we can trust them with our goods. Even if they have no wine to ship us now, the French have always been pretty good winemakers and we can depend on it they will make shipment against any trucks they may take now. Olive oil from Italy would indeed be welcome on any American table whenever it comes. The petroleum interests tell us our domestic supply of this commodity is dwindling to a point of national danger, and yet a tariff on petroleum prevents the importation of the vast supplies offered by South American wells, owned, incidentally, by these same interests. There is no nation in the world which does not have an overabundance of something which we can use, and which would make pretty good specie for the automobiles we are equipped to send them.

WHY SCUTTLE OUR NAVY?

The inclination is strong to extend this argument for preparedness through free trade to other industries. We have seen how all sorts of plants were turned almost overnight into war machines, and since free trade must increase the productivity of all industry by the simple expedient of widening the market, it is evident that free trade is the best assurance of a ready-made, well-oiled and superior defense potential. But, there is one industry which merits special attention, since its need in time of war is most essential, and which our protective policy threatens to extinguish. That is our merchant marine. In any war which we can envisage our navy must play an important part, and what kind of a navy would we have without a merchant marine? The common carrier which plies the seas in peacetime is immediately convertible into an auxiliary of the fighting ship, while its personnel are graduates of the most important naval academy.

The maintenance of a merchant marine is so necessary for defense purposes that we have resorted to subsidization to keep it from folding up. Yet there was a time when the American merchant marine was the envy of the nations of the world, and that was when this nation was poor both in population and in capital. The American Clipper was the cockiest ship on the high seas simply because it had cargoes to take home as well as to deliver. It had no tariff wall to impede its progress. The men who manned the Clipper were a comparatively opulent crew, and therefore enterprising, hardy, and resourceful; and all this because there were practically no political impediments to their business. Then came the protective tariff lunacy, about the time of the Civil War, and the American merchant marine began to decline. When World War I came, it was necessary at great cost to build merchant ships in a hurry; as soon as the war was over this vast accumulation of capital had to be scrapped because our protective tariff made shipping a profitless one-way business. Since we as a nation are addicted to this protective lunacy, we were incapable of learning the lesson, and when the second war came we had the same job to do all over again. Unless we come to our senses and realize that ships which carry cargoes out must have cargoes to bring back, we shall have to scuttle a second great and expensive navy. Free trade is the only means of saving it. Imagine what would happen to our railroad system if the various states put quotas and tariffs on the importations from the other states. That is what has happened to our merchant marine.

Now, this vast arsenal which an expanded international business would build up would cost the nation nothing. On the other hand, the wealth it would bring into the country, the wealth it would create by the employment of labor, would strengthen the nation financially in time of need. An army and a navy are all expense. Industry not only supports itself but also supports the army and the navy. The colossal French army collapsed at the first test because it rested on a decadent economy, a tax-corroded industrial establishment. As a consequence the morale of the people was far below fighting pitch and the productive capacity of the country was no match for the extra task put upon it by war. The experience of France should warn us against the stupidity of taxing industry to death to support a standing army. With a flourishing economy, we can build an army when we need it; with a tax-ridden economy, no army can stand up.

USELESS STANDING ARMIES

Rumor has it that Russia has a standing army of three million—a semitrained army of millions more. If this is so, Russia is getting weaker day by day. The cost of maintaining a nonproductive institution of anything like that size must be debilitating. But, more than that, every man who marches and drills is a man who not only is not producing, but because of lack of training is incapable of producing when production is most important. In the last war, the comparative technical skills and capacities of the two sides told off in the end. In the next war this factor will be of even more importance. The wags speak of it as the "pushbutton" war, meaning that mechanical gadgets will be relied upon more than personal fighting. Mechanical gadgets are made and operated by men who know how, and that knowledge can be gained only in designing rooms and shops, not in barracks. In the final analysis the nation with the biggest and most productive factories will be superior to the one with the biggest and best drilled army. Those factories are the product of a free economy—in which free trade is an essential element.

The final argument for free trade as a measure of preparedness is that it tends to minimize the irritations which lead to war. A free-trade nation is a nation of buyers, and on the recognized principle that "the buyer is always right," such a nation is looked on with favor by its neighbors. So, the most effective good-neighbor policy we could pursue is that of buying from our neighbors that which they have in abundance, and which we can use to advantage, selling them in return the things we have lots of and want least. They would not expect us to buy from them what we can produce more cheaply, nor would they consider buying from us anything of which their natural advantages or skills provide all they want. But, if we have automobiles and cotton which they need, we should not refuse payment in steers or minerals we could use. It is time we quit taxing ourselves to support our inefficient producers or to protect such "infant industries" as the United States Steel Corporation. It is time we stopped irritating other countries by refusing to do business with them on an equitable basis. Thus, both for preparedness and as a preventative of war, free trade commends itself.

Part X

When War Comes

A Jeremiad

The Korean affair is not The War. That was evident from the beginning. Just as every fistfight can end up in murder, so this bloodletting in the Orient has possibilities; but the weight of economics, as well as military considerations, is against Korea as the locale for man's next spasm of total madness.

When The War comes we will know about it, unmistakingly, by the peremptory suspension of all traditional and constitutional restraints on political power. That will be the true signal. The war powers still on our statute books will be dusted off and put into operation again and the administration will ask for, and be promptly granted, whatever else it deems necessary for a free hand.

In a word, when The War comes the individual will cease to exist as an individual. His body, his property, and his mind will be merged into the mass battering ram. The regime of totalitarianism that our recent history has been pointing to will have arrived.

It will be asserted that to carry on an effective war with the USSR we must match her methods. Our military, like hers, must be possessed of every drop of energy in the nation; any

This short article appeared on the front page of the August 1950 issue of analysis.

small concession to freedom will be weakening. Her law will be our law, which means that the will of the supreme command will be the only law.

This transformation of our political setup into an absolutism will be accomplished with little warning and practically no social opposition. For, unlike the war with Hitler, we will be in this one knee-deep from the very first shot, even before a formal declaration of war is perfunctorily passed by Congress.

The very first step will be the seizure of private property. The right of property will not be abolished in theory, but it will be enunciated as a principle that the government may without question lay its hands on anything that can be put to the war effort. Every factory will fall into its appointed place in the war machine; ownership will consist in obeying orders. Every worker will be a soldier. To facilitate the latter transition, union leaders will be drafted into the bureaucracy and their organizations put on the shelf.

The traditional economic forms of wages and profits will be retained, but the fiscal machinery will be used to rid monetary returns of material meaning. Taxes will liquidate purchasing power.

The fiction of borrowing will be maintained, but the "lenders" will accept the bonds under duress. Since every issue automatically depreciates the value of all preceding issues, the increasing worthlessness of these bonds will be reflected in a lowering of the value of money. Thus, through taxation and depreciation the danger of diverting production from war purposes to consumption will be avoided.

There can be no question that the economy will be put on a military footing, just as there can be no question that every man and woman able to contribute in any way to the fighting will be pressed into service. There will be no private life. Total war must be total in every respect.

The liquidation of social power will be facilitated by mass fear of the consequences of military defeat; in the face of common danger the herd instinct is to follow bold leadership, blindly. This psychological support of its program will be furthered by the high command through its control of information. The censorship of thought is a military necessity.

It follows that writers and publications endeavoring to keep alive prewar values must be rendered inarticulate, for the duration at any rate. The frightened public will enter no demurrer.

All wars come to an end, at least temporarily. But the authority acquired by the state hangs on; political power never abdicates. Note how the "emergency" taxes of World War II have hardened into permanent fiscal policy. While a few of the more irritating war agencies were dropped, others were enlarged, under various pretexts, and the sum total is more intervention and more interveners than we suffered before 1939.

If The War lasts long enough, long enough to become a habit of mind, the totalitarianism will have lost its initial disfavor. The will to freedom can be broken by adjustment to subservience. Besides, the economic conditions resulting from The War will be difficult enough to make continuation of control a compelling plausibility. In their general bewilderment the people will ask for direction, and direction means control.

There will be reason enough for the bureaucracy to insist on continuance of a politically managed economy. The debasement of the currency and the burdens of taxation could well turn the people to direct barter; barter is not taxable, and the state's recourse, for its own security, is to control and tax production at its source. Under the circumstances, the factories and the farms will not be returned outright to the former owners, except under conditions that will prompt the latter to offer their properties at bargain rates. The government can print bonds.

Will not the former labor leaders, now well ensconced in the bureaucracy, favor the nationalization of industry? What interest will they have in restoring the traditional labor-versus-capital controversy?

The workers will not find the riskless life, with subsistence assured, hard to take. A fetal sense of security will have submerged the will for maturity; there will be little demand for the free marketplace.

The aristocracy of the country will be the bureaucracy. They will be a class apart. Because of their prerogatives, to say nothing of their comparative opulence, they will have attracted to themselves the sharpest wits and the most skillful technicians, and it will be to the interest of the group to encourage a reputation for near divine capacities. This vested interest in rulership, spawned during The War, will flourish in the general enervation resulting from its consequences.

In short, the net profit of The War will be a political setup differing from that of Russia in name only. The very effort to oppose that form of absolutism will require our adopting it and, despite the best intentions, the resulting economic and social conditions will tend to perpetuate it.

There will be a resurrection, for the spirit of freedom never dies. But its coming will take time and much travail.

Warfare Versus Welfare

The welfare state is headed for the mothballs. What with the concentration on the business of war, the tradition (built up during the past twenty years) that the function of the state is to provide for us will be set aside. Whether or when it will be taken out again and put to use depends on the turn of events. At this writing, the welfare state can be written off.

Welfarism presupposes a condition of relative peace. Estimates of what can be taken out of the general economy for handouts, or for the administration of handouts, are based on what can be produced for consumption. Since, however, war has first call on the productive capacity of the country, and can demand all above mere subsistence, these estimates are thrown out of kilter by it.

This is not to say that the welfare state will be deliberately scuttled; it will simply fall into disuse. The laws, offices, desks, clerks, and officials set up for the dispensing of old-age pensions, educational subsidies, unemployment insurance, and the rest will remain in being; and even though new machinery for the control and regulation of the economy will be set up during

This article appeared in Human Events *(January 10, 1951).*

the emergency, the existing plant will not be dismantled. Operations will slow down for lack of appropriations.

Certainly, no new enterprise in welfarism will be undertaken. You will hear no more about socialized medicine, what with the doctors being drafted into the army, and the crusade against racial discrimination in employment will be forgotten in the manpower shortage.

It has already been suggested (by the New York State authorities) that the high school period be cut from four to three years, so as to facilitate earlier conscription; the corollary effect of diverting taxes from education to war purposes is obvious, even if not intended. This must be taken as a hint of things to come. The administration will surely drop its program for the subvention of elementary schools. From now on what is spent on education will be with an eye to its contribution to war; physics will be a desirable subject of study, philosophy will not.

The entrenched bureaucracy will certainly try to maintain unemployment insurance at its present level, but the need for labor will offset the bureaucrats' demands. Some use will be found for the productive power of those drawing old-age pensions. The national emergency will make a shambles of the handout business.

The recent withdrawal of price support for eggs will be followed by the dropping of subsidies for other farm products. The war-created shortages will boost prices to the point where "parity" becomes ridiculous. Moreover, the need for agricultural products will make necessary the dropping of that part of the program that calls for paying farmers for not producing. Every acre in the country will be put to work.

In short, the claims of welfarism on the tax dollar will lose all importance. Warfare comes first.

Speculation on the future of the welfare state is weighted by the conditions brought on by the international situation. It is possible that the all-out war with the Soviets can be put off for some time; the communists may not want it just yet. But, nothing is more certain than that we shall be for a long time on a war footing, that our economy shall be geared to military preparations for years to come. During that time, or during the war, a new way of thinking and a new social order will replace the tradition of the welfare state.

The idea of the welfare state is rooted in the all too common desire for manna from heaven. It is because of this strong demand for something for nothing that the do-gooders and the planners are able to do business. But, however strong is this demand, it is overshadowed by the will to live. If the conditions of war threaten existence, the urgency for safety will drown out the urgency for "security."

In a small way, we have had an indication of this instinctive emphasis on existence. In the past year the newspapers have recorded a rise of land values in sparsely settled and even in desert and mountainous areas, indicating a strong decentralist tendency. This development is explained on several grounds: as a hedge against inflation by investors, as making provision for subsistence when jobs become scarce, as an escape from the dangers of the atom bomb. The last reason will gain in importance as war becomes more imminent; we can expect this trek to the hinterland to gain in volume.

A basic economic principle is at work. When industrial and commercial wages fetch less in satisfactions than what can be extracted from the soil, the latter becomes more attractive than the office and the factory. One must live. The back-to-the-land movement today is basically economic. Well, then, as taxes combine with shortages to reduce purchasing power, factory workers turn to their garden patches to supplement income, while others go in for farming as an occupation.

If the war is long drawn out, if the bombing of our cities becomes more than a threat, the search for a haven of safety and a certainty of subsistence may well become the national habit. The transplanting of women, children, and the aged will be undertaken as a war measure, but the economics of it will accelerate the dispersal of the population. Keeping in mind the lowering of our economy by a war of attrition, the disruption of our productive machinery, and a ruinous inflation, we may be on our way to a new tradition: self-sustenance and self-reliance. Out of the war can come a habit of living that will have no place for the welfare state.

It is true that England, despite the bombing of her industrial centers, took up where she left off with welfarism. But, could England have done it if she had not had help from the outside? Without this help she could not have attempted a return to antebellum fancies; she would have had to go to work. Who would help us?

During war, of course, the omnipotent state takes over. The welfare state rests its case on the *paterfamilias* concept of society; the political establishment undertakes to alleviate disabilities by confiscating and distributing wealth, but in theory it does not deny the right of private property or violate personal prerogatives. The omnipotent state, on the other hand, puts its own purposes above those of the individual, and therefore must deny not only private property but all freedom of action; society becomes a tool, not a concern, of the state. When national existence is at stake, the latter idea gains in ascendancy; society abdicates in favor of the state as a matter of necessity.

History indicates that the powers acquired by the state during a national emergency are not usually relinquished when it is over. Absolutism is the product of war. Thus, if we go by the evidence of history, it may be that our welfare state will be transformed by the war into a continuing omnipotent state.

On the other hand—again assuming that the war, or mobilization lasts long enough to establish new ways of life and new traditions—it is entirely possible that economic decentralism will be followed by political decentralism. The dispersal of the population on a large scale will automatically make for a weakening of the central authority, partly because a self-sustaining citizenry resents interference, partly because the large centers will lose their dominant position. The city has always been the backbone of the strong state, the country has always been the opposition. Consequently, if the war draws large chunks of our population to the land, an American state after the pattern of Orwell's *1984* may be averted.

The sinews of the state are taxes, and taxes are limited by the productive capacity of the people. The productive capacity of the people is, in turn, in proportion to the capital structure at hand; the more and better tools at the disposal of the worker, the greater his output. So, if the war absorbs and destroys a considerable part of our capital structure, our productive capacity will be diminished and the revenues of the state will dwindle accordingly. A war of attrition, therefore, is a threat to the state itself. And if, during such a war, we acquire the habit of self-sustenance, it is a certainty that the state will have hard going to reestablish its position. An agricultural economy yields little in the way of taxes.

If this is so, it may be argued, then Russia is in no position to carry on a war of attrition. Her economy has been on a war footing since the communists took over in 1918, and her capital structure must be only what slave labor can yield under the lash. That is true. She probably has squeezed out of her slaves a striking force of considerable strength; having spent it, she would be hard pressed. There is reason to believe that a continuing threat of war, with sporadic demonstrations by her satellites, would suit her purposes better than an all-out struggle. Meanwhile, a continuing threat of war will have the same effect on our economy as a war of attrition.

For the time being—and that is the point of this argument—the welfare state is out. In the immediate future the direction of the American state will be toward the acquisition of power for war purposes, not eleemosynary purposes. The tendency will be more and more toward totalitarianism. That is unavoidable.

The ultimate is difficult to foretell. Will totalitarianism settle down on us as a continuing way of life? The pessimists are of that opinion. On the other hand, we cannot underestimate the power of tradition. Maybe the American tradition of individualism will rise up and smite totalitarianism hip and thigh. All the totalitarianism of the past finally succumbed to the will for freedom.

A War to Communize America

We are again being told to be afraid. As it was before the two world wars so it is now: politicians talk in frightening terms, journalists invent scare lines, and even next-door neighbors are taking up the cry: the enemy is at the city gates; we must gird for battle. In case you don't know, the enemy this time is the USSR.

There is no question about the sincerity of these good Americans. And I admit that the evidence they adduce to support their fears cannot be easily dismissed. As a matter of fact, the history of nations is a continuous story of enemies at the city gates, and it can be conceded without further argument that a rich country like ours would be a tempting morsel for any gang that thought itself strong enough to make a try for it. Perhaps it would be good for us to "keep our powder dry."

But how? What is "defense"? There is a wide divergence of opinion in this area, probably because it involves an understanding of strategy and defense, and who is there that has the

This article appeared during Chodorov's editorship of The Freeman *(November 1954) and at the height of the controversy over what to do about communism that was raging in the conservative movement. It was his last passionate reaffirmation of the isolationist, Old Right tradition.*

right answers in either field? Some say that the way to get rid
of the Red menace is to knock it off wherever it shows its head.
Others would avoid the sideshow and get to the big top, in
Moscow. Even the experts are in disagreement on tactics: some
say the foot soldier will win the war, others maintain that air
power has made the infantry obsolete, while the navy presses
its claim to preeminence. Nuclear physics has confounded the
confusion, while the reliability of presumed allies blurs the
picture still more.

The ordinary citizen, the fellow who will do the fighting and
paying, is certainly scared by all these arguments over "defense," all of which are based on the assumption that the war
is inevitable, which alone frightens him. Before he goes ber-
serk, he might review the whole situation in the light of experience, and maybe the common sense of it will give him
some light.

In the first place, as these articulate fearers readily admit,
the war being talked about will have to be fought with con-
scripts. That is taken for granted, is not even argued, because
it is inconceivable that enough Americans would volunteer to
fight a war with Russia on foreign soil. I am sure that if Americans were convinced that their country were in imminent danger of being invaded, they would rush to the ramparts. If I am
wrong, then the whole question is meaningless; for a people
that will not defend its homeland is of no account. But if conscription has to be resorted to, is that not evidence that the
proposed war with Russia is not wanted?

NO ARMY WITHOUT CONSCRIPTION

Let's belabor this matter of conscription, for I believe it
points to the heart of the question. In all probability we would

not have been able to raise a volunteer army to send to Europe in 1917; the fact that it was not even tried indicates that the politicians knew it would not work. In 1942, the armies sent to Europe and Japan were also conscript armies. I don't think a single division could have been raised by the volunteer system for the Korean adventure.

That raises the pertinent question: If Americans did not want these wars, should they have been compelled to fight them? Perhaps the people were wrong in their lack of enthusiasm for these wars, but their right to be wrong cannot be questioned in what we call a democratic system. Those who presume to compel people to be "right," against their will, are taking unto themselves a mandate for which there is no warrant other than their own conceit. Did God select them to do the coercing?

I could go into the results of these wars to show that the instinct of the people was sounder than the judgment of the politicians; a good case could be made for the thesis that if we had not been forced into these wars we would not be facing another one now. But that is not the present point. We are told that we must fear the Russians. I am more afraid of those who, like their forebears, would compel us against our will to fight the Russians. They have the dictator complex.

The conscript wars were all fought on foreign soil. And each was preceded by a campaign of fear such as we are now experiencing. The kaiser and Hitler each planned to invade the United States, it was said, and there are some who maintain that if we had not fought the communists in Korea we would have had them on our hands in California. That is, the rationale of these wars was invasion, which was another way of admitting that the soldiers would not have even reluctantly accepted involuntary servitude if they had not been convinced that their homeland was threatened. Postwar research reveals that neither the kaiser nor Hitler even contemplated the impossible task of crossing the Atlantic with an army, suggesting that the fear campaigns were manufactured out of whole cloth. What reason have we to believe otherwise of the present campaign of fear?

This time, we are told, things are "different." The kaiser and Hitler were only partly deranged: now we are dealing with a crowd of honest-to-goodness maniacs. I might accept that designation of the Moscow communists simply because I have met Americans of like persuasion and have found them to be off base. Also, I am acquainted with the literature of the communists in which they proclaim their intention to conquer the world. But I am not frightened because I am not convinced of the world-conquering potential of the Moscow gang, or of its ability to invade my country. If I were, or rather, if the youth of my country were, we could dispense with the "selective service" bunkum.

There is only one difference in the present urgency for war and that which preceded the others, and it is a frightening difference. The proponents frankly admit that if this war eventuates, Americans will be rushed into a condition of involuntary servitude not unlike that which obtains in the Soviet Union. Such soothing syrup as the "war to end all wars" will not go down this time. Even the most gullible American cannot be fooled by moral platitudes. Too many Americans now realize that war adds power to the state, at the expense of liberty, and there is a strong suspicion that the next war will just about wipe out whatever liberty we have. That is, we will be infected by the same virus that we set out to exterminate.

EITHER WAY, IT'S SLAVERY

Admitting all this, the fearers come up with a "clincher"— the argument that is supposed to leave no escape for the prospective buyer. "Would you not prefer to give up your freedom temporarily to an American than to a Russian dictator?" Let's examine this either-or gimmick.

The "clincher" only seems to suggest a choice. But there is none. In either case, the chooser has only one choice: a condition of slavery. The selection is limited to the nationality of the master, or between Tweedledee and Tweedledum. Why go to war for that privilege? (Parenthetically, it is easier to stir up a revolution against a foreign invader than a native dictator.) The suggestion that the American dictatorship would be "temporary" makes this whole argument suspect, for no dictatorship has ever set a limit on its term of office; it is by nature precluded from so doing.

Let us keep in mind that the advocates of war do not propose to exterminate communism; they only hope to exterminate a communistic regime. No doubt they would like to do both, but they admit, as they must, that the war would not exterminate it but would rather saddle communism, or something very like it, on America. The only way to avoid that consequence is to avoid war, and the question at issue is whether it can be.

Assuming that we do not bring the war to Russia, can the Russians bring it to us? That is, can they invade the United States with an army? I know of no responsible military man who maintains that they can.

If they cannot invade us with an army, can they invade us with hydrogen bombs? It is said that they can; but why should they? The experts agree that it would be a hazardous venture, involving an expenditure of men and material of fantastic proportions; the Soviet leaders are not crazy. Nor are they unaware of the probability of a retaliatory delivery which, because of their reportedly weak productive capacity, might do them more harm than what they did to us. If they started a mutually destructive war of bombs, it could only be as an act of desperation and an admission that they were licked anyway. Also, some military men hold that a bomb war would not be decisive; there would still be the problem of transporting an army to hold the territory of the destroyed country. (Here I am getting into strategy and tactics, about which I know only what I read; but in that respect I believe I am on a par with the proponents of war.)

REVOLUTION IS IMPROBABLE

Well then, can Moscow foment a successful revolution in this country and take possession through its American agents? That is a possibility. But, if a successful revolution occurs in this country, it will indicate that our security officers have either been asleep or in cahoots with the Kremlin. Either situation seems highly improbable. Anyway, war will not prevent the revolution, if one is in the making, but would rather help it along, for it would divert our soldiers from the job at home.

What then have we to be afraid of? The hysteria of fear. There is no doubt that the warmongers of Moscow are as fearful as our own. Neither group knows what the other is up to, and the misapprehension could trigger a "preventive" war by either side. So the only way to prevent a conflagration is to remove the tinder. The Soviets could do it very easily by simply reversing their position, that is, by moving their troops back to within the borders of their country and indicating an intention to keep the peace. But they are not likely to do that, for ideological reasons, and because a dictatorship is impelled by its inner workings to be on the warpath all the time.

America is not a dictatorship. Presumably, its government has the interests of its people at heart, and their interests in the present instance would best be served by the avoidance of war. That is the only way to preserve whatever freedom we still have. Therefore—and now I am assuming that our leaders are not imperialistically minded—if we withdrew our troops to the Western Hemisphere and abandoned our global military commitments, the danger that is now threatenting us would be minimized, if not removed.

IF WE LEFT EUROPE

To this suggestion that we come home and mind our business the fearmongers pose an objection taken from the graveyard of propaganda. Before World War II we were told that if we did not go to Europe to stop Hitler, he would come to us. "Our frontier is on the Rhine." Now we are told that if we get out of Europe, the communists will overrun the Continent, get hold of its productive machinery, and prepare themselves for an invasion of America. We must stop them before they move an inch farther West.

If the Russians, after we had left, did move into France and Italy, it might be because they were invited or met only token resistance. If I read the newspaper dispatches correctly, I must conclude that large segments of the populations of these two countries are favorably inclined to a regime of communism. In that case, our presence in Europe is an impertinent interference with the internal affairs of these countries; let them go communist if they want to.

On the other hand, if we moved out, and the Muscovites followed on our heels, it could be that the countries of Europe which now show little inclination to defend their national integrity would put up a fight; they would not have to resort to conscription. And even if they could not stop the Russians, their resistance would be an assurance that the invaders would get little production out of them; the vast productive capacity might be sabotaged and become useless to the invaders. In short, we might have real allies in Europe, which we don't have now.

My history books tell me that the weakness of a conqueror increases in proportion to the extent of his conquest. If that is true, then the overrunning of Europe might be the death-knell of the Soviet regime; it could collapse without any effort on our part. Then again, if communism should solidly establish itself in Western Europe, it would be because it is in fact a sound economic and political system, one under which the people like to live and work; in that case, we ought to take it on ourselves, willingly and without getting it by way of war.

There is a more important reason for our getting out of Europe and abandoning our global military commitments. We would be strengthening ourselves, even as the Soviets were weakening themselves by extending their lines. The vast military equipment which we are sending abroad, and much of which might fall into the hands of the Russians, would be stockpiled here for the ultimate struggle. The manpower which is now going to waste in uniform could be put to the task of building up our war potential. Our economy would be strengthened for the expected shock. We would become a veritable military giant, and because of our strength we would attract real allies, not lukewarm ones.

Of course, it would be hard on the Europeans if they fell into Soviet hands; but not any worse than if we precipitated a war in which their homes became the battlefield. It is bad for the Hungarians, the Czechs, the Latvians and all the other peoples who have to live under the commissars. We are sorry for all of them and wish we could help them. But we are only 160 million people, and we simply cannot fight for all the people in the world. Maybe we could be of more use to them if, while they carried on an underground movement, with whatever matériel we could get to them, we built ourselves up for the final knock-out blow, provided it became necessary.

The important thing for America now is not to let the fear-mongers (or the imperialists) frighten us into a war which, no matter what the military outcome, is certain to communize our country.

Part XI

It's Fun to Fight

On Doing Something About It

E very diagnostician is faced with the demand for a cure. Readers of *analysis* have found fault with its lack of a "constructive program" of some kind, of a proposal for action leading to a correction of the incongruities which it points up month after month. The editor here meets the demand, although he insists that the charge of critical aloofness is unwarranted; every issue, every article, every item has insinuated the remedial measure. The demand, however, is for a specific program.

THE DIAGNOSIS

Let us first sum up the diagnosis. Society is sick, we say, because it is divided into those who live by their own production and those who live by the production of others. This we put down as an injustice, because we postulate the unquestionable right of every man to himself, and therefore to the results of his labor; the transfer of such property from one person to another, without adequate compensation, violates our sense of correctness.

This article was written for analysis *(April 1946). Parts of it appeared in chapter 10 of* Out of Step.

Leaving aside charity, gifts and family obligations, nobody willingly relinquishes possession of that which he produces without obtaining possession of that which he prizes as highly. Therefore, we are compelled to the conclusion that where such transfer does take place force or fraud, which is the same thing, must be present. This is so even when habitual acquiescence to force has dulled our power of perception, even when custom has regularized the robbery; inurement to slavery does not deny its existence.

What, then, is the nature of the force causing the economic injustice at issue? All inquiry along these lines leads to the law. The law is the flux through which political coercion works, and hence we trace the cause of the trouble to our political organization. It is by the power lodged in this political organization that some men aquire property at the expense of those who produce it. Those thus advantaged we call the privileged classes.

First among these classes is the group that exercises authority. We place it at the head of the list for several reasons. The total of the group's appropriations comes to an astounding half of all we produce; then, its power of enforcing exactions increases with every draught, putting us more and more under its domination in all matters; finally, it is on the authority exercised by this group that all privileges rest. For these reasons the politician must be put at the head of the predatory hierarchy.

Taxation is the lifeblood of political authority. If political authority were deprived of this method of exacting "dues and charges," it would collapse. But, this collapse would also bring down the entire structure of privilege supported by the power of the law. Hence every privileged group, consciously or unconsciously, and even though it grudgingly makes its contribution, favors the general scheme of taxation. The economic tie-up between privilege and political power is strong. This tacit partnership, which is rooted in historic practices, is called the state. However, usage correctly limits the name to the political branch of the partnership, for its power of coercion is the keystone of the entire business.

The privileges handed down by power are various, and the identity of the groups enjoying them changes with the need of the political arm for support. Some participate directly in the returns from taxation; among these are subsidized industrialists and farmers, bondholders, pensioners of all sorts. Then there are the indirect beneficiaries of the tax system, primarily manufacturers and merchants who in the course of business pyramid profits on the taxes they are entrusted to collect, while those who are protected from foreign competition by our tariffs exact higher prices for their products. Others profit from legally made patent and franchise monopolies. Those who gain most from the tie-up with the law are the few, estimated at five percent of the population, who hold title to the "eminent domain" over which the state exercises authority; their privilege of collecting rent from producers, for whom the use of natural resources is a prime necessity, makes them, in the final analysis, the residuary legatees of all privilege.

This is the condition which causes the injustice complained of. The only way to correct it is to do away with the cause; that is, to abolish the state. Any attempt at reform is ruled out on the ground that there is no way of transmuting a malignant growth into a healthy one. It is abolition or sufferance.

PREPARATION

If we are agreed on what must be done, the next question is: How? Before we go into the matter of method, let me say that

I assume the willingness of those readers who have asked for it (and to whom I shall refer as "you"), to carry their share of the load. My experience with many who demand social action is that they speak for others, not themselves, being content to limit their cooperation to "moral support." I am sure that such are not among those who have criticized *analysis* for its lack of a program.

You will admit that the force of resistance must be considerable to be effective; the number of those who recognize the antisocial character of the state must be enlarged. Many minds must be brought to the common purpose, and the only known means of accomplishing this is education. It is a laborious job, but it must be done. That you may be an effective educator, carrying conviction as well as knowledge, it is necessary that you be in full command of all the arguments and facts which bear on your thesis. Are you familiar with the historic genesis of the state? How well grounded are you in economic theory, so that you can demonstrate how political coercion channels goods from producer to nonproducer? Can you explain how the cost of social services, necessary for organized living, will be met when taxation is done away with? Are you prepared to prove that justice will be better served when individual integrity replaces political power? Unless you know all this, and more, your job must begin with self-education.

Satisfied that you are well enough along to tackle the job of disseminating knowledge, you seek minds capable of absorbing it. That I assure you, and I speak from long experience, is a fishing expedition that will yield picayune results; you must console yourself with the quality of your few recruits and hope that your movement will make progress because it is all wool and a yard wide. You pummel your students with arguments, you put them in the way of reading (and please don't forget *analysis*), you convince them that the state is the root of all evil. They, in turn, carry on likewise, and in time you have a roster respectable enough to make its influence felt.

POLITICAL THERAPY

Meanwhile you consider strategy. The historical pattern for doing something about it is to confront political power with organized opposition, which is, of course, political power. While vengeance is sometimes satisfied by this head-on collision of forces, the record shows that the principles of justice remain exactly where they were before. And this is so whether the conflict takes the form of violent revolution or a battle of the ballot box. The reason for this invariable outcome is found in the technique necessary to political action.

Leadership is the first requirement, for an army without direction is a mob, easily dispersed by the first concentrated charge. I nominate myself for the job, not because of any particular qualifications, but because I know myself and believe I can prognosticate my behavior as leader. Well, then, we have brought the opposition to terms, under my leadership, and it is now my duty and desire to carry out the mission entrusted to me. But, I know I am a human being, with the usual run of desires and the usual aversion to labor, and these impulses keep tugging at me while I am carrying out the common purpose. If in putting this purpose into practice the opportunity to barter power for self-betterment presents itself, I am afraid I might be tempted; it has happened with other leaders, and why should I deem myself exempt? Under the head of "realism" I will find justification enough for swerving from my appointed course. Or, I might be pushed into expediency by the self-interest of those who share power with me, for they too, despite their devotion to principle, are human.

The failure of every political movement to bring about social betterment is thus inherent in its technique, and we are forced to the conclusion that politics can never do the job. Something else must be tried. The state itself suggests an alternative.

THE VULNERABLE STATE

The weakness of the state is that it is an aggregate of humans; its strength lies in the general ignorance of that fact. From earliest times the covering up of this vulnerability has engaged the ingenuity of political power; all manner of argument has been adduced to lend the state a superhuman character, and rituals without end have been invented to give this fiction a verisimilitude of reality. The divinity with which the king found it necessary to endow himself has been assumed by a mythical fifty-one percent who in turn ordain those who rule over them. To aid the process of canonization, the personages in whom power resides have set themselves off by such artifices as high-sounding titles, distinctive apparel, and hierarchical insignia. Language and behavior mannerisms—called protocol—emphasize their separatism. Nevertheless, the fact of mortality cannot be denied, and the continuity of political power is manufactured by means of awe-inspiring symbols, such as flags, thrones, wigs, monuments, seals, and ribbons; these things do not die. By way of litanies a soul is breathed into the golden calf and political philosophy anoints it a "metaphysical person."

But Louis XIV was quite literal in proclaiming, "L'etat c'est moi." The state is a person or a number of persons who exercise force, or the threat of it, to cause others to do what they otherwise would not do, or to refrain from satisfying a desire. That is, the state is political power, and political power is force exerted by persons on persons. The superhuman character given it is intended to induce subservience. The strength of the state is Samsonian, and can be shorn off by popular recognition of the fact that it is only a Tom, a Dick, and a Harry.

THE ONLY CURE

We must disabuse our minds of the thought that the state *is* a thief; the state *are* thieves. It is not a system which creates privileges, it is a number of morally responsible mortals who do so. A robot cannot declare war, nor can a general staff conduct one; the motivating instrument is a man called king or president, a man called legislator, a man called general. In thus identifying political behavior with persons we prevent transference of guilt to an amoral fiction and place responsibility where it rightly belongs.

Having fixed in our minds the fact that the state is a number of persons who are up to no good, we should proceed to treat them accordingly. You do not genuflect before an ordinary loafer; why should you do so in the presence of a bureaucrat? If someone high in the hierarchy hires a hall, and with your money, stay away; the absent audience will bring him to a realization of his nothingness. The speeches and the written statements of the politician are directed toward influencing your good opinion of political power, and if you neither listen to the one nor read the other you will not be influenced and he will give up the effort. It is the applause, the adulation we accord political personages that records our acquiescence in the power they yield; the deflation of that power is in proportion to our disregard of these personages. Without a cheering crowd there is no parade.

Social power alone can bring down the top layer of political skulduggery to its moral level. Those whose self-respect has not dropped below the vanishing point will get out of the business and put themselves to honest work, while the degenerates who remain will have to get along on what little they can pick up from a noncooperative public. Below the top layer there are the millions of menials who are more to be pitied than scorned; you find it difficult to censure the man whose incompetence forces him to the public trough. Yet, if you take the "poor John" attitude toward him you keep him reminded of a higher moral standard, and you may thus help him save himself.

A government building you regard as a charnel house, which in fact it is; you enter it always under duress, and you never demean yourself by curtsying to its living or dead statuary. The stars on the general's shoulders merely signify that the man might have been a useful member of society; you pity the boy whose military garb identifies his servility. The dais on which the judge sits elevates the body but lowers the man, and the jury box is a place where three-dollar-a-day slaves enforce the law of slavery. You honor the tax dodger. You do not vote because you put too high a value on your vote.

THE DOCTOR'S RESPONSIBILITY

Social power resides in every individual. Just as you put personal responsibility on political behavior, so must you assume personal responsibility for social behavior. It is your own job. You think poorly of legislator Brown not because he has violated a tenet of the Tax Reform Society to which you belong, but because his voting for a tax levy is in your own estimation an act of robbery. It is not a peace society which passes judgment on the warmaker, it is the individual pacifist. All values are personal. The good society you envision by the decline of the state is a society of which you are an integral part; your campaign is therefore your own obligation.

You are ineffective alone? You need an organization before you can begin? Individuals think, feel, and act; the organization serves only as a mask for those unable to think or unwilling to act on their own convictions. In the end every organization vitiates the ideal which at first attracted members, and the more powerful the organization, the surer this result. This is so because the organization is a compromise of private values, and in the effort to find a workable compromise, the lowest common denominator, descending as the membership increases, becomes the ideal. When you speak for yourself you are strong. The potency of social power is in proportion to the number who are of like mind, but that, as was said, is a matter of education, not organization.

Let's try social ostracism. It should work.

Freedom Is Better

Too bad you never knew Grand Street and its cafés in the old days. The coffee was mostly milk, or it might be tea with lemon, served in a glass, but the chunk of sponge cake was quite liberal in size. The whole cost a dime, and thrown in gratis, whether you liked it or not, you got a dissertation on truth. You always got it, in polysyllabic dosage, from some co-customer who had established himself as the custodian of truth in this particular "coffee saloon."

Grand Street, on New York's Lower East Side, was no mere thoroughfare; it was the symbol of an era. Before Tovarich Lenin had got himself boxcarred into dictatorship *over* the proletariat, and thence into mummified immortality, Grand Street typified the eternal search for the Absolute—the Holy Grail containing the positive specific of the good society. In one coffee saloon the Sir Galahad of dialectical materialism would dilate on its inevitability to those who were already convinced of it, while next door a Knight of Kropotkin would diagnose the case of "direct action." Each eating place had

"Freedom Is Better" appeared in Plain Talk *(November 1949).*

its own philosophy—which was the Only Truth in every case—
giving the impression that the philosophy and not the food was
its stock-in-trade.

Characteristic of the Grand Street era was the certainty of
each protagonist that only his doctrine was on the side of the
angels, that all others were frauds, to say the least. Objectivity
was looked down upon as a weakness of character, and questioning as a manifest expression of innate sinfulness. All of
which gave life exhilaration and charm. People who are sure
of themselves, downright sure, are always exciting. It is only
when they abandon argument and proceed to "do something
about it" that they become dull. In the Grand Street days there
was a lot of talk about action, but you got the impression that
for these delightful exponents of truth, action would be the
most distasteful thing in the world. They enjoyed talking too
much. Action does to a philosophy what a kitchen does to a
beautiful woman, and then there is nothing to talk about. Action
killed Grand Street.

Every doctrinaire dreams of "doing something about it"—
of demonstrating his truth in the field of human affairs. If only
he could try it out! There is no question that the good society
is guaranteed by his mosaic of words, for he has checked and
cross-checked it at every point and nowhere has he found a
logical leak. It must work. It is truth. The obstinacy of selfish,
ignorant, and sinful people who deny it is all that stands between the cure-all and the sick world.

Well, something was done about it in Moscow. To be historically exact, Grand Street, the era of dreams and discussion,
was murdered on the battlefields of World War I, for there was
nothing to palaver about after the Brest-Litovsk treaty. The time
for action had come. Truth would now prove itself.

Thirty years of experience have somewhat diluted the Truth According to Marx; the promise of Grand Street has not been fulfilled, for Moscow seems to have fallen short of the expected Eden. Evidently there was a flaw in the mosaic.

When we go back over the argument, applying the Moscow experience to it, we find that the neglected and defective element in it is the human being. The basic assumption of the Moscow truth—and of every truth that ever came down the pike of social science—is that the human being is absolutely and indefinitely malleable. There is nothing in him that can resist the force of environmental influences. When he is fitted into the ideal mold, the institutional pattern of truth, he will come out the ideal man. He is the putty, not the sculptor.

From this assumption follows another, which is never expressed but always implied. And that is that some sculptor of society is needed. Who shall fill the bill? Quite obviously, one whose capacity for understanding truth automatically raises him above the level of human being. He is something special, endowed with gifts that are denied the run-of-the-mill anthropoid, picked by nature to do the work of truth. His anointment both qualifies him and puts upon him the obligation to "do something about it."

These two assumptions, absolutely necessary in Grand Street to make the truth stand up, tend to show up its deficiency when put to the test. At Moscow and Berlin and Rome the absolute truth came crashing to the dust simply because the sculptors did not measure up to the assumption of infallibility, while the human being denied the assumption as to his plasticity. *They* proved incapable of ridding themselves of the very inadequacies which *he* was supposed to shed in his new environment. *They* wanted material satisfactions without end and advantages over their fellow men. *He* was not malleable, at least in his inclination to hold on to what he produced, and proved it by lying down on the job when his claim to property was denied; and *they* lost all their lofty pretensions simply because their resignation from the human race was not accepted. They were human beings, after all.

The spirit of Grand Street lingered on after World War I, even though sickish and apologetic, and kept cracking that "something be done about it." Between wars, the truth underwent some alterations, in the light of its European experience, and its perfection was undertaken by the London School of Economics and Harvard University. Statistics replaced coffee and cake. But the two assumptions that wrecked the experiments in truth were retained; that was necessary, for if it is recognized for a moment that the human being has something to say about it, or that omniscience is denied to the oracles of truth, how can one make "progress"?

After World War II, when the consequent confusion gave them the opportunity to "do something about it," the Back Bay successors to Grand Street set up their polished versions of truth in London and Washington. For the selfsame reason that truth failed in Moscow, Rome, and Berlin, it is proving itself quite fallible in a "democratic" locale, and despite its statistical veneer. Far from bringing about the good society, it is again turning out to be a pattern for disharmony. Even its advocates admit by constant revision that it is not what it was cracked up to be in the erudite Grand Streets.

The spirit of Grand Street is eternal; it never dies. For it is man's treadmill search for the key to happiness, yearning for the monistic principle of the good life. Every one of us, deep down, is certain that the "mess we are in" could be cleaned up with one application of the perfect formula, and so anxious are we to get at it that a good peddler has only to buttonhole us at the propitious moment to make a sale. We are suckers for the infallible.

Seeing how the market is never oversold, this writer, a confessed Ancient Mariner, comes at you with, believe it or not, the truth and nothing but the truth. It is all wool and a yard wide and carries the money-back-if-not-satisfied guarantee. It is called—freedom. Now, counterfeiters have helped themselves to this label only too often, and since you have been fooled before, you may be inclined to pass my booth with a sneer. However, if you will but listen to a short sales talk, a few hundred words, you will realize that my elixir is genuine, entirely different from the ersatz you have tried.

First, I am compelled to violate the first principle of good salesmanship; I must talk about my competitors' products, by way of contrast. Take them all down the line—socialism, anarchism, communism, single tax, prohibition, monetary reforms, controlled economies, ad nauseam—and you find a common essential ingredient: political power. In that respect they are all alike; not one of them can stand on its own feet, not one can work without a law. When their proponents say "let's do something about it," they mean "let's get hold of the political machinery so that we can do something to somebody else." And that somebody else is invariably you.

Freedom has nothing to do with political power. Freedom makes concessions to the law, as a matter of necessity, but always with the reluctance of a child taking castor oil. The ideal of freedom is a social order without law, but since the nature of man is not prepared to live in so rarefied an atmosphere, since he will on occasion covet his neighbor's property, which is a denial of freedom, it is necessary that the ideal be somewhat watered down with law. A free man is one capable of non-interference in the affairs of his neighbor, while the legally conscious man is consumed with a desire to control or dominate his neighbor. When a man says "there ought to be a law," he confesses his incapacity for freedom.

It is obvious that a free society is one in which the law concerns itself with minimizing the interferences of men in one another's affairs, and never presumes to interject itself; and it is obvious from that rule that freedom is quite unlike the various reforms that are being peddled on any Grand Street. Every one of them is labeled with a "legal directions for taking."

Freedom is essentially a condition of inequality, not equality. It recognizes as a fact of nature the structural differences inherent in man—in temperament, character, and capacity—and it respects those differences. We are not alike and no law can make us so. Parenthetically, what a stale and uninteresting world this would be if perfect equality prevailed. When you seek the taproot of reform movements you find an urgency to eradicate these innate differences and to make all men equal; in practice, this means the leveling-off of the more capable to the mediocrity of the mass. That is not freedom.

However, we must not be too hard on the spirit of reform. Every social integration fosters practices and institutions that deny the adequacy of freedom; envy, cupidity, and ignorance fertilize these weeds of the social order, and the impulse of reform is to root them out. But experience has shown that the law is ineffective in that purpose, that the law is in fact the instrument by which these iniquitous institutions came about. Whatever may be said of it as an expedient, as a steady diet castor oil is no good; the dosage of law is important.

The reforms will come of themselves, automatically, when instead of asking for a law we learn to shout, "Let us alone." For then we will have assumed the responsibility for our behavior; we will ask no favors, seek no advantages over our neighbors. We will get along with the capacities with which nature has endowed us and make the best of it. In the final analysis, freedom is an individual experience.

Let's Try Capitalism

B abies born out of wedlock—the original custom—did not acquire a secondary position in social life until the right of inheritance loomed large. Just as the offspring of promiscuous quadrupeds are not estopped by the accident of birth from winning championships, so bastards even as late as the eighteenth century could attain positions of prominence. The odium came upon the descriptive word by way of profit.

That is a way with words. When someone has an end to gain, a purpose, he attaches a moral connotation to some altogether descriptive symbol; its original meaning is lost in the emotional coloration which, by usage, becomes its definition. Take the word *capital* or, particularly, its derivatives, *capitalist* and *capitalism*. Before Karl Marx hooked onto the morally loaded idea of exploitation, capital described an accumulation of wealth. It was a thing, utterly amoral. It was not a man or a class of men. It was a herd of cattle, an ax, a stock of goods or gold, a house, a machine, or store fixtures. The word was used to differentiate wealth which satisfied the immediate needs of the owner from wealth he set aside for further production. The

This article was written for analysis *(October 1945).*

shoes which the cobbler offered for sale constituted his capital, while the shoes he wore were not in that category. His anvil was the blacksmith's capital, but not the nails he used to fix his wife's cupboard. When a man spoke of his capital he referred to the surplus he had accumulated for the purpose of increasing his output. That was all it was. That is all it is today.

The germ of capital is man's capacity for taking thought. The fellow who domesticated the wild animal was a simon-pure capitalist. He put himself to that trouble in order to profit by an abundance of milk, or to reduce the labor of hauling firewood. The one who first made use of the wheel was the archcapitalist of all time, for he fathered mankind's most important labor-saving devices. A capitalist was he who observed nature's fecundity at certain times of the year and, recalling the unpleasantness of scarcity, thought up the principle of storage. Nor can we overlook the first trader, the man who learned that he could better his lot by giving up some of his abundance to obtain possession of what he lacked; thus arose the cooperative system known as the marketplace.

We cannot know when capitalism began, but we can be sure it is rooted in the gift of reason which identifies *Homo sapiens*. Therefore, it is probably as old as man. Let us say it began when the first human being went in for "overtime" work. Aiming to shortcut the irksomeness of labor, or seeking to better his enjoyment of life, he put in effort over and above that required for his immediate necessaries in making devices which would lighten tomorrow's chores or yield him an increased output for the same exertion. He stored up labor in what he called capital, with the intent of bettering his circumstances. Anything immoral in that?

Marxist usage has twisted this human tendency to save for increased enjoyment, for delayed and greater consumption, into something reprehensible. This it accomplished not only by the misuse of words but more so by unscientific inference. Observing the prevalence of poverty when capital came into great use, Marx made the ready inference of cause and effect. The enigma of accumulations and destitution existing concurrently had to be explained, and what was more obvious than that the means for accumulating was the cause for the destitution? It was easy to infer that the instrument by which labor increased its output is the instrument by which labor is deprived of its output. Capital, then, is exploitative. The plausibility, by providing a culprit, fitted in with the bitterness which involuntary poverty induces. Something definite, visible could be blamed and hated.

The purpose served by this perversion of words was to prove a hypothetical notion—namely, that socialism is inevitable. It is predestined in a theory of history. According to this theory, the story of man is a succession of "modes of production." Each mode results in a conflict between the haves and have-nots; the conflict is resolved by a new mode. The machinery mode is capitalism, and the conflict is between those who own capital and those who do not. Out of the conflict between these two will come socialism, the final mode, in which there will be no conflict; that is, the millennium.

Capitalism was not a "new" mode of production, as the Marxist thesis contends. The use and ownership of capital, as has been noted, began when man first learned how to employ means toward ends; it is a mode of production indigenous to man and will continue to be his method of getting along until he ceases to be man.

Furthermore, poverty prevailed long before machinery (and trade) came into great use, and exploitation, which is the robbery of the producer's products, was common practice long before the Marxist "discovery." What is the essence of slavery, a very ancient institution, but the exploitation of labor? Ages before the invention of the steam engine, which to Marx definitely dated the advent of pure capitalism, the custom of collecting tribute for permission to work on land had been in use. And since earliest times armed bands collected tolls on controlled highways. Exploitation, as Marx himself finally saw, antedates by untold centuries the widespread use and private ownership of "the means of production and distribution." The association of exploitation with capitalism was gratuitous and unfounded in fact. It was done by legerdemain in logic, by giving descriptive words moral values, by appealing to passion rather than thought—and all for the purpose of proving an historical theory.

In the final, predestined mode of production there will be no conflict because by substituting public for private ownership of capital its exploitative power will vanish. Here again words are used to confuse thought and moralisms are used to obscure facts. What is "public" ownership? Is it not in practice the control of property by persons wielding political authority? If capital has the capacity for exploitation, cannot these persons use it to better themselves at the expense of others? What warrant have we that a political person is more moral than a private person or is, in fact, a different kind of person? Is man in the mass—the "public"—transformed into an all-wise, all-good being? That is the ethical thought which socialism implies in its defamation of capitalism. The evil of it is transmitted into good by a mere transference of title from private to political persons. What could be simpler—or more appealing to the exploited? Let's steal from the thieves and stop thievery.

Socialists, however, have not been alone in this befuddlement of language; they have had some powerful, though *sub rosa,* confederates. As might be expected, the confederates took to the socialistic jargon because it suited a purpose of their own, which happens to be—exploitation. When we define exploitation as any means of robbing labor of its products we can see how nonsocialists find socialistic usage convenient; it diverts the attention of the robbed from the real culprits. Now robbery involves the use of sufficient coercive power to overcome resistance. The quintessence of coercive power is vested in the state. It follows that every kind of effective and continuing exploitation must in some way make use of that power; occasional illegal robbery does not count in the long run because it cannot compete with the state. The exercise of state power is regularized by the law, acquiescence in which becomes habitual by the common inclination to let things be. Thus, exploitation in the final analysis is legalized robbery, and the exploiters are those who gain control of the power vested in the state.

These are the allies of socialism. Like Bismarck, the wily aristocrat who recognized in socialism an instrument useful to his purpose, the fellows who profit by use of state power are strong for any increase of it. Since they are not essentially owners and operators of capital, although that may be a sideline with them, the scapegoat provided by socialistic usage has proven quite convenient.

In the first instance, the gang that lives on taxes is by trade the vanguard of socialism. How can it suffer by the proposed transfer of title into its hands? Then there are those who by virtue of legalized deeds hold possession of natural resources and are thus in position to demand tribute from laborers; for life without access to land is impossible. Since what they own is not capital, they can well go along with the socialists. Those who profit by monopolies or subsidies of one sort or another, are to that extent in favor of the centralized power; state capitalism, whatever it may do to them ultimately, is in line with their present interests. When we see how during the last fifty years the growing acceptance of socialistic usage has kept pace with an increase in the emoluments of those who profit by privilege, it is easy to understand why capital and its derivatives have fallen into disrepute.

True capitalism—the undisturbed ownership and use of capital—has never been man's lot. For never, except among primitive peoples, whose employment of capital is extremely limited, has the human race been free of the political means of acquiring economic goods. We ought to try out capitalism and see how it works. As a preliminary step, we should rid our minds (and our schools) of its Marxist bastardization.

About Revolutions

It is agreed that the world is knee-deep in a social revolution. What is not so obvious is that embedded in the present revolution are the seeds of another. Yet that must be so simply because it was always so. No sooner do men settle down to a given set of ideas, a pattern of living and thinking, than faultfinding begins, and faultfinding is the taproot of revolutions.

Many reasons are offered in explanation of this historical restlessness. One reason that will serve as well as any other is that we are born young, very young. It is the natural business of the young mind to ask *why,* and since nobody has answered that question with finality, the field for speculation is wide open. And so, as soon as youth finds flaws in the going answers he makes up his own, and because they are new, as far as he is concerned, they are guaranteed against flaw. Somehow, the flaws do show up and another generation mounts its hobbyhorse in quest of the Holy Grail, the Brave New World. Revolution is inherent in the human makeup.

Suppose we came into this world with all the disabilities and disillusions of, say, the age of sixty. In that event, mankind would never have moved out of its cave apartments, never

This article appeared on the front page of the last issue of analysis *(January 1951).* *It was reprinted in* One Is a Crowd.

would have heard of the atom bomb or the New Deal. The only function of old men—or, at least, their only occupation—seems to be to find fault with the panaceas that possessed them in their youth. The price of experience is loss of faith. With disillusionment comes resistance to change, and the obstinacy goes so far as to find fallacies in the infallible panaceas of their sons. Nevertheless, youth hangs on to the ideas in which it has a proprietary interest, and change does come.

A revolution is a thought pattern born of curiosity and nurtured on an ideal. Every generation thinks up its own thought pattern, but because the preceding generation hangs on to what it is used to, the transition from the old to the new must be gradual. From the perspective of history it seems that on a certain date one revolution died and another was born. We think of the nineteenth century, with its tradition of natural rights, and its laissez-faire doctrine, as suddenly ushering in a reversal of the feudal tradition. But Voltaire, Adam Smith, Rousseau, and others were plowing and planting some time before 1800, and if you do some digging you'll find the roots of the nineteenth century in much earlier times. Even so, while we are enjoying, or rueing, our own revolution, it is a certainty that youth is critical of it and is building its successor.

There is a measure of fun, if you are inclined that way, in trying to discern in the prevailing current of ideas the direction of the next revolution. It is an interesting game, even if you know you cannot be on hand to say "I told you so." It is a game that takes the bitterness out of disillusion and robs pessimism of its gloom.

THE CURRENT TRADITION

Our own revolution, the one that seems to have started on the first day of January 1900, is identified by the doctrine of collectivism. Briefly, the doctrine holds that improvement in our way of living is attainable only if we discount the individual. The mass is all that matters. The doctrine does not deny the existence of the individual, but relegates him to the status of a means, not an end in himself. To support itself, the doctrine insists that the individual is only the product of his environment, which is the mass, that he could not exist outside of it, that he could not function except as an accessory to the mass.

The mass, on the other hand, is lacking in self-propelling force, and needs pushing. For this purpose a political machinery comes into existence, presumably by way of something called the democratic process. The individual serves the march of progress by submitting himself to the direction of that device. In the end, the doctrine holds, the individual will prosper because of the equal distribution of the abundance that comes from collective action.

That is the central idea of our current tradition. It is the idealization of the mass and the negation of the individual; its panacea, its method of realization, is political direction; its goal, as always, is the undefined good society.

So dominant is this doctrine in our thinking that it amounts to a dogma. It is implied, if not explicitly stated, in every field of thought. The aim of pedagogy today is not to prepare the individual for his own enjoyment of life, but to enable him better to serve the mass machine; the psychologist makes adjustment to mass thought the measure of healthy thinking and living; jurisprudence puts social responsibility ahead of individual responsibility; the concern of the scientist in the discovery of principles is secondary to his preoccupation with mass production; the economist studies institutions, not people; and philosophy rejects speculation as to the nature of man or the purpose of life as effort that might better be put to the practical problems of society. Ours is the culture of "the all," rather than "the one."

The end result of this kind of thinking, the practical result, is the worship of the state. This is a necessary consequence of the idealization of the mass, for since the mass can operate only under political power, then that power becomes the necessary condition of all life. It is a self-sufficient agency. It operates on a plane higher than not only that of the individual but also that of the mass. It is not only superpersonal, it is supermass. Without the state the mass could not function, even if it could exist. The state, then, is the modern golden calf, with this essential difference, that its power is demonstrable, not assumed; it can and does guide, direct, and harbor all of us. Hence, we adore it, make sacrifices to it, and never question its infallibility, even if we detect imperfections in its hierarchy. The current president may be in error, but the state can do no wrong.

OUR FATHERS' TRADITION

Just how far our revolution has gone along this path is seen when we make comparison with that of the nineteenth century. The dominant doctrine of that era held the individual to be the be-all and end-all of all life. He was the only reality. Society was not a thing in itself, but merely an agglomeration of individuals working cooperatively for their mutual betterment; it could not be greater than the sum of its parts. The individual was not the product of his environment, but the responsible master of it.

The nineteenth century had a dogma too, and it went by the name of "unalienable rights." These were held to be personal prerogatives, inhering in the individual by virtue of his existence and traceable to God alone. Government had nothing to do with rights except to see that individuals did not transgress them; and that was the only reason for government. Its functions were entirely negative, like a watchman's, and when it presumed to act positively it was not minding its business; it should be called to account.

In the practical affairs of life, doctrines and dogmas have a way of losing their virtues; even integrated philosophies fall apart when men start applying them. The individualism of the nineteenth century suffered considerable mayhem, even from those who paid it most homage—the advocates of laissez-faire. Their insistence on their right to do as they pleased turned out to be the right to exploit others, a right they could not exercise without the help of the very state they were pledged to hold in leash. They built up the power of the state by demanding privilege from it.

By the middle of the nineteenth century, this privilege business had given individualism a bad character. The reality was far short of the earlier dream. Youth was quick to detect the fallacies in individualism as it was practiced, condemned it, anc went to work on a replacement. The cure-all they hit upon was the doctrine of egalitarianism. Curiously, they promoted this new idea in the name of natural rights: if we are all endowed with an equal amount of natural rights, then it follows that we all have an equal right to what everybody else had. That was, at bottom, not only a revolt against the injustices of privilege, but also a rationalization of covetousness. At any rate, egalitarianism called for an extension of privilege, not the abolition of it; and since privilege is impossible without political enforcement, the egalitarians turned to state power for help. All kinds of reforms were advocated, and all of them strengthened political power at the expense of social power. It never occurred to those who, like Dickens, struck a blow for bigger and better "poor laws" that they were preparing the ground for social security, which reduces the individual to wardship under the state. Meanwhile, Karl Marx was developing his rationale of collectivism. The collectivistic revolution was born in the matrix of individualism.

REVOLUTIONS BREED REVOLUTIONS

That is the point to keep in mind when we speculate on the future, that revolutions are born in revolutions. And they are always being born. Curious youth never fails to detect inadequacies in the tradition it inherited and is impatient to write a new formula. On paper, the formula is always perfect, and perhaps it would work out just as predicted if the human hand did not touch it. Take the case of liberalism, which was the political expression of the individualistic thought pattern. At the beginning of the last century, when liberalism was emerging from adolescence, its only tenet was that political intervention in the affairs of men is bad. It traced all the disabilities that men suffered from to the power of the state. Hence, it advocated the whittling away of that power, without reserve, and proposed to abolish laws, without replacement. This negativeness was all right until the liberals got into places of power, and then it occurred to them that a little positive action might be good; they discovered that only the laws enacted by nonliberals were bad. The fact is—and this is something the state worshippers are prone to overlook—that the comforts, emoluments, and adulation that go with political office have great influence on political policy; for the state consists of men, and men are, unfortunately, always human. And so, liberalism mutated into its exact opposite by the end of the nineteenth century. Today it is the synonym of statism.

Who knows what revolutionary ideas youth is toying with right now? We live entirely too close to the present to judge the direction of its currents. We are either pessimists or optimists, and in either case are poor witnesses. Those of us who are enamored of "the good old times" point to the prevalence of socialistic doctrine, particularly in classrooms and textbooks, as evidence that the "world is going to hell," while the proponents of socialism take the same evidence as proof of the immediacy of their millennium. Both sides are probably in error. It should be remembered that the present crop of teachers, who are also the textbook writers, are the product of the socialistic tradition built up during the early part of the century, and are necessarily convinced of its virtue. Their denial of natural rights, for instance, is as natural as was the espousal of that doctrine by the teachers of 1850. However, the pessimists can take comfort in this fact, that though the professors do exert some influence on their students, they cannot stop curiosity. If the history of ideas is any guide as to the future, we can be sure that a change is in the making, that youth is brewing a revolution; it has been at the job throughout the ages.

To predict with any accuracy the tradition of the twenty-first century would require the equipment of a prophet. But, and here again relying on the evidence of history, we are on safe ground in anticipating a renaissance of individualism. For, the pendulum of sociopolitical thought has swung to and fro over the same arc since men began to live in association, and there is no warrant for believing that it will fly off in a new direction. Modern absolutism—going by the various names of communism, fascism, nazism or the less frightening "controlled economy"—is in many superficials quite different from "the divine right of kings"; but in their common rejection of the individual the two frames of thought are alike. Or, the individualistic doctrine of salvation that tarnished the glory of Rome had none of the economic overtones of nineteenth-century individualism;

but, though the theologian might object to the observation, the underlying idea of salvation is the primacy of the individual, not the collectivity, and that is the underlying idea of any form of individualism. A discarded tradition never returns in its former garb; in fact, it takes a lot of disrobing to recognize it. Only a historical expert can trace the New Deal of modern America to the New Deal of ancient Rome, or recognize Sparta in Moscow.

THE INEVITABLE FUTURE

Whatever the character of the coming revolution, it will not show itself until the present revolution has run its course. There is some disposition to try to stop it in its tracks, but that is in the nature of things a futile occupation. Even the opposition to the present collectivistic trend is tainted with it, as it must be. Those who fight socialized medicine tooth and nail would fight equally hard against a proposal to drop socialized education, unable to see that both institutions are cut from the same cloth; and those who view with alarm the teaching of collectivistic doctrine in our public school are simply plugging for a politically managed curriculum more to their own liking. Likewise, the "free enterprisers" rail against the subvention of farmers but are strong for the subvention of manufacturers through protective tariffs. We are immersed in the prevailing tradition, and until it wears itself out and is replaced by another, nothing can be done about it. The best we can do is to find fault, which is the necessary preliminary to the coming revolution.

Of this, however, we can be sure: enrolled in some nursery or freshman class right now is a Voltaire, an Adam Smith, a Locke, or a Godwin, some maverick who will emerge from the herd and lead it. Youth, as always, is in a ferment, is dissatisfied with things as they are. Well, since the only direction youth can go is away from the current collectivistic tradition toward its opposite, those who cherish individualistic stock of values must try to peddle them to these embryonic revolutionists. We must polish up our ancient arguments, apply them to the current scene, and offer them as brand new merchandise. We must do a selling job. Youth will not buy us out, lock, stock, and barrel, but will be rather selective about it; they will take what seems good to them, modernize it, build it into a panacea, and start a revolution. God bless them.

A Legacy of Value

A man of means and goodwill said: "But, if we put into office men who believe in private property and the sanctity of the individual, would not the trend toward statism be stopped? After all, it is only a matter of the right legislation."

The legislation is the product of the general will. What with the common passion for confiscation, contrary-minded men could hardly be elected to office; and, if they happened to slip in, they would be ousted if they tried to oppose the trend.

"Is the case for the free development of the personality in a free society hopeless?"

Yes—unless a demand for it can be generated. Statism is a state of mind, not an historical necessity. There was a time when Americans were opposed to the income tax, to conscription, to public doles, to political intervention in private affairs. They believed in themselves, not the government. They came to collectivism by way of education. The socialists reshaped the mind of America by hard work, by self-sacrifice, by looking always to the future.

"A Legacy of Value" appeared in analysis *(August 1950) and perfectly represents many key elements of Frank Chodorov's thought.*

"Then, it is a matter of education?"

Only education. And the education must be directed at the mind of the future. The present generation is the product of collectivist thought propagated during the past thirty years. The job of reeducating it is well nigh impossible. It would be far more profitable to work on the mind of the future.

"Where would you start?"

In the kindergarten, if possible. Surely at the college level, where there is an avid market for "something new and different."

"But, the professors and their textbooks seem to lean to the collectivist philosophy."

True. The professors and their textbooks are the product of their times, like the rest of the population. Fifty years ago the campus was singularly free of collectivist doctrine. Nevertheless, and in the face of official opposition, the socialists invaded it. They worked on the students.

"There is nothing 'new and different' in individualism; it is as old as man."

It is quite new and quite different these days. And it is, in the true sense of the word, revolutionary. If it is presented that way, as an ideal worth fighting for, it will capture the imagination of youth.

"You are advocating a long-term project."

What's your hurry? You have only a few years to live and cannot hope to remake society in so short a time. Nobody now living will see a free society in America. But, in fighting for it one can have a lot of fun. Consider the effort as a legacy to your great-grandchildren. What else can you bequeath them? You know that confiscatory taxation will increase, not diminish. You will leave your children part of what you have accumulated. Have you any doubt that your grandchildren will get a smaller part, or that their children will get nothing? In the circumstances, what better heritage could you bestow than some understanding of the principles of freedom and, perhaps, a will for freedom?

Selected Bibliography of Chodorov's Works

BOOKS

The Economics of Society, Government, and State. New York: Analysis Associates, 1946. Only a limited number of this title were distributed. It is mimeographed and is apparently an early draft of *The Rise and Fall of Society* but with a stronger Georgist emphasis.

One Is a Crowd: Reflections of an Individualist. New York: Devin-Adair, 1952. Introduction by John Chamberlain.

The Income Tax: Root of All Evil. New York: Devin-Adair, 1954. Foreword by J. Bracken Lee.

The Rise and Fall of Society: An Essay on the Economic Forces That Underlie Social Institutions. New York: Devin-Adair, 1959. Foreword by Frank S. Meyer.

Out of Step: The Autobiography of an Individualist. New York: Devin-Adair, 1962. Introduction by E. Victor Milione.

PAMPHLETS

"From Solomon's Yoke to the Income Tax." Chicago: Human Events Associates, 1947.

"Taxation Is Robbery." Chicago: Human Events Associates, 1947.

"The Myth of the Post Office." Hinsdale, Ill.: Henry Regnery Company, 1948.

"Private Schools: The Solution to America's Educational Problem." New York: National Council for American Education, n.d.

"Source of Rights." Irvington-on-Hudson, N.Y.: Foundation for Economic Education, 1954.

"Flight to Russia." Colorado Springs, Colo.: Freedom School, 1959.

"Debunking the State." Alexandria, Va.: Audio-Forum, n.d. This is an audio cassette of a talk Chodorov gave.

PERIODICALS

(Frank Chodorov was a political journalist and wrote hundreds of editorials and articles. A full listing would be cumbersome. The following are the major periodicals he wrote for, and often edited. Those dates given indicate the length of his major involvement.)

The Freeman (monthly, November 1937–March 1942). Chodorov was initially the publisher and then the editor of the magazine of the Henry George School of Social Science.

analysis (monthly, November 1944–January 1951). Chodorov was editor and publisher.

Human Events (1947–60). Between March 1951 and June 1954 Chodorov was associate editor; thereafter he wrote less frequently as a contributing editor.

Plain Talk (1949–50).

The Freeman (1950–54). This reincarnation of the workhorse of the libertarian movement was edited by Henry Hazlitt, Suzanne La Follette, and John Chamberlain.

Faith and Freedom (1951–52).

The Freeman (1954–60). Published by the Foundation for Economic Education and edited by Chodorov from July 1954 until 1956.

National Review (1956–60). For this biweekly Chodorov wrote a number of articles and book reviews. He was listed on the masthead from the founding of *National Review* until his death in 1966.

Fragments (1963–66). Chodorov was an editor of this magazine started by friends. Although he did contribute a few small original pieces, his participation consisted mostly of reprints of his articles and "being there." *Fragments* was largely inspired by his writings over the years.

Chodorov also wrote in a number of other periodicals, including:

American Mercury
Economic Council Review of Books
Ideas
Saturday Evening Post
Scribner's Commentator
Spotlight

INDEX

action
  constructive, 383–91
  education for, 386
  leadership and, 387–88
  thought and, 214–16
Adams, Mrs. John, 290
Agricultural Extension Service, 264
Alexander the Great, 335, 339
America
  advent of communism to, 186–89
  communism and, 163–89
  communizing, 371–79
  empire building in, 342–49
  natural rights in, 301–5
  revolution in, 376–77, 406–10
  saving, 193–96
  Soviet invasion of, 375–76
America First Committee, 332–33
Americanism, 166, 172, 175–78, 302
  communism by means of, 175–77
American Revolution, 255
  1913 revolution undoes, 259
  second revolution compared with, 408–9
analysis, 23, 383
  end of, 19
  founding of, 18
  Nock on, 19
anticommunism, 23–27
army, standing
  production and, 356–57
Arnold, Benedict, 63
Articles of Confederation, 178, 255
Attlee (prime minister of England), 63
Austrian school of economics, 133

authoritarianism, 120, 124, 125. *See also*
  communism; government; socialism;
  state; statism

Bazalgette, Leon, 311
Bentham, Jeremy, 212
Bible, 243. *See also* God, Word of; Ten
  Commandments
Bill of Rights, 256
  1688, 300
  Virginia, 307
Billson, 310
Bismarck, 403
bonds, 334
Brest-Litovsk treaty, 154, 393
British Empire, 120, 337, 338, 339
Browder, Earl, 188
Buckley, William F., Jr., 12, 19, 26, 30
  Chodorov vs., 23–24
  God and Man at Yale, 218
bureaucrats, 53–54
  attitude of, 218
  politicians compared with, 50–51
  See also collectivism; state
Byzantine Empire, 338

Calhoun, 266
capitalism, 34, 112–13, 399–404
  definition of, 404
  Marx on, 142–43
  Marxism and, 400–404
  monopoly in communism and, 170–71
  private property in communism and, 168–70

This book was set in Times Roman. The face was designed by Stanley Morison to be used in the news columns of the London *Times*. The *Times* was seeking a typeface that would be condensed enough to accommodate a substantial number of words per column without sacrificing readability and still have an attractive, contemporary appearance. This design was an immediate success. It is used in many periodicals throughout the world and is one of the most popular text faces currently in use for book work.

Printed on paper that is acid-free and meets the requirements of the American National Standard for Permanence of Paper for Printed Library Materials, Z39.48-1992. ∞

Book design by JMH Corporation,
Indianapolis, Indiana
Typography by Weimer Typesetting Co., Inc.,
Indianapolis, Indiana
Printed by Thomson-Shore, Inc.,
Dexter, Michigan